# Table of contents

*WITHDRAWN FROM THE RODMAN PUBLIC LIBRARY*

---

***Sections beginners should read <u>first</u>***

Note: All prices in this book are for Spring, 1991. Please adjust them for inflation.

**\* Sections beginners should read first**

# 1. The audience comes first

**P**icture the typical reader you need to reach. Then think about all the other people you can't afford to snub.

Those readers will influence every task discussed in this book, from picking the type size to arranging meetings. If the audience isn't foremost in your mind, you'll publish something you and your close friends can enjoy, but which will strike most people as just the mumblings of a clique.

Consciously reach out to all potential readers. Only when you meet them halfway will they be convinced your message is relevant to them.

Are you reaching a broad audience or a clique?

## How would readers feel about that?

Every so often step back, look at your publication and ask yourself that question. If, when you flip through a couple of issues of your paper, you see pictures of nothing but fifty-year-old white men, the paper will make young people, women, minorities and senior citizens feel your group simply isn't for them. Or do you have a habit of using "in-group" words the whole audience can't follow?

When you identify an important minority among your readers, whether it's senior citizens or tool room workers, write some articles about them. Sometimes those articles get a special page or column, and sometimes you'll write them for everyone's benefit. Not all readers care when the elderly lunch program is held, for example, but they should be told why old people complain.

## Writing for a limited audience

A group sponsoring women's rights might publish a paper just for women. A furniture workers' union will publish newsletters only for members – workers who build furniture.

Publishing for a limited audience gives you free rein to appeal directly to that group. For example, an engineers' newsletter can throw around technical engineering terms, and a neighborhood paper can refer freely to well-known local landmarks.

Yet with every publication, you risk limiting the audience more than you intend to. For example, a women's paper might raise issues important to professional women, but thoughtlessly forget file clerks, secretaries and homemakers. Avoid that pitfall by defining your audience and thinking about everyone that audience might include.

This brochure is aimed at an audience of teachers

Lawmakers Deserve D- for cuts in education

"Is throwing spitballs at teachers the answer?" – Krell

## Audience checklist

Here are factors to consider when defining your readership.

### Families

People tied down with family responsibilities have precious little time to wade through a long newspaper or answer every plea for help. So choose your issues carefully.

To appeal to parents, discuss child-rearing issues. And occasionally write articles directed at the kids.

On the other hand, don't assume

everyone's married and has kids. More people than ever live alone. Don't assume the wife does all the housework, or that the husband has a job. Single workers raising kids alone are often neglected – and remember, some are men.

## Jobs

Do you include readers who work in offices as well as factories? How about shift workers, retirees, students, homemakers and the unemployed? Do you assume readers hate their jobs, when many are proud of the work they do?

Do you refer to work rules not everyone is familiar with?

## Beliefs & attitudes

Avoid carrying articles full of a religious faith all readers don't share. Don't assume all readers are liberal or even interested in politics. Do you imagine everyone likes to down a few beers when many are really reformed alcoholics or teetotalers?

Don't assume people identify with each other, or that they agree with what you think are obviously good goals. Instead, anticipate prejudices, fears and gripes that keep people from relating better to your group and to each other.

And what do readers think about your opposition? If many are awed by bad-guy politicians or the boss, go easy. Instead of railing at those "villains," start by quietly proving that the rest of us deserve a piece of the action.

Remember, people have conflicting feelings. Appeal to their shared interests, without needlessly insulting other cherished notions.

## Age

Each generation has its own language, so this is a hard gap to bridge. To include older readers, avoid fine print a farsighted person couldn't read. Do you refer to things that happened three years ago, when many younger people weren't around? Explain them. Does your paper discuss issues important to each age group, from job training to retirement?

## Racial & ethnic groups

Here too, each group has a distinct way of looking at things. And it's *much* easier than you think to innocently use a word some group will mistake for an ethnic or racial slur. If many people read another language more comfortably than English, carry key articles in their own language.

## Education

These days, even high-school graduates may not read well; if you suspect your audience isn't crazy about reading, keep every article short. And use cartoons, photos and charts to tell as much of the story as possible.

## Women & men

Include the female or male minority at work, plus the spouse at home who reads the paper. Don't thoughtlessly exclude men when discussing child care or the kids' schools. And don't assume all dentists are men and all nurses are women.

Could your language make women readers feel left out? When possible, use words like "chair" or "chairperson" instead of "chairman." (More on p. 111.) In cartoons and jokes, do both women and men have well-rounded personalities? Or are women alone portrayed as silly and scared or big spenders? Do you refer to grown women as "girls" while the guys are "men"?

## Where readers live

Do readers of a workplace paper live in the same communities, so you can discuss those issues too? Or do different neighborhoods set up barriers you must bridge? Are readers both homeowners and tenants?

# The committee

To appeal to all potential readers, there's no substitute for a broad committee that includes all kinds of people. As they help plan and edit the paper, they'll reflect the subtleties of how various groups think; and someone will catch misunderstandings before they're published and the harm is done.

Keep their different needs in mind when setting up meetings, too. For example, avoid scheduling meetings at places and times women and oldsters wouldn't dream of traveling to alone. And provide child care when possible. Above all, don't let one clique, whether they're men, college grads or youngsters, dominate the decisions and put down other people's ideas.

# 2. How to make a leaflet or brochure

**Y**ou have an important meeting to announce, need to get out the facts during an organizing drive, or want to rally people during a crisis. Or maybe you need something handy to explain what services your organization offers. What you need is a *flyer, leaflet* or *brochure.*

## Leaflets & flyers

These are short, often urgent, written messages you'll usually hand out or post on a bulletin board, hallway, etc. Something at the top must look so striking and important that harried passersby who take a quick glance from 20 feet away will stop dead in their tracks, drop everything, and read it.

Everything should be on one side only of a sturdy sheet of paper – It's remarkable how few people flip over a leaflet to see what's on the other side. The message must be so short and easy to read that people will finish the whole thing before they look up or get wherever they're going.

## What's a brochure?

A brochure is a glorified leaflet. It may still be a single sheet of paper, but it's longer, folded up, and printed on both sides. A brochure is handy for long-term use or mailings, and it's less likely to get mangled or thrown away. You can cram more into a brochure.

## Where to start

Take a few moments to think about the audience you must reach, reviewing Chapter 1's list of considerations. What on earth would interest these people in your message?

## Printing & typesetting

Decide how many copies you'll need (always figure in a few extra), how sturdy they should be, and what resources, such as typewriters, are available. How much time and experience can you devote to the job? How much money can you scrounge up? All this will help you pick the typesetting and printing that makes the most sense. Make arrangements now, so you'll be clued into scheduling problems or technical limits right from the start. Chapters 5, 6 and 7 help you compare costs and advantages of various methods.

## Make a list

What do you want to say? Make a list of key ideas and then rate them, from the information most crucial to your audience to points that could be left out.

## Outline the main points

Narrow your focus down to one basic theme, or idea, per flyer or brochure,

Brochure

Leaflet or flyer

### Example A

We need to lobby for a national health plan.

1. Health costs are going through the roof;

2. Companies are making workers pay more for health insurance;

3. Millions of Americans have no health insurance

### Example B

Why is health insurance so expensive?

Are you paying more for health insurance and getting less?

Can you afford the health care you need?

Company threatens to cut our health benefits

### Example C

Let Senator Hairdo know you care;

We need a national health plan.

### Example D

Support the Campaign for National Health

and then develop two to five points or examples that explain the main idea. For a longer brochure you could include as many as ten points. Example A shows how your outline might look.

This simple outline is written first from your point of view. Then you'll rework it, so the leaflet will appeal to people who haven't thought about things the way you do – and may not feel like reading a flyer to start with.

# Flesh out your ideas

### Find a good picture

Pictures aren't just decorations. Find the right picture (called a *graphic*) for the top of a leaflet or front of a brochure, and it'll hook casual lookers. Look for one with emotional appeal that's hard to resist. Other pictures help illustrate key points, so people can tell what you're concerned with just by looking. Chapters 12 and 18 give tips on finding the right photo or other graphic.

### Write a headline

The headline should always stand up to the all-important question: "Why should your audience bother with this?" If it doesn't, most people won't read another word.

Put yourself in the shoes of the people you're trying to reach. How does the issue touch them? How does it relate to things they think about every day? What's the biggest problem you're aiming to solve, or the biggest question people might have about it?

Then write a headline that will grab readers who aren't yet convinced of your message's importance. Start where readers are at. If you've got a great picture, make the headline flow from the picture, connecting it with the points that follow.

P. 118 gives tips on writing headlines. Questions make great headlines, because they invite people to think – or at least get them curious. A leaflet pushing a national health plan could have any of the headlines in example B, depending on the audience you're aiming at.

Once you've written the headline, reorganize your main points so they flow nicely from the headline.

## Make it snappy

Pruning your list of important points down to what's essential for now is the hardest part of writing a leaflet. When you're in the thick of things, everything seems crucial. Resign yourself to putting aside vitally important information for a future leaflet. Even for old pros, that's painful. Keep going over your list and outline, crossing out what's less important for the moment.

### Turn each outline point into a subheading

You can see a leaflet or brochure's outline when you look at it. A headline (plus a graphic) attracts people; subheadings outline the key points; and a short paragraph or two explains each point. When a leaflet's well organized, people can see what it covers before they read all the details. The leaflet looks inviting, and it's easy to refer back to the main points and remember them.

### Put the main idea or action last

That's your punch line, the idea you leave with people once you've gotten them in the mood for it. Put it at the end, bold enough to stand out but not so big it distracts attention from the top headline.

In the health care example, the last two lines could be example C or D.

### Make a sketch

Even before you've written it, sketch how the leaflet or brochure will look – how long you want it to be, where pictures might go, and how big the headline should be. Write out the headline, subheadlines, and the punch line at the end. Then draw lines where the explanation for each point goes, so you'll know about how much room it gets.

● **To sketch a brochure,** fold one or more sheets of paper the way you want it to look. Example E shows all the ways one sheet of legal-size (8½" x 14") paper can be folded. Pick your favorite, decide where everything goes, sketch it out, and then test it by folding and unfolding the sketched brochure the way a typical reader would. If it gets confusing, pick a different format.

Don't pick a format just because it's cute; pick one that lets you make the headline and pictures the right size and bunch material that belongs together on the same page. "B" subheadings should fall at the top and not bottom of pages. In other words, the format can complement your message or confuse and crowd it. It's your choice.

How you put out a brochure or flyer also influences its look – read on. For example, must you leave a space for mailing labels? Will you try to get mailing discounts that require the publication or mailing area to be a certain size (p. 171)?

• The name of your group. You want people to notice this, but it won't be the "draw" that attracts strangers to the flyer. Put it at the end. Then consider adding a phone number and address.

# Fill in the outline

## Explain each idea

Once you've sketched the leaflet, write a paragraph or two explaining each point in the outline. A brochure might explain things in more detail. The key is to start with something exciting or important to readers (the headline), and then move people to the punch line at the end, giving them evidence along the way to prepare them for it. These paragraphs are your *body copy*.

## Leaflet writing

• Write & rewrite. Keep refining the exact wording of each subhead and explanation, and be merciless in cutting every unneeded word or phrase (p. 115). Chapter 13 gives tips on writing.

• Stick to the point. No matter how truthful you are, a good leaflet or brochure comes across as simpler and more orderly than life actually is. You must simplify some points and leave out others to make information fit neatly into an outline. That's why a leaflet that comes across as clear and obvious to readers takes time and sweat to write. It's much easier to put out a leaflet that will confuse or overwhelm readers.

• How many words can you fit? If the flyer is short and simple and full of space, you can pretty much tell by looking at your sketch whether the copy you write fits where you want it to go. If it's long and space is tight, you must *copyfit* – see p. 131. But first, pick the exact type you'll use – see Chapter 5.

Example E — Folds for an 8½" by 14" brochure

Graphic attracts attention

Pencil sketch

Example F — Finished leaflet

Format hurts message

Format complements message

A-level head

B-level
subheads

Hodge-podge design

Consistent design

# Put it all together

## Label each subheading

Organize your leaflet by labeling the big headline at the top "A." Label each of the main subheadings from the outline "B."

For a brochure, look over the copy. Any explanation that gets long and involved should be divided into smaller sections, so it's inviting to read. Introduce each with a little sub-subheading, and label them "C."

If you want to highlight the name of your group, label it a "B" subheading. If you just need to make sure the name can be found, label it "C." The same goes for the time, date, place, etc. Label details that should pop out at people, such as the date, with "B." Those that are less important, like the address or phone number, are labelled "C."

This ranking system will help you pick the right type style and placement for each subheading.

# Design the leaflet or brochure

## Pick your type

• Whenever possible, type or typeset every word. Handwritten words are hard to read, look messy, and tell everyone you're a fly-by-night, bush-league group they shouldn't take seriously.

• If you're using a typewriter or word processor, that's fine for body copy. P. 132 gives tips on how to make the most of any typewriter. You'll still need large, bold type for the "A" headline and (if possible) "B" subheadings. P. 38 tells how to make the big stuff.

• If you use a typesetter or computer, you have a wealth of type styles and sizes to choose from. But don't get greedy, and try to use every option you can get your hands on. Pick no more than two styles – one for the body copy, and one that goes well with it for the "A" headline – maybe just a big, bold variety of the body type style. Use a different size and/or variation (p. 72) of the same typestyle(s) for "B" and "C" subheadings (if any). That's it.

• Chapter 15 shows how to type up copy yourself or tell a typesetter what you want.

## Space

No leaflet or brochure should be jam-packed with type. Plan to leave at least a ½" margin of space all around each page, and leave extra space around the headline. Space makes things look relaxing and easy to read, and empty areas attract attention. P. 142 tells how to make space work for you.

## The body copy

All copy is typed into columns of the exact same width. If you have room, just put one column on a page, with plenty of space on one side or both, like example F on p. 7. But don't let the type column get so wide it's hard to read (p. 70). To fit more copy, try two or more columns of type on a page (but don't fill the whole page with type). P. 131 tells how to figure column widths. Type should be at least 9 points tall – p. 67.

## Headline & subheadings

• The "A" headline should be big and bold, so it jumps out at people. Use 24-point or bigger type for brochure headlines, and between 36-point and 60-point type for leaflet headlines. The fewer words there are in the headline, the bigger the type can be.

• "C" subheadings should be barely big (or bold or underlined) enough to stand out a bit from the copy. They're usually the same type style as the body copy, but could be bolder (p. 72). Leave a little space above each subheading – just *2 points* (p. 67) may be enough. If you're using a typewriter, just skip a line (or half-line) and underline and/or center type for C-level subheadings – like example H on p. 9.

• "B" subheadings are bigger and bolder than the copy, and could stick out into a wide margin or space (example G). They should be around twice the size of the body copy, but no more than half the size of the "A" headline.

• Be consistent. The type for all B-subheadings should be exactly the same. If one sticks out to the left of the type column, then they all should. If one B-subheading is centered in the middle of the column, center them all. If one is underlined, or has a band of space above it, all of them should.

Likewise, C-subheadings all look the same. This makes your leaflet or brochure seem orderly, so the words and ideas dominate it. If it *isn't* orderly, the chaos will overwhelm the message.

## Design tips

Skim Chapter 8, looking for other categories, such as photo captions, that should look distinct. For each, pick a variation (like *italics* – p. 36) or different size and placement of the same type used for body copy.

Until you get the hang of designing flyers from scratch, scan the examples in this book. Pick one that suits your purpose, and copy its design. Keep your eyes peeled for brochures and leaflets that work, and use them as models, too.

• If you've already written the text, *copyfit* (p. 86) to see if it fits. If it doesn't, either chop it down, leave out a point or two, or redesign the leaflet or brochure. (But *don't* continue anything on the back of a leaflet.)

# Types of leaflets

Which of the leaflet types below suits your purpose?

## Come to a rally, meeting, hearing, etc.

You're planning an event and asking people to come. Maybe it's a political rally, a voting registration drive or a party. If it's something fun like a picnic, announcing the event right off the bat in a screaming "A" headline could do the trick. But unless everyone's hopping mad, few people get excited about sacrificing free time to attend a meeting or rally. You must convince them the issue's so important they can't ignore it.

Pick the most concrete, pressing and/or widespread needs you're tackling, like how hard it's been to get a raise or the lack of nearby playgrounds. Start with these. Or maybe there's a crisis on people's minds like a firing, electric rate hike or health-care cutback.

To show a sense of urgency, make the "A" headline huge and super-bold, with space above and beside it. In the headline, appeal to people's stake in the crisis or their unmet needs. After they're hooked, mention the meeting, hearing, etc. in a "B" subheading.

Such leaflets must be pared down to the bare bones. Since success depends on involving as many people as possible, you can't afford to lose anyone by being

Brochure heads & subheads

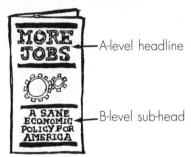

A-level headline

B-level sub-head

Inside the same brochure

B-level head

C-level subheads

wordy. You'll walk a tightrope, not belaboring what everyone knows, yet not assuming they know more than they do, or share your commitment. Prune out all thoughts that aren't needed to mobilize people for the immediate event.

When the leaflet's written, check that you've included: what the meeting, hearing, etc. is (briefly); where; when (date and time); why it's important; who your group is; who to get in touch with; and a phone number to call. Who will be there, topics of discussion, available transportation and child care, refreshments and possible action following the meeting may also be important. A simple map showing how to get to the event could help. Include only what you can easily fit onto one side of paper.

## Educational leaflets & brochures

You need a flyer or brochure that outlines your group's services, shows the benefits of a new contract, or gives people a rundown of their legal rights. Or maybe you're walking a picket line and want something to hand out explaining why you're there. Or you want to ex-

Headline & graphic work together

Example H

Many parents are plagued with worry over where their kids are while they're at work.

**What we won** C-level head
The child-care debate was peppered with veto threats from the President, who didn't want

"Come to a meeting" leaflet

Educational brochure

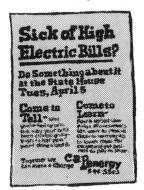

"Come to a hearing" leaflet

Educational leaflet

Fact sheet for organizers

plain your group's views on an economic problem or political issue.

In many cases, a well-funded publicity blitz has already hit people with the other side's point of view – whether from management, the landlords' association or right-wing politicians. Often they've distorted the facts in an appealing way. Keep in mind what they're saying, what people are likely to believe, and questions they've left unanswered. On key issues, you might have to poke holes in their distortions.

Design these with special care, so they'll have lasting appeal. Whenever possible, use charts and pictures to help explain complex ideas (p. 157).

Don't overestimate the power of the written word, however. Few people will miraculously change their whole view of the world after reading one brochure. Educational literature can supplement personal contacts, but it can't replace them. A good flyer gives you an excuse for talking to people, and gives them a concrete reminder of the discussion. It puts the facts down in black and white, so people will take them seriously and remember them.

For an educational leaflet, you may need more than one side of paper to do the necessary explaining. If so, make it a brochure, and add pages as necessary. But remember, if the subject can be divided up, two short brochures are more apt to be read cover-to-cover than one long one; and if you've got two brochures, you'll have something new to hand out the second time you show up.

## Join the campaign

This is a cross between the first two kinds. You're aiming to solve a long-term problem, not one crisis. You may want to recruit new members, fight unjust property taxes, or organize a union.

● **One issue at a time.** You can't say everything in one leaflet, and there's no point in trying. If you plan a step-by-step campaign now, you're less likely to cram too much information into your first leaflet or two. Pick one simple issue per flyer, starting with ideas that have the widest appeal. The first leaflet will give you credibility if it says one thing well. If the leaflet's a garbled flop instead, people may not bother to read your next attempt.

Trying to win people's trust is a tricky business. Again, flyers can't replace person-to-person organizing.

● **Keep issues local and specific.** Even if it's beautifully done, a vague leaflet on why people should organize just doesn't hit home. It can sound like so much pie in the sky. Show you understand specific problems the way people feel them, so they'll be convinced you aren't just a bunch of naïve outsiders.

● **Don't get defensive.** In planning a campaign, get a clear grasp on your most meaningful arguments. That can save you from being thrown into a panic and put on the defensive.

Your opposition could make you so furious, you'll be tempted to rush out a leaflet to answer every nasty lie or distortion. But hold on. Once you start fighting every twisted idea, you've let the opposition pick the battlefield and the rules of the fight. And although each lie can drive you crazy, a stormy battle over trivial issues could make your audience get disgusted with both sides and give up trying to sort it all out.

In every campaign, take a good, hard look at your audience. What issues are most important to them, and what distortions of your group or goals are likely to influence them? If you don't know, talk to as many "typical" members of your audience as you can. Only when the other side messes with key issues should you go all-out to fight back.

● **Timing.** How much printed information can people absorb? Don't swamp them with too many leaflets. An organizing committee firmly rooted in the community or workplace you're aiming at can help you constantly take their pulse, to make sure you aren't overdoing it. Timing is also important. Keep a few trump cards up your sleeve to throw on the table in the last days of a campaign, taking your opposition by surprise and upsetting their strategy.

● **Accentuate the positive.** Beware of seizing upon every issue people gripe about. For every problem you raise, suggest a convincing solution. Read each flyer over to see if the overall impression is optimistic, not depressing. You want people to believe your activities can brighten their futures, not encourage them to take up the bottle, quit their jobs, or move out of the city.

● **Develop a style,** a consistent "look" for each series of leaflets or brochures. Then people will recognize your literature at first sight. It will seem like an old friend, or at least an acquaintance. And when your style helps identify you, you won't be tempted to put your name too big (disrupting the message). To get a distinctive look, make rules for the type style, sizes and placement, column width, etc., and follow them for each flyer.

• **Think up a slogan** for each campaign, a catchy phrase ending each flyer that captures the spirit of your goals. It can be as long as "Rothschild never let us down; don't let him down" or as simple as "Raises, not Roses," a slogan for organizing women office workers.

• A **tear-off coupon** could encourage people to get in touch with you.

### Vote for so-and-so

The best way to offend readers is to throw at the top of your flyer a screaming headline saying, "Vote for Tom Gallagher!" People who agree with you will nod their heads and walk on, and those who disagree will shake their heads and move on. Many will mumble to themselves: "Who do they think they are, telling me how to vote?!"

The top ("A") headline should instead convince people that the election and/or Gallagher is meaningful to *them* – try something like Example I. The right picture could drive home that point. At the end, a B-level subheading says something like: "Tom Gallagher deserves your vote on Nov. 6."

The best campaigns don't suddenly appear a month before the election. Consider publishing a newsletter that educates people about the issues and all the great things Gallagher does for them, month after month.

This leaflet's too vague

It Pays To Vote Union (TRU)

This leaflet's too defensive

**Mr. Bingly Lied!**
• Our Raise Was 2¼¢, Not 3¢.
• Our Organizer Comes From Montclair, Not Orange.
• Only 211 Employees Got Merit Raises, Not 240.
• There Are Not Any Blondes in the Accounting Dept.!

**Listen to the Truth-Vote Union!**
—Employees For a Union

Example I
Tom Gallagher is fighting for your safety

Poor leaflet timing

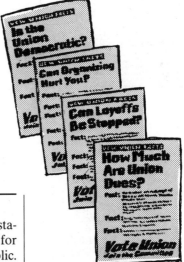
A leaflet campaign

Answering the opposition

## How will you distribute it?

Decide that *before* you put together the flyer. Be realistic about the audience, how much money you can spend, what public places are available, how many people you can recruit to help, and how fast the information must get out. Here are the main options:

### Handouts

If you don't have money, this could be your only option. It also makes sense if you don't have a ready mailing list and have a logical place to pass flyers out. For example, plant gate, doorway or lunchroom distribution makes sense for

a local union. Downtown or subway-station handouts may be a good way for community groups to reach the public. If you're urging people not to cross a picket line, you'll pass out leaflets then and there.

If you plan to blanket a neighborhood with flyers door-to-door, recruit a loyal troupe of members who are ready to confront snarling dogs. Since it's illegal to put handouts in the mailbox in the U.S., slip them under the door or sandwich them between doors. P. 33 gives other legal dos and don'ts.

The big advantage to handing out flyers personally is that it gives you a chance to talk with people – to discuss their doubts about what your group is up to, to get feedback and suggestions, and to convince them you aren't weird

Envelopes are boring

Self-mailer with "tease"

Back

Front

For a bulletin board or hand-out

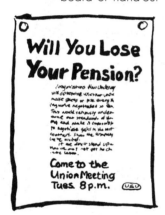

Example J

Only the brochures on the left were designed for a literature rack

or dangerous. That means well-informed members should hand out flyers. If a member looks wildly different from the image you want to project or is prone to start a violent argument at the drop of a pin, don't ask that person to help you leaflet.

## Mailings

To get out a mailing you may not need scads of willing volunteers, but you do need money. Mailing costs have skyrocketed. When deciding whether you can afford it, figure in the cost of making and keeping up a mailing list, as well as postage. To get the lowest rates, get a non-profit permit and take the time to fold and bundle the mail just the way the post office likes it (Chapter 19).

Consider mailing long brochures that can't be read within a few minutes, or ones you want the whole family to see. But avoid mailing controversial educational pieces to the public. Few people trust utter strangers.

If your flyer is a one-shot deal and you haven't developed a mailing list, look into borrowing some other group's list, or even buying one. A magazine whose readers you'd like to reach might sell or trade subscription lists. For fundraising, look into commercial brokers. Their specialized lists can be narrowed down to groups like teachers of sex education in Rhode Island.

• A mailed flyer should look its best the moment it arrives. That rules out stuffing it into envelopes, so it looks like junk mail. Some people won't bother ripping the envelope open at all; others won't tackle their pile of junk mail until long after your event is over.

To mail a leaflet, fold and staple it, and stick the address label and stamp directly on its back, so it becomes a self-mailer. If you can afford printing both sides, add a "tease" to the back of the leaflet, a phrase or two that hints at the urgency of the message and gets people to open up. But make sure it's in the right place if you want special mailing discounts (p. 170). And use paper heavy enough to keep the ink from showing through – p. 61.

If you're designing a leaflet to be

mailed and not handed out or posted, make it a self-mailing brochure instead. Then people will see the front page and "A" headline as soon as they pick up the mail, and many will start reading at once. Leave a space at least 3" tall and 5" wide on the lower right-hand corner of the back for the mailing label, and print your non-profit mailing *indicia* (p. 168) in that space – check with your post office or mailer to make sure you've designed the space right.

## Literature shelves & bulletin boards

Are there bulletin boards everyone walks by in your office or plant? Does the lounge, supermarket, laundromat or health clinic offer a bulletin board or literature rack to the public? Must you ask permission to get access?

• Bulletin boards. A leaflet that'll be posted should have big, simple headlines, lots of space, and very little wording. To make it stand out clearly from the mass of paper pinned up alongside, try printing the leaflet with colored ink and/or on bright colored paper. To make it durable, try a heavy paper.

• Literature racks. This is the laziest and least effective way to get a message out quickly. All too many people will pass by the literature rack without so much as giving it a glance.

But if you've got useful long-term information that isn't controversial, it could be worth a try. A list of services, information about veterans' benefits, or a brochure on how to avoid a heart attack might fit this category.

Look for places where people hang out or wait in line with so much time to kill they'll read anything.

You'll need a tall, sturdy brochure. If it's just one sheet, use 8½" x 14" paper and fold it like example J. The "A" headline must be super-simple and short enough to fit into the top third of the front page, so it won't get covered by the rack. One or two key words printed in huge type within the top third might do the trick. Heavier paper will keep it from flopping over, and attractive colored ink and paper can make your brochure look different from the rest.

## Lay it out & paste it up

When everything's planned and typeset, you're ready to fine-tune the layout

and get the whole thing ready to be printed. For guidance, see p. 137. But first, proofread everything – p. 135. To paste type and other pieces of the flyer together, consult Chapter 17.

# 3. Why your newsletter or paper is special

**W**hy is your newsletter or paper published? Answering that will help you decide what to include and how to handle it. Don't just use the daily press and TV news as models: the companies that own the commercial media have very different goals from yours.

## How most media operate

*The New York Times* says it carries "all the news fit to print." But who decides what's "fit to print"?

The media are, first of all, Big Business. We have 750 TV stations, 1,600 daily papers, and hundreds of magazines bombarding us with messages; yet most of these media are owned by 25 giant, powerful companies. That's *half* the number that controlled the media in 1983. A dozen newspaper chains control access to over half the nation's readers.

The biggest of these media giants, Time-Warner, had by 1990 amassed $20 billion worth of TV stations, newspapers and other media companies, including over 40% of the nation's magazine business. Gannett, the biggest newspaper chain with 88 dailies, also owns 8 TV stations, 18 radio stations, *USA Today*, the Louis Harris poll, and McNeil-Lehrer productions.

Rupert Murdoch, the Australian who bought control of Fox Broadcasting, 20th Century Fox studios, TV Guide, and more than 100 newspapers on three continents, also owns Australia's biggest airline. To amass this huge empire he had by 1990 taken on debts totaling $8.7 *billion*. To get cash to pay creditors, etc., owners like Murdoch squeeze as much profit as possible from their media "properties." But that's not the only corporate influence.

### Consumers or consumed?

Who are the *consumers* of the commercial media? And what is the *prod-*

*uct* they consume? The answers aren't as simple as you may think. In fact, each question has *two* answers, depending on who you ask.

If you ask media workers (reporters, technicians, writers, actors), they tend to see us, the audience, as the consumers of their work, and the product is the newspaper story or TV program. But this isn't how corporate management sees things: For the owners, the real consumers are the ones who pay the bills – the advertisers. Three out of four dollars a daily paper makes and *all* of a TV or radio station's income comes from selling advertising. The product they sell to advertisers is us, the audience.

For media owners, the newspaper or TV/radio program is the advertising bait, not a final product. If the bait

draws a big audience with above-average incomes and puts them in a receptive mood, they can charge advertisers top dollar for a half-page ad or commercial. For a popular extravaganza like the Superbowl, networks can charge $800,000 for a 30-second spot. But if such "bait" attracts a smaller audience, or an audience with less money, or an audience depressed or angered by controversy, they've failed. Advertisers will pay less money because the audience contains fewer likely shoppers.

To bait their media hooks to snag the biggest fish, corporate managers invade every dimension of the communications process, narrowing the range of accept-

able messages. Yes, there must be *some* good writing, acting and reporting to attract an audience. And some media companies pay more attention to this craft agenda than others. But in a private media industry, advertisers, not the audience, are the bottom line.

The sad truth is, most media professionals actually make their living producing ads. TV ads in particular employ more actors and have more lavish budgets than the programs. Sometimes the ads are funnier, more entertaining and more seductive than the programming "bait" we watch between the commercial interruptions. That isn't a mistake; it's what the advertisers want.

# Do we have a choice?

On your TV or radio, you can tune in more channels than ever before. When you stop at the newsstand, you can buy a paper and a huge variety of magazines.

On the surface there seems to be a lot of choice; but in many ways such choices are remarkably limited. Do we, for example, have much say over whether we get bombarded with commercials every five or ten minutes during our favorite shows? Most TV shows are broken into a predictable format of

small segments, each building up to a moment of drama – "tease," as TV producers call it – that will keep us tuned in during the ads.

Why are newspapers *always* skinny on Mondays and Tuesdays, and fatter the next three days? It's not because the first two days of the week have less news. It's because stores advertise more heavily on days when readers plan weekend shopping.

A paper decides how many pages to make each edition by how much advertising it sells. It sets aside most of the space for paid ads, then fills the "news hole," as they call it, with stories to attract the readers advertisers want.

*Out of 519 pages in these two magazines, only 98 were not ads or ad-related*

# Yes, the news is censored

### The heavy hand

The hand of censorship can weigh heavily on writers and performers in the commercial media. The fact that General Electric, maker of jet engines, home appliances, and nuclear reactors, is also the owner of NBC Television may not mean that *every* news story is tailored to fit GE's perspective; but editors do feel the heat. Why else would NBC, the first network to show a tragic Iowa plane crash, be the last to report that the plane's jet engines, made by GE, contained inferior parts? Is it a coincidence that NBC News also failed to mention a report saying that GE sold nuclear reactors it knew to be faulty? Or that the producer of David Letterman's "Late Night" show lost his job right after a guest blasted GE on the air?

Newspaper editors often feel the same pressure. When the American Society of Newspaper Editors asked its members if they'd feel free to publish news that might hurt the company owning the paper, one-third admitted they would not.

Advertisers sometimes dictate what kinds of stories go alongside their ads, and they expect to be favorably mentioned in many of these stories. Procter and Gamble, the nation's biggest packaged-goods advertiser, peddles everything from Tide to Folgers Coffee. It tells editors its ads can't be placed in any magazine that mentions gun control, abortion, the occult, cults, or the disparagement of religion. Instead of controversial issues that distract some readers and antagonize others, P&G wants upbeat stories.

### They're really ads

Advertisers even demand "bait" that contains the advertising message within the story. By 1990, more than 75 kids' programs were actually marketing tools – "G.I. Joe," "My Little Pony," "Masters of the Universe" and others were all designed to make kids beg their parents to buy the toys. Movies and prime-time TV shows also contain advertising "props" – the hero's racy Chevrolet or the newscaster's wardrobe – that advertisers pay to have included.

Over 2,000 half-hour TV shows are 100% advertising. Detroit's Channel 4 bumped the public affairs show "Inside Washington" to run "Builder's Open House," a series of real-estate commercials. The "Due Process" legal-affairs show was produced by lawyers, and "Health Matters" came from the hospital industry. Of the hundreds of new magazines launched every year, many are little more than marketing tools – ski magazines to sell sports equipment, or health magazines to sell vitamins.

Newspapers also blur the line between ads and news, especially in the back sections. Stories in Travel or Real Estate sections rarely go beyond buyers' tips and cheery hype. Exposés of slumlords or descriptions of, say, the police state running "Sunny Mexico," are rarer still. "Features" like Your Next Latin Holiday or a luscious cottage cheese salad are fed to the paper for free by the industries selling those products.

"As journalism becomes more marketing oriented, the task of what it is to be a journalist and what it is to be an advertiser becomes more and more similar," warns the chair of Hunter College's communications department.

## The hidden hand

The government used to limit TV and radio advertising. (It never regulated newspapers.) But in 1984, the Federal Communications Commission (FCC) dropped all time limits on TV commercials. TV is "just another appliance," said the FCC chairman. "It's a toaster with pictures." The FCC also killed rules that made stations respond to community needs, air public affairs programs, and present all sides on controversial issues.

In the absence of *publicly* defined standards, advertisers can "regulate" the commercial media unchallenged. "We insist on a program environment that reinforces a corporate point of view," the TV ad buyer for General Foods once put it. To control this program environment, the "hidden hand" of spon-

Huge media chains

sorship often does the trick. If advertisers don't like a show, their "boycott" quietly drives it off the air.

Censorship often takes subtle forms. Reporters know the narrow range of "acceptable" stories – and many make these standards their own to advance their careers.

● Why did CBS's "Lou Grant" show die? It had a loyal audience, but the Kimberly-Clark Corporation led an advertiser boycott to punish star Ed Asner for his stinging criticism of U.S. policies in El Salvador – where Kimberly-Clark had a factory.

● *Ms. Magazine* failed in late 1989 for much the same reason: despite a readership that grew steadily to 550,000, advertisers shunned the magazine. General Foods wouldn't advertise because *Ms.* didn't carry recipes. Revlon was turned off by a cover story about Soviet women who "weren't wearing enough makeup." Clairol was outraged that *Ms.* briefly mentioned a congressional investigation into dangerous hair-dye chemicals. (Clairol was happy, however, to sponsor the ABC News special, "Blonds

Freedom of choice

Video news release on tourism in Jamaica

All these "programs" are really paid commercials

Have More Fun.")

• The TBS cable network's "World of Audubon" show on endangered forests was aired with no paid commercials – after all eight sponsors were strong-armed by the logging industry to pull out. A similar fate dashed *The New Yorker* magazine's plans for a 16-page environmental section on Earth Day 1990: The piece was cut in half because it didn't attract enough ads. When the marketing department complained that the writing was too "abrasive," the editor let them "fix" the article. They turned it into "a piece of pap," says author John C. Mitchell.

• Newspapers also pay a heavy price if they ignore such pressures.

When Seattle's two newspapers finally covered a dispute between the big Nordstrom clothing store and its workers, Nordstrom pulled out advertising worth over $1 million a year from the papers. Until then, the papers had published "a seemingly endless string of stories about Nordstrom's successes, rising stocks and profits, and the release of another line of fashions or fragrances," said a *Seattle Times* columnist. And that's what Nordstrom expected.

# What you see in today's news

News reporting is more effective as "bait" when it has lots of quick melodrama, action and sex appeal – and doesn't step on corporate toes. Advertisers welcome newscasts that focus on crime, scandal, disaster and celebrities, since channel-clickers will stop to watch a burning building or a drug bust – and linger for the ads if the newscaster promises more.

## It's like M-TV

Newscasts are becoming as fast-paced as M-TV videos, and even Presidential campaigns have deteriorated into a parade of emotional images and one-line "sound bites" created by candidates for the evening news. In the 1988 campaign George Bush refused to answer questions on issues, so the media just showed his carefully staged appearances at Disneyland or a flag factory. Many viewers couldn't tell the difference between news reports and commercials, reveals *AD Week*.

Newspapers like *USA Today* ape that quick-paced TV coverage, and other newspapers ape *USA Today*. What gets lost in all that flashiness is the news. A 1989 study revealed that Americans don't know much about political issues, and those who read the paper and/or watch TV news every day are slightly *worse* informed than those who aren't so addicted to the "news."

## News slips through

Journalists and TV writers still struggle to produce work that's honest and challenging. And sometimes they do report stories that offend corporate interests, including advertisers. Editors toler-

ate this to a degree, because extreme censorship would demoralize journalists, and because the credibility of the newspaper or newscast depends on including news that comes across as "objective" reporting.

## It's "objective"

Since reporters are supposed to be unbiased observers, they aren't allowed to be actively involved in issues they might cover. "Out of our manic concern about being compromised, we sometimes piously keep the community at arm's length . . . So we come off as distant, unfeeling, better at criticizing than celebrating, better at attacking than healing," admits the head of the Knight-Ridder newspaper chain.

That "distance" doesn't apply to the news corporation itself, however. Media companies lobby heavily for their corporate agendas.

## The official sources

Just to be safe, the news sections of most newspapers and TV shows ignore the private economy.

Many stories that deserve front-page headlines – such as a festering dump that could poison the community – don't get covered. But if the *government* has a big investigation underway – or groups are visibly pressuring authorities to act – that can attract media attention.

Flip through today's paper, and you'll find it's full of government actions and scandals, plus things the government investigates.

The media covers official government actions closely, and that makes it easy for government to decide what's covered and what isn't.

Why did the media close its eyes to the outrageous looting of HUD housing programs by rich political cronies throughout the 1980s? Because the feds didn't put out a news release on it. The media decided "nothing was happening with HUD," says that era's *New York Times* Washington Bureau chief, because they dismissed HUD chief Sam Pierce (the only black in the Reagan cabinet) as "someone who just was not important." Over the same years Education Secretary William Bennett got plenty of attention for doing little but make controversial statements.

When a Kansas reporter published news that a top official told a racist joke in the statehouse, other reporters clicked their tongues. Many, explained a Wichita reporter, believe "that unless something is formally on the record, you don't report it." Why? For one thing, reporters don't want the official sources they depend on to get mad and dry up. And accepting official statements without comment makes the media appear "neutral."

Newspapers often present stories that seem to conflict without investigating which is right. Examples A and B are based on two U.S. government reports issued the same day.

Example A
Feb. 5, 1991
P. 1 Business Section, *Detroit Free Press*

## Rust Belt ready to weather recession

New York Times

In the last recession, America's aging industrial heartland was widely considered to be incapable of saving itself.

But a government report issued Monday suggests that the Rust Belt has staged a renaissance on the factory floor. Thanks to a wrenching contraction in payrolls and plants, <u>productivity – the measure of output per hours worked – climbed to a record level in 1990.</u>

That . . . matches the level of output achieved in the 1960s, when American factories hummed at a feverish clip. The new data put U.S. manufacturers on a par with those of Japan and Western Europe . . .

Example B
Feb. 5, 1991
P. 2 Business Section, *Detroit Free Press*

## Productivity off for 2nd year in a row

Associated Press

WASHINGTON – <u>The productivity of America's non-farm workers fell 0.8 percent last year</u>, the worst decline since 1982 and the first back-to-back reversal – coupled with the 1989 drop of 0.7 percent – in a decade, the government said Monday . . .

The latest showing, said Jones, shows the United States is continuing to lose its competitive edge in international markets and threatens a long-term reduction in living standards . . .

Reporters sometimes do important stories like this one – but usually they don't have time

# Cheap & easy

Media workers are brought to heel by still another goal of commercial media: keep it cheap. As media companies boost profits by slashing budgets and laying off staff, real reporters don't have time to run around town, investigating as if they were Murphy Brown. Editors must find ever-cheaper ways to fill the "news hole."

Check the sources at the beginning of stories and photo captions in your local paper, and you'll find that most are clipped from a few major services, such as AP. Opinion columns and cartoons are supplied by national syndicates. Local news gets harder to find.

Since fewer than 20 American cities have more than one newspaper, there's not much competition for local readers to turn to.

## Is it news or a news release?

News media lift stories directly from the press releases of corporations and the government, often with no editing.

It's cheap, it's easy, and it gives them news or features they need. Viewers aren't aware that the TV news story they see on talking dolls or artificial voice synthesizers, for example, is really a video news release supplied by the company making the product.

In the 1980s, TV viewers heard Mike Mansfield, the U.S. ambassador to Japan, assure them on local news shows that "Japanese markets aren't as closed as we might think," while the screen showed American farm produce being shipped to Japan. Viewers weren't told that the "news report" was produced for the government of Japan by a Washington public relations firm. This was not an isolated incident: Three out of four TV stations surveyed in 1988 by Nielson admitted that they regularly put on the air video news releases sent them by companies and PR firms.

Sometimes the "cheap and easy" agenda means the media will also pick up stories from alternative groups who've done the expensive footwork. News of nuclear weapons at sea and the global trade in toxic wastes, for example, appeared after the environment-

Example C

## The Costs Of Cleaner Air

# Law to touch everyone in U.S.

Another flourish of the presidential pen, another 700-page pile of congressional compromising committed to law.

Will it matter to you and me?

In the case of the Clean Air Act that President Bush is scheduled to sign today, the answer is a yes. It will change our lives, eventually affecting almost everything we make and every breath we take.

For some companies the new law is a potential death sentence. For others, it's an automatic boom. For the rest of us, it's cleaner air – and thousands of less profound changes in our daily lives.

For example:

Expect to pay more for anything made in a factory that has a smokestack. The White House estimates that businesses eventually will spend $25 billion a year complying with the law, costs that will be passed on to consumers of everything from typewriters to toasters.

Small businesses won't be spared.

For the first time, government regulators are going to tell dry cleaners what kind of machines to use – the kind that keep the chemical soup of cleaning compounds from evaporating into the air.

Birmingham dry cleaner James Munson already has spent $500,000 preparing his two shops for the changes. He expects he'll have to spend hundreds of thousands more in . . .

– continued

Typical media image of workers

al group Greenpeace dug up the facts and staged actions to dramatize their importance. (Even then, such stories may be buried in the back pages or get just a 30-second once-over.)

## No time to think

When the story in example E showed up in the *Detroit Free Press*, one local reader got angry. How come they write about the *inconvenience* of a strike, but don't discuss the *issues* that led to the walkout?

When the reader phoned the reporter to complain, he learned that this bias wasn't really the journalist's fault. An editor had assigned a reporter to cover the story who wasn't a labor reporter, and he already had two other stories to complete by a 4:30 p.m. deadline. The editors told him to focus on the "idlings," and the copy editor wrote the headline. He had no time to research the issues, but it was easy to get quotes from GM's huge public relations department.

# Where are the rest of us?

Regular folks are more likely to appear as victims of a fire or other disaster than as workers or parents. A 1990 study of 1,000 network evening news broadcasts discovered that just two percent of news time was devoted to worker issues – including child care and wages. Even the workplace hazards that kill up to 70,000 workers each year weren't considered news. Almost two-thirds of the limited worker coverage focused on one strike. Stories about business – without workers – got twice as much coverage as worker concerns.

Example C shows a page-one story about the Clean Air Act of 1990. The whole story devotes just three words to the life-saving benefits of clean air. Not until five days later did example D appear – buried far inside the "D" section of the paper.

In Boston, almost nine out of ten mainstream news stories on two largely black neighborhoods were about crime or violent accidents, a month-long 1987 survey showed. In contrast, the two African-American papers covering the same neighborhoods showed a community thirsty for education and striving to remedy poor living conditions.

## The rich & famous

You'll rarely find anyone you know – or would run into – in the "people" or lifestyle sections of the news or daily paper. And why are there all those daily pages of stock prices and Dow Jones updates on the nightly news? Four out of five Americans own no stock at all.

In dramatic TV shows, two out of three characters are men, and most are white-collar and well-off. Yet in real life, only 15% of male workers have professional white-collar jobs. The only blue-collar workers around are usually cops whose main function is to keep the action rolling.

TV heroes are beautifully dressed, they have huge, clean kitchens, and they never fail to solve their problems in less than 25 minutes. A 17-year study from the University of Pennsylvania reports that most viewers feel this TV world is more "real" than their own.

## Why are we left out?

Some say that's what people want, that we want to escape through television. Yet when the "Roseanne" show appeared, it rocketed to the top of the ratings almost overnight. "Despite the size – and spending power – of working-class America, most marketers don't want their products associated with the masses," explains *The Wall Street Journal*.

It's hard for groups of average Americans to even *buy* a hearing in the media. Frustrated by poor coverage during their 1989 Pittston strike, the United Mine Workers produced an ad explaining their goal was to save health care and pension benefits. Only one Washington TV station would air it. Others made the union take out the company's name, and one station wouldn't even take the censored version.

Why would the media refuse paid ads? WHDH-TV in Boston found out in 1990, when it ran a 30-second spot produced by Neighbor to Neighbor that 28 other stations had refused to air. The ad, which called for a boycott of Folgers coffee, so enraged Procter & Gamble that the company yanked ads for all its products (worth $1 million a year) from WHDH.

## What about public stations?

Even non-commercial options like the Public Broadcasting System (PBS) are so hobbled by cuts in public funding that they cater to the elitism of rich sponsors. A two-year City University of New York study discovered that the upper crust gets ten times more prime-time program hours than workers do on PBS, and that two out of three of the few workers you see have British accents. Some PBS stations make direct appeals to snobs: "Narrowcasting to serve your rare and sophisticated tastes," is how one PBS station promotes itself.

## Where you fit in

Although grassroots groups and unions can sometimes attract media attention or develop friendly relations with a reporter, the deck is stacked against us. The public desperately needs an alternative. And that's where you come in.

No matter how inexperienced you are as a newspaper or newsletter editor, you're filling a vacuum. When people want news about people they know, neighborhoods they live in, places they work, and their own organizations, they have to turn to you. They'll be grateful to find out what's behind political or economic news, or to discover that other people share their frustrations and burdens.

Recent revolutions in printing and typesetting now make it possible to turn that potential into reality with very little training and a modest budget. Chapters 5, 6 and 7 give the lowdown.

### You're the alternative

The alternative media, whether it's community groups, clubs, agencies or unions, can and should do more than just tell what your organization is up to. The gap only you can fill includes:

• **Take on news that goes beyond** your group's normal activities. Subscribe to as many alternative publications (p. 88) as possible, so you can pass along their news.

• **Offer well-rounded coverage of** people's lives, not just "news." Community and shop or office papers are published by folks who care about and understand their readers. What makes

Why your newsletter or paper is special

Example D

## Clean Air Act aims to limit pollution-related health risk

Risk of cancer, respiratory disease, heart ailments and reproductive disorders will drop, but it will cost about $25 billion a year in higher consumer prices, say experts on the landmark Clean Air Act that President George Bush signed last week.

Dirty air has been killing at least 50,000 Americans and Canadians a year, putting millions of children and the elderly at risk of respiratory ailments, boosting child asthma cases and costing billions annually in health care costs and lost time at work or school, health experts have told Congress.

– continues

Example E

## Delco strike's impact grows, idling 33,385

A continuing strike at General Motors Corp.'s Delco Electronics subsidiary in Indiana will close or partially idle six more GM facilities today, doubling the number of employes laid off nationwide to 33,385.

GM Chairman Roger Smith has warned that the four-day-old UAW work stoppage in Kokomo could shut all of GM's 31 U.S. car and truck assembly plants if it continues much longer.

"If the strike is allowed to go too much longer, we'll be completely shut down," Smith said. He placed no time estimate on a complete shutdown.

The Kokomo plant, which was struck this week by 7,700 workers, makes car radios and electronic engine components.

Detroit area plants shut down by the strike earlier this week are the Clark Street complex, which has 5,500 workers and was shut down Wednesday, and the Detroit-Hamtramck assembly operation, which has 3,500 workers and was shut down Thursday. Today the Orion Township assembly plant will be idled, affecting 5,600 workers.

In addition to Orion, other plants newly affected by the strike are assembly plants in Linden, N.J. and Wilmington, Del., which build Chevrolet's new Corsica and Beretta models.

About 5,600 workers were told not to report today at Linden and Wilmington, and an extended shutdown at those plants could affect the introduction of the new models.

Though the nationwide launch of the new models is not scheduled until March 12, GM had hoped to make several thousand available to car rental companies in hopes of having the new compact models serve as rolling billboards.

Other GM shutdowns will affect 5,000 workers at GM's Fairfax, Kan. plant and 1,032 employes on one shift at the company's Lordstown, Ohio facility, who were told not to report to work today. Another 153 workers at a GM component facility in Anderson, Ind. will also remain off the job.

The company's Bowling Green, Ky. and Wentzville, Mo. plants will remain closed, idling a total of 7,000 workers.

Company officials met with representatives of UAW Local 292 at GM headquarters for the second consecutive day Thursday.

"We're still hopeful that General Motors will make some moves soon, and we can resolve the situation," said Reg McGhee, a UAW spokesman. The strike began after a dispute between company officials over transferring some work to Mexico.

Because of GM's "just in time" inventory system, which is designed to eliminate costly inventory by having parts made and delivered as needed, the effect of the strike was felt early.

About 3,000 workers were idled Tuesday, only one day into the strike.

That number doubled to 6,000 Wednesday, then more than doubled to 16,200 Thursday. It is to double again today.

them popular is that people can see their own lives fairly represented: their jobs, their activities, their history, their concerns. The heroes of your publication are co-workers and neighbors, people who never normally get the recognition they deserve.

Give other folks a fair shake too. Even a neighborhood on the other side of town might deserve a story every so often. If your readers never hear about those people except when there's a brutal murder or other disaster, it only heightens the fear and suspicion that pits one working-class group or neighborhood against another.

● **Show how everyone's involved in the economy**, not just executives. Economics isn't just "business." Nor are economic problems just dry facts and formulas to be discussed by the "experts." Economics is dramatic news that profoundly affects us all. And whether we're at work or at home, we all play economic roles that have an impact.

Help your readers understand that mysterious world with down-to-earth stories and explanations.

● **Don't be afraid to go after business.** Since you don't have large corporate advertisers breathing down your neck, you can report what actually goes on. Although keeping tabs on the government is important, keep a leery eye on business, too.

# Journalistic myths to avoid

Like it or not, most journalists must work for the commercial media to make a living, and must accept its commercial standards. But the alternative press can afford to question them. Here are ones to steer clear of:

## Myth #1: All reporting must be "objective"

To be "objective," you'd give equal weight to all sides of every issue, and only take sides in editorials. Such objectivity can help commercial reporters resist the power advertisers and publishers exert. Since a commercial paper's bias leans toward corporate owners and advertisers, trying to avoid bias is a fine idea – for them.

No reporting is really objective, however. Who you quote, the words you use, what facts you pick, how much space you give different stories, all reflect a point of view about what's true and what's important. A reporter can appear "objective" merely by sticking to official sources, avoiding controversy and not drawing any conclusions.

The alternative press, however, can be proud of its bias. A union newsletter doesn't represent supervisors and managers; they already have their say in day-to-day control, and can publish their own newsletters whenever they want. Likewise, a community paper doesn't have to pander to the politicians and business leaders who already have enormous influence over the economy and commercial media.

Don't waste your group's meager resources giving them equal time. Only by catering to "forgotten" people and their groups and ideas can you correct the tremendous imbalance all around you.

When your bias favors people and public interests, don't hide it. Just make sure your opinions flow from facts and experiences, and that you give readers the evidence to arrive at similar conclusions themselves (Chapters 10 and 11).

## Myth #2: You can say anything in editorials

Commercial papers supposedly reserve the editorial pages for all opinion and commentary. But divorcing opinion from fact isn't such a noble goal even if it were possible.

Once editorial opinion is freed from fact, it can center around prejudice, self-interest and guesswork. You'll get a lot closer to the truth by combining fact with opinion in all editorial comments, as well as articles.

Don't be tempted to throw around ideas you can't prove just because you wrote "editorial" above the column. And consider how your opinions fit the goals of the group you're writing for. Use the paper to inform people, bring them closer to each other, and support their interests, not just blow off steam.

## Myth #3: "Human interest" vs. hard news

In commercial papers, "hard news" stories report on the decisions leaders make. And "human interest" stories about people often center on the bizarre, the trivial and the strictly personal

Hard news vs. human interest

Human interest          Hard news

side of people's lives.

The commercial media fragment the world around us. Just as divorcing news from editorials discourages us from drawing conclusions from the facts, separating "human interest" from news encourages us to think there's nothing human about the news. That makes politics seem abstract and untouchable, while human events seem unimportant and private. It downplays the effect political events have on living and breathing people, as well as the effect people can have on political events.

In your paper, don't separate life into cubbyholes. Features about your readers should reach beyond their hobbies, quirks and private lives. Bring out the human aspect to all news, showing what it'll mean to the average person. And report on how your readers react to the news, how they think, and how they shape events, both great and small. Show them as the backbone of powerful groups, not just isolated individuals.

### Myth #4: Anything from official sources is news

Whenever the mayor holds a news conference it gets front page headlines, even when he doesn't say anything at all. Since the mayor is well covered, it's your job to show what's going on with the rest of us, or what's fishy about the official line.

### Myth #5: Any change makes news

Real change is news, but day-to-day reality is more important to most of us than meaningless changes. For instance, if the mayor appoints a new tax assessor, that's supposed to be news, even if the new assessor does just what the old one did. The real news is how assessors do their work, and which property owners or tenants end up paying more taxes. Don't ignore long-term trends like global warming that have no "hook" to lure the commercial media.

### Myth #6: Shoehorn facts into the opening

The biggest commercial papers come

out every day. The typical first paragraph of a news article tells the facts of what happened or what was said yesterday: who, what, where, when. A few more paragraphs elaborate on it; by the time you turn to page 20 to read the end of the article, they're discussing the Secretary of State's necktie.

Reporters must structure articles this way so the editor can chop them off anywhere after the first few paragraphs. That way, the editor can quickly adjust each article's length to the amount of advertising, and no one will know the difference. Few people are expected to read beyond the first couple of paragraphs anyhow, especially if you have to flip through the paper to find a continuation. It's called an *inverted pyramid* style of writing.

Don't mimic the inverted pyramid, especially that first paragraph, just because it's what you're used to. You don't publish every day, and yesterday's who-what-where-when isn't the meat of your articles. Instead, start by convincing readers that the information is important to them (p. 116) so they'll read the whole article. And keep each article short enough to fit on a page or two, rather than continuing it on a back page.

"Objective" reporting

## Setting an editorial policy

### Why you need a policy

Every TV network or commercial paper has a purpose: to make a profit.

Every shop, office, community or other non-profit paper also serves a purpose: to strengthen your group, its members and its goals.

To fulfill your goals, you'll be forced to make tough editorial decisions. When a member writes something that con-

## Our Editorial Policy

*To our readers:* This paper is the voice of your local and international union. This is our *only* vehicle for bringing to you, on a regular basis, the views and actions of the leaders you elected, so you can evaluate them. Through the paper we explain union policies and show how your dues are spent.

The paper is also the voice of the members. We welcome articles from members· and stories about members.

While we welcome your contributions, we ask that they be constructive. All articles should contribute positively to the welfare of this union and its members, and we will accept no attacks on any union leader or member. We will accept a thoughtful discussion of all related issues in the letters column, and reserve the right to reply to those that seem to reflect a misunderstanding of the union and its policies.

We look forward to hearing from you.

---

tradicts your program or criticizes the leadership, will you print it? Will you ever give targets of criticism a chance to reply in your paper?

If you don't control the range of viewpoints your paper presents, it won't help anyone sort out the confusions and contradictions all around us, or inspire people to join together and act. And people tend to judge the whole group on the basis of what each article says.

On the other hand, if your readers don't get a chance to contribute various opinions to the paper, it risks becoming the voice of a small sect; and whether your positions are right or wrong, your paper will become boring and irrelevant if people feel it leaves them out.

The best papers solve this dilemma by striking a balance midway. They print a range of views, so long as they come from the shop floor or grassroots, are based on evidence, and aren't destructive to the group. They establish an editorial policy that highlights the purpose the paper must serve. By outlining your policy and distributing it to people who want to write for the paper, you'll avoid confusion and arguments.

### Guidelines you might include:

• **No article should insult any member** of your group or your allies. Nix slurs on women, government workers, students, tenants, blacks or whites, oldsters, etc.

• **Don't let people dump** on the group's leaders and its basic goals and strategies, especially when your publication is used to recruit new members. Let your enemies handle that. And avoid catering to powerful people and institutions whose influence you're trying to counterbalance.

• **All controversial ideas** must be backed with evidence.

• **Don't use words and expressions** that'll turn your audience off unnecessarily. Use Chapter 1 as a guide to develop specific dos and don'ts.

• **Where your paper has its own style rules**, like how to abbreviate the organization's name, spell it out in the Editorial Policy.

### Bylines

Each paper also sets a policy for how an author's name will appear. Giving each writer credit at the beginning of an article makes the publication look like a group project (unless one person wrote all the articles). It also makes the individual writer responsible for what the article says.

When you print an article without an author's name, the reader can assume the article speaks for the entire group. However, a paper full of such articles can seem cold, and controlled by too few people.

### Be realistic

Setting a clear policy doesn't mean every article is a puff piece. If you pretend everyone agrees on everything and success is easy, it'll seem about as real as a pink steel mill. If your group is basically on the right track, a little honesty about failures and problems won't kill you; it'll make your paper lively and realistic. Just don't let it get nasty.

On issues where your group has no clear policy, like whether to raise dues or how well the child-care center is working, feel free to air several sides.

### Letters, we get letters

Let it all hang out on the letters page. There you might even print articles that don't conform to your policy – criticisms of your group, debates on issues, or a demand for different priorities. But don't print lies (p. 29).

Here's your chance to print gripes that represent the private feelings of many readers. By making them into letters, you bring the debate into the open. If it's a worthy criticism of your group, follow it up with a thank-you or explanation, and tell how you're working to fix the problem. Answer some letters with an "editor's reply," explaining in a friendly way why your group doesn't go along with this or that point.

Many groups insist that all letters be signed, even if the name won't be printed. Then a union paper, for example, can make sure the letter was written by a member, not a supervisor.

# 4. The basics: staff, money & the law

## Staff

**M**ost community, church, club, activist, workplace and union papers are at least in part a labor of love. Grassroots writers, cartoonists, reporters, photographers and editors are the lifeblood of such papers and newsletters.

You may also need at least one staff person to work full-time, but that has its dangers. If one person controls the whole show, other people figure it's not their job, and may not be willing to lend a hand. Some local unions solve that dilemma by dividing money to hire staff among a whole committee. Then several people get time off work to devote to the paper. That can lead to a top-quality paper, because the editors don't lose touch with members at work, and with conditions readers are up against.

But other groups may have to choose between scrounging up money for a full-time editor or having no paid staff at all.

## Organizing your work group

Organizing is the hardest part of publishing a newsletter or paper.

First of all, recruit a newspaper committee. The only way to publish a paper that truly represents your group is to have a group oversee it (p. 4).

### Beware of depending too much on one editor

As soon as the paper becomes a one-person job, it becomes a headache; it's just not much fun working all by yourself. The lone editor who becomes isolated from the rest of your group becomes bitter about all the unappreciated work he or she does.

The lone editor often complains that no one will lend a hand, that no one else can be depended on. Yet often it's the same editor who makes it impossible for anyone to join in because the editor won't share decisions, follows a hectic, impossible schedule, and doesn't communicate well (except in writing).

Because the lone editor puts so much into the paper, he or she begins to feel it's personal property, and not really the group's. And if that editor moves, dies, loses interest or goes crazy, there's no one to step into those shoes, and the paper will either die or have to start again from scratch.

No matter how talented and dedicated your editor is, one person just can't produce the publication your group needs all alone.

### Recruiting the committee

If you wait for volunteers to sign up, you'll never get going. To recruit your committee, flatter people ("You know more about what's going on in this neighborhood than anyone else". . . "You have a great way with words and

Poorly organized group

are just the person we need"), lure them with promises of fame and good company, appeal to their self-interest ("It'll be much easier to get re-elected if people see your name in the paper each month"). Hold contests to find the talents you need.

Not everyone who writes for the paper or hands it out needs to be on the newspaper committee (although you should give them all credit in the paper). The committee sees the paper through, beginning to end. If you've got a full-time editor, the committee gives the editor valuable feedback and input.

Look for people with skills, but don't just fill the committee with your most educated members. You'll do better with a cross-section that can truly represent your group and its members, and who understand the purpose the paper serves. At least one officer of your group, perhaps the vice president, should serve on the committee, so it won't stray from the priorities of the elected leadership.

Once you've cleared the first hurdles of launching a committee, it will start to run itself. If the editor's sick, out of town or just plain pooped, someone else will know the job well enough to fill in. When someone new wants to join the committee, there'll be several people who can train the newcomer, depending on who's free at the moment.

### Beyond the core committee
• Involve as many people as you

can. Even the person who has only one evening a month to spare should be given something concrete to do that one evening. Divide up tasks into their parts so, for example, one person can make up headlines, another is a "stringer" reporter, and another hands out the paper or delivers it to the supermarket. If each wants to do more, fine.

Making the paper a group project will at first mean more work for the harried editor and committee. It requires a sane schedule that everyone can adapt to. It requires recruiting and training people. It requires sensitivity to everyone's often exasperating personalities, and a willingness to appreciate and develop each person's abilities.

Yet the rewards are well worth the trouble. As more people are involved in putting the publication together, more feel it's their paper. They'll read it avidly themselves, and they'll encourage others to read and appreciate it. They'll have a stake in wanting the paper continued and improved. You'll have transformed many from passive, lukewarm supporters of your group to active, enthusiastic members.

• **Find reporters** for each area your paper covers, people who serve as eyes and ears in the neighborhood, office or plant. They can pick up interesting happenings you'd never find out otherwise, such as the story of someone who fought an unfair speeding ticket in court and won. Reporters find out what people think of the paper, what they read and enjoy, and what they don't.

Overambition

# Problems you might encounter

## Overambition

If you try to accomplish too much in too little time, you'll likely end up with a few people running around, going crazy and being cross with everyone else.

Overambitious goals place inhuman burdens on a group and discourage people from joining in. When your own work pace is insane, people might start wondering about your ideals of a just society. They might rightly feel they're being sacrificed to your ego(s).

## Not enough help

This is the opposite side of the coin. Fit what you're doing to your resources,

even if it limits you to a four-page newsletter every other month.

Publishing every other month is the least you can do and still pretend to be putting out a paper. When the paper comes out less often, everyone will forget it exists between issues, and they won't look forward to it. Much of the news will be embarrassingly old hat, and not at all exciting.

Some editors wait for the first issue of the paper to be published before pulling together a full staff. It's often easier to get people involved in something they can see, than in an idea that's still rumbling around in your head.

## Leadership

A good leader inspires others, but a bad leader ends up with no followers.

Good leadership means someone sets up a coherent strategy and organization which others join, try out, and modify to their liking. A good leader discusses ideas and is willing to share credit and glory as well as work. The best leaders are even wrong once in a while.

## Volunteer work

It's hard for people to take their work with you as seriously as their jobs and families. And no busy person can avoid occasional crises which cut into volunteer work. You can make volunteer labor easier:

• **Have a clear schedule** (p. 77), and stick to it. The more likely it is that the newsletter will come out two weeks late anyhow, the more likely it is people will put off doing the work.

• **Don't waste people's time.** No one wants to give up a valuable Saturday, perhaps going to a lot of trouble to get a sitter, just to sit around and watch you try to figure things out. If someone commits time to your publication, set

aside something for that person to do.

• **Take their work seriously.** If you don't, people will realize that their names in the staff box are just a token gesture. Don't rewrite people's articles behind their backs, no matter how little time you think you have. Instead give them enough guidance to do it right themselves (p. 122).

• **Adjust to volunteer problems.** Since most people have jobs and/or families, organize work around those responsibilities. Arrange babysitting possibilities before you ask people to help. Schedule the heaviest work for weekends or other times when people are likely to be free. To keep to your schedule, you should never have to stay up all night before the deadline.

• **When helpers lose interest** and drop out, find out why. Someone might unintentionally be pushing them out by giving them more work than they're comfortable with, or by not giving them enough guidance to do the job well.

Poor leadership

# How much money do you need?

Plan a budget now, so you won't be caught off guard when you need cash.

## Typical expenses:

• **Staff**, if any.

• **Printing.** Chapter 7 discusses the alternatives and their costs. Even when you're using another group's machine, budget money for supplies like paper, ink and staples (p. 57).

• **Typesetting.** Chapters 5 and 6 give typing and typesetting alternatives. Even when you just peck away on an old office typewriter, you need to buy new ribbons and correcting tape and pay for occasional repairs.

• **Taxes.** If you're non-profit or get a resale number from the state, you pay no sales tax on expenses like printing.

• **Reporting expenses.** When reporters cover far-flung stories, they may need money for travel and other expenses. Researching some stories will involve long-distance phone calls.

• **Photographs** make the paper look worth reading. You can probably find a group member with a good camera, but plan to pay for film, paper and develop-

ing. And the printer will likely charge extra for each photograph used.

• **Office space** – unless you work out of a kitchen or donated area.

• **Paste-up and layout equipment.** See p. 150 for the bare bones needed to put the paper together.

• **Distribution.** Chapter 19 gives the options, from mailing to handouts.

• **Sanity.** When members spend long hours at editorial meetings or laying out pages, have refreshments on hand to keep them going.

## Raising money

If you're non-profit, get legal tax-exempt status so you don't pay taxes on whatever you raise (p. 170).

However, just because your group couldn't make money if you fell over it doesn't mean the state or feds will consider you tax-exempt. The guidelines get tighter every year. If you're close to an existing tax-exempt group, it might sponsor your paper as its own project; but that could muzzle you – see p. 29.

The ideal way to publish a paper is to set aside a portion of dues money. Then you can concentrate on making it a top-notch paper, free from daily worries about the green stuff. The other ways can be extremely time-consuming. Here they are:

Too much advertising

# Supporting your paper with ads

This may be the way to go for a community paper. It provides a steady flow of funds, while it can also give neighborhood merchants a plug. But before you take the plunge, see if you can answer "yes" to these questions:

## Questions to consider

• Do you have a decent computer or typesetter? Most merchants expect you to design and typeset ads for them.

• Do you have a reliable distribution system? Merchants will buy ads only when they know the paper's getting out. Ask members to keep records of how many papers they distribute.

• Is at least one responsible person willing to sell ads? If you think the editor can solicit ads on the side, you may be in for a big surprise. It's a hefty job and will seriously cut into the editor's essential work.

• Does your paper come out on a strict schedule? Merchants will sign on the dotted line only if they know the paper is published regularly.

• Will the money advertising yields be worth the time spent drumming up ads, designing and typesetting them? To get a member off work to hawk advertising space, a union may end up spending more on "lost time" than the ads themselves take in.

• Will advertising jack up your

40% ads is a lot

One column-inch

Six column-inch ad

## How much should you charge for ads?

Base your rates on how many *column-inches* they take up in the paper. A column-inch is one inch tall and one column wide. Charge the same for a ten column-inch ad, whether it's two columns wide and five inches tall, or one column wide and ten inches tall. Give discounts for bigger ads, and ads that run for several issues of the paper.

Here are things to consider when setting your ad rates:

**1.** How much does it cost to publish your paper? Take into account every item from p. 25, plus expenses drumming up ads and typesetting them.

**2.** How much of your total budget must you raise through advertising? Let's say your eight-page paper costs $680 to produce. But since you get a $205 subsidy from member dues, you need only $475 from ads each issue.

**3.** How much of the paper can be filled with ads? Set a strict limit, reserving no more than 20% to 40% of total space for ads. Although commercial papers are up to 60% pure advertising, don't model your paper after them. Chapter 3 explains why.

**4.** How much ad space will you sell? Suppose you publish an eight-page paper with three columns of type per page, and each page is 17" tall. Measure the maximum height for a column of type. If you leave a ½" margin on both top and bottom, each col-

umn will be 16" tall.

Multiply the column height times the number of columns per page to get total column-inches per page. Three columns times 16" gives you a total of 48 column-inches.

Multiply that times the number of pages. In our example, eight pages would have 384 column-inches of room (48 per page times 8 pages).

Multiply total column-inches times the percent ads are allowed to occupy. If up to 30% of that 8-page paper can be ads, don't sell more than 115 column-inches of advertising. (30% of 384 column-inches = 115.) If you can't resist selling more, expand the paper.

**5.** Make sure you'll get the money you need from available space. If you must make $475 from 115 column-inches of advertising, you'll charge over $4 per column-inch. Boost your standard rate so you can offer discounts for bigger ads or long-term contracts. Tack on a few cents extra to cover slow periods and bad debts – merchants who buy an ad on credit and then don't pay. And either charge extra when you're asked to typeset and lay out an ad, or include those expenses in your basic rates.

**6.** Check out advertising rates for other small papers in your area. If they're a lot steeper, raise your prices too. Circulation is a key factor. If you distribute only half as many papers as the local community paper does, don't charge nearly as much for ads.

mailing rates or taxes? If ads take up more than 10% of the paper and you mail Second-Class (p. 169), your mailing rates go up. Also, if your group takes in $1,000 a year in advertising and other income *unrelated* to the basic non-profit mission stated in your charter or articles of incorporation, then a non-profit group must pay taxes on profits the ads bring in. (Ads for your group, its T-shirts, or other activities don't count, however, as *unrelated* advertising. For unions, neither do small ads for opticians and other providers of union-won benefits.)

Once your *unrelated* income tops $1,000, your life changes. You must keep track of all income and expenses (including printing costs and staff time) devoted to advertising separately from income and expenses for the rest of the paper. If the paper's a money-loser, you may not owe taxes. But if just reading this gives you a headache, then don't cross that $1,000 threshold.

• **Will you limit how much of the paper's space is given to advertisers?** If you go along with commercial norms, the ads will take up most of the paper, overwhelm your articles, and destroy your group's image. To keep your paper from becoming an ad rag, don't rely exclusively on ads for money. If too much advertising comes in, are you prepared to either say no or write more articles and expand the paper?

• **Can you work out a reasonable "code" for advertising?** Even commercial papers have standards – most won't take gun ads, for example.

• **Can you resist advertising pressure?** Advertisers are spoiled and can be very demanding (p. 15). They're used to getting their way with commercial papers, which bend over backwards to please them. They'll demand to be given the choice spots in the paper and threaten to pull out their ads when you criticize them or their allies. You may have to take a financial hit to say, "No, this is our paper, not yours." Remember, your first aim is to inform readers, not sell lawnmowers.

## Why you need an advertising code

As a grassroots publication, you have a responsibility not to send readers to a place that'll rob them blind. Nor should you advertise companies involved in a nasty labor dispute or banks that refuse

An ad you wouldn't accept

to loan in your neighborhood. That means you must check out all advertisers.

Beyond that, your paper should *never* accept "issues" advertising, like selling space to Turnoff Light & Power company so it can justify another electric rate increase. Such ads are professionally designed and so flashy they'll overwhelm the rest of your paper. Then all your hard work will be serving the light & power company, not your group's goals. Some groups refuse all ads except those from members and local merchants you know.

Every group must also make strict rules for where ads can go and where they can't. Never allow advertising on the front page, for example. See p. 140 for more.

## Special rules for unions

U.S. law says union papers must either steer clear of union politics or give all sides equal coverage (p. 34), and that applies to advertising, too. If you accept ads from one candidate, you must offer similar ad space to all candidates for the same office. If you carry ads, you may have to accept ads from members disputing union policy.

### Selling ads

Don't expect to break even the first few issues of the paper. To get a new paper off the ground, throw in a number of big public-service or "good will" ads. Then merchants can picture how their own ads will look.

Print your rate structure on a little card, or in a brochure with the sizes of available ads sketched out for merchants to look at. Put your strong points in writing – number of readers (does more than one person read the average paper?), their incomes, etc.

Merchants will tire of dealing with a new ad representative each month; you need a regular salesperson to build good relations with each advertiser. Consider offering a commission of 10%-30% to steady ad salespeople. Hawking ads is such frustrating work that a financial reward may be needed to keep a dependable person on the job.

# Grassroots fundraising

Raising money from readers is time-consuming, but it can be lots of fun. A good fundraiser can help build a spirit of camaraderie within your group, plus recruit new members.

### Be careful

Beware of planning big extravaganzas, however, like an all-day festival or a concert. Such events need a dedicated crew of workers who know what they're doing and will hammer out every detail. You may have to lay out big money up-front, and you can never be sure you'll get that investment back.

Look for fundraising ideas that bring in the most money with the least work and up-front cash.

### Suggested fundraisers

• **Sell subscriptions to the paper.** Even if it's normally free, ask loyal readers to pay to get the paper mailed to their homes.

• **Hold a sale.** Bake sales, auctions and flea markets are all tried and true money-makers.

• **Regular sustainers.** Your wealthier fans could "sponsor" the paper by contributing a hefty amount each year. Reward sustainers by inviting them to fundraising events free of charge.

• **Make something to sell.** Advertise your group's special T-shirt, poster, calendar or holiday cards in your paper. But remember, seasonal items like calendars must be sold out within a short period, or you're stuck. Think of a catchy slogan that will entice readers to display your poster or wear your T-shirt. It may be the best publicity your paper gets.

• **Benefit plays and movies.** A sympathetic theater group or movie-maker might offer you a free or inexpensive showing. Invite people to stick around and socialize after the show, while you sell them drinks and other items.

• **Parties, picnics and dinners.** Show people a good time, and don't overload the program with dull speeches. Once guests arrive, pick up a few bucks beyond the admission price by selling raffle tickets. Or, after one freebie, charge for drinks. Sell those T-shirts and subscriptions. Then auction off a year's subscription.

At a picnic, hold a sports event and sell "chances" on who will win or how well each person will finish.

• **Walk-a-thons and races.** Ask members who enter to get buddies and co-workers to pledge a donation for each mile they complete.

• **Raffles, bingo, etc.** Even if no one really expects to win that big TV, they'll be quicker to donate when there's a chance. Pick lots of second- and third-prize winners who'll get free subscriptions to the paper or your group's T-shirt or poster. (But first, ask your printer or the state lottery or gambling division if state law requires you to get a raffle or bingo permit.)

Get local businesses to donate stuff for you to raffle by treating them right. If possible, someone they know (maybe a regular customer) should approach each business and cultivate a friendship. Have a pamphlet you can drop off, explaining what you'll do with the gift.

After they've given, thank each one with a personal note, plus a copy of your paper that lists and thanks each donor. Put them on your mailing list, and keep in touch.

### More information

For more about grassroots fundrais-

ing schemes, get a copy of *The Grass-roots Fundraising Book: How to Raise Money in Your Community,* by Joan Flanagan for the Youth Project. (Write Contemporary Books, 180 N. Michigan Ave., Chicago, IL 60601.).

## Applying for a grant

This isn't the gravy train it once seemed to be. It probably isn't worth going after big foundations, and you won't find a sugar daddy who'll take care of everything. Your best bets are people and small foundations who are already committed to your goals; for them, you might write just a letter, not a formal proposal.

### Looking for a patron

A typical foundation wants to fund something new, and isn't the slightest bit interested in paying your overhead. If you think it's worth a shot, start looking in your community. Visit a public or special "foundation" library and thoroughly research local foundations.

Look at the 990-PF report each one files with the IRS, and see what kinds of groups it gives to. Look up its guidelines, and read something on how to write a proposal. Get a list of foundation libraries called "Cooperating Collections Network" from the Foundation Center, 79 5th Ave., N.Y., N.Y. 10005.

### Tax-exempt status: 501(c)(3)

Donors expect to deduct gifts from their taxes. But here's the hitch: They can only deduct gifts to groups with special 501(c)(3) non-profit status. To get that, you may have to sell your soul – you can no longer back political candidates or take a stand on ballot issues.

## Your legal rights & limitations

Since your paper serves a cause and a grassroots audience, you must aggressively pursue readers' interests. Yet many editors beat around the bush because they're afraid of being sued. In reality, your right to freedom of the press gives you considerable leeway.

### You could be sued

No amount of respect for the law will guarantee you won't be sued. That means someone filed a lawsuit, even when there isn't a legal leg to stand on. Suing can be a grandstand act by a bruised ego who'll drop the case later. It can be mostly harassment.

Being sued is scary and can be expensive; it could take an appeal to get justice in a borderline libel case. But a free press is basic to democracy, and your rights are guaranteed by the U.S. and Canadian constitutions. If you don't know and use them when necessary, you could lose them.

Remind anyone who threatens to sue that the publicity over a phony libel case can hurt them. What's more, they may be told to pay all your legal expenses. In the U.S., you can turn around and sue the harasser for malicious prosecution and abuse of your constitutional rights. In 1986, a lawyer for the plumbers' union won $5.5 million from Shell Oil after the company dragged him into court for revealing that a plastic pipe Shell made could cause cancer.

### Canadian vs. U.S. law

While your basic rights are similar in both countries, Canadian libel law varies from one province to another. Key differences, such as who has to prove what's true (see below), make it easier for someone to successfully sue a Canadian paper for libel. And Canadian labour law doesn't spell out special rights and duties of union communicators, as American law does.

## Your rights under libel law

Telling the truth for a good reason is your best defense against libel lawsuits. Don't print rumors. Check out the facts on controversial statements and get details like dates exactly right. Don't exaggerate and don't hint at something that isn't true. Attack only when it serves the group or public interest. And use only information that comes from sources you can trust.

When you stick to the truth for a valid purpose you're always safe (except in Quebec). What's "valid?" That depends on state law, but any situation that gets a "qualified privilege" (p. 31) should be okay.

• **In Quebec,** you must not only prove you're telling the truth, but also that your statement is in the public interest, and you weren't being malicious.

### Telling the truth

• **Who's to say what's true?** You or the person suing? In the U.S., the person who feels unjustly attacked has to prove what you said is *un*true. The U.S. Supreme Court confirmed that in 1986 (*Philadelphia Newspapers Inc. vs. Maurice S. Hepps*). Don't let this be an excuse to get lazy, however. You must show that you had good reason to believe you were telling the truth – that you have reliable witnesses, documents, or other evidence to back up controversial attacks.

In Canada, the burden of proof is on the editor. You must prove your statements *are* true.

• **You're in hot water if a false or unfair statement damages or destroys** someone's "reputation" – if your words lower that person in the eyes of others, expose him or her to ridicule, or cause him or her to be shunned or avoided. That person can successfully sue you for libel if it's also proved that you're wrong on matters of fact, not opinion – or said it just to be mean.

• **Naming names.** There's no point in hinting about who's who when you go after a foreman who's harassing women or a landlord who won't clean the back hall. If that person can be identified by your hints, it's the same as if you said the name outright. Go ahead and say what you want directly, protecting yourself by making sure it's true.

• **Name-calling.** This can be dangerous. Don't call a supervisor or developer a villain or a liar if you aren't prepared to prove it. Rather than attack someone's whole character, pick out a specific time you know for sure the person lied, and talk about that.

Even worse are exaggerations – calling someone an idiot or a fascist. Those charges can be tough to defend.

### Other dangerous false or unfair statements

These can get you in hot water, even when you don't damage anyone's reputation. They are:

• **Saying people can't do the job** or profession at which they earn a living. Don't call the store manager or supervisor a stupid incompetent. Say instead Mr. Gonzo caused chaos in the department by a specific stupid thing he did.

• **Calling people crooks,** frauds, murderers or anything else they could get jailed for. If it isn't proven in court yet, say they're charged with a crime, not that they actually did it.

• **If you accuse someone** of having a contagious disease like AIDS, or if you question a woman's chastity(!).

### Check everything

The group is responsible for everything that's printed, including letters to the editor and articles by various writers, the same as if the editor wrote them. If you quote an untrue, libelous statement like example A, your paper is guilty of libel too.

(However, the U.S. Supreme Court in 1989 ruled that you can quote libelous accusations against a government official, so long as you get the quote right and it's clearly presented as opinion, not fact.)

### Absolute privilege

You can reprint what's said in court, in Congress, in the legislature, or by the president or governor's office with an *absolute privilege* in the United States. That means you can't be successfully sued, even if the words you quote are out-and-out lies. Canadians don't get an absolute privilege, but in Ontario you now get a *qualified privilege* (see below) to quote false, libelous statements people make in public bodies like parliament and the courts, so long as your quote is fair and accurate.

### Qualified privileges

When a *qualified* privilege applies, you can escape a libel lawsuit (even when what you said was damaging and untrue) if you didn't lie *maliciously*. You're considered legally malicious (defined in the 1964 *New York Times vs. Sullivan* case) when you spout off about something you *know* isn't true; or when you show "reckless disregard for the truth" by not checking questionable statements you publish.

What's more, the person suing

The only creature you should call a vulture

must *prove* that you were being malicious, not vice versa.

The U.S. Supreme Court confirmed that definition of "malice" in 1990. However, in Canada malice can simply mean you're out to "get" someone. If you are, be especially careful.

## When you get a qualified privilege

In these situations the person suing has to prove that your printing something damaging and untrue was done with *malice* (defined above):

● **Coverage of elected officials and prominent people.** In the United States, writing about public figures – people whose names often appear in the news – gets the same qualified privilege as coverage of public officials. In Canada, however, you have a qualified privilege only when discussing the public acts of public officials.

● **Discussing matters of public interest.** In 1964 and again in '86 the U.S. Supreme Court stressed that "debate on public issues should be uninhibited, robust and wide open, and that may well include vehement, caustic, and sometimes unpleasantly sharp attacks." This helps you target big-time wheelers and dealers, especially when politics or the public safety is involved.

● **If you have a "common interest"** with your readers. For example, if you all have the same landlord, work at the same place or belong to the same union, you get a qualified privilege when you talk about what you have in common. Canadian courts just confirmed that this protects unions. But you have to limit circulation to that particular group to enjoy this privilege; if you distribute the paper publicly you lose it.

● **When you discuss the self-interest of the publisher.** This further protects papers published by a union or a community group.

## Fair comment

If you're caught in Canada printing an opinion you can't prove is true, your best defense may be "fair comment" – that you're discussing matters of public interest and draw your conclusions from provable facts. In example B, if you have proof that Nogood dumped the chemicals, then you can call him "one of the most hated citizens" even if it isn't true – so long as an honest person could have that opinion.

## Added help for U.S. labor editors

Union editors in the U.S. get legal shelter under the National Labor Relations Act (NLRA – covering private workers), the Public Employment Relations Act (for most public workers), and an executive order covering federal workers. State law could give state workers the same coverage – but check to make sure.

Labor law guarantees your right to "the free debate required in employer-employee relationships" and protects "derogatory" language related to union activities. That gives union editors a *qualified privilege* (explained above) when you criticize the company, labor relations and supervisors, so long as the criticism serves a union purpose.

If company officials file a "knowingly frivolous" libel lawsuit to shut you up, the labor board can keep it from going to trial. In a 1985 case, the labor board sued American Motors for helping foremen sue union activists for libel, saying the company was trying to suppress dissent, "chill" collective action and "exact reprisals" against workers. American Motors had to fork over $238,000 to the workers it tried to silence.

## Can you get fired?

In the U.S., editors and writers can't legally get slapped with discipline for what they write in a union paper or flyer, so long as it's related to hours, wages and working conditions. If a supervisor tries to punish someone for such writings, file a grievance or unfair labor practice charge with the National Labor Relations Board. If you get personal or unfairly attack company products, however, you could be in trouble. In other words, feel free to attack the company's absentee policy, but don't unfairly ridicule the widgets you make or the supervisor's bad taste in clothes.

## The law's no barrier

As you can see, the law doesn't limit you beyond good sense. For the reputation of the paper, as well as your legal peace of mind, your top concern is always to print the truth for valid reasons. When you've got a hot potato on your hands, check it out so you can defend yourself before readers and the community, as well as the law. That's the bottom line.

<u>Example A</u>
The supervisor at Greedtown said Suzie Q was a lazy drunk who didn't deserve to have a job.
If Suzie isn't a drunk, it's probably illegal to print the supervisor's accusation.

<u>Example B</u>
Nick Nogood has been caught dumping over a dozen dangerous chemicals into Babbling Brook, making him one of the most hated citizens in Montclair County.

Stealing graphics from another paper

## Do you need permission?

### Taking photos

Normally people want to see their pictures in the paper. But whether they like it or not, you still have a legal right to snap photos and, in most cases, to print them.

Here are exceptions to watch out for:

• **Courts, local laws or private owners** can bar your camera from courtrooms, museums, factories or other private property. When in doubt, ask permission of whoever's in charge.

• **Military installations** are off-limits, and photographing money is limited (so the photo won't look like the real McCoy).

• **Don't publish** photos of private situations if it would offend a reasonable person.

• **If you plan to use a photo for advertising** or other commercial purposes, ask everyone pictured to sign a *release*. You do *not* need a release, however, for a photo used for current news, educational or informational purposes. A typical release is shown on this page.

• **If you add a caption or touch up** a photo, avoid libel by following the guidelines on pp. 29-31. If the caption damages someone's reputation, it had better be accurate and fair.

• **Use common sense.** Printing a photo of someone at a rally who's supposed to be at work may be legal, but it's not wise. When in doubt, ask permission.

### Reprinting photos & articles

No editor depends 100% on original articles and graphics. You'll occasionally reprint interesting articles and cartoons from other papers and magazines. As for whether you need permission, the rules are a bit muddy. Such reprints are policed by the Copyright Act.

## Copyright law & you

According to law, all feature articles, cartoons, and photographs are copyrighted whether or not they say so, and even if they aren't yet published.

Although the work is supposed to carry a copyright notice, it still can be registered as copyrighted as late as five years after it was first distributed. But if it isn't, it's then fair game.

Whoever owns the copyright has exclusive rights to reproduce the work, distribute and display it. You can't reprint it without permission. However, there are sizable loopholes:

### Helpful loopholes

• **Facts** can't be copyrighted. If an American wants to reproduce part of an article that's mostly fact, without opinions or original thought, that's okay. But in Canada, you can't just copy it word-for-word; you have to rewrite it.

• **"Fair use" for educational purposes** is exempt from American copyright law. Reprinting a cartoon, poem or feature story one time for non-profit educational purposes (regardless of whether your purpose is nonpartisan) will likely be considered "fair use."

Although the definition of "fair use" is vague, you're probably safe when your reprint of part of a cartoon, photo or article wouldn't damage its commercial potential. If it's a month old, it has less commercial potential than when it first appeared. The more you borrow, the greater the danger.

You're also safest when you have a limited readership and you're honest about where you took it from. Show the source with a *credit line*.

In Canada, copyright law is stricter. Educational materials can be reprinted without permission *only* if they're used mostly in schools. Canadian law applies to everything you want to reprint in Canada, even if it was originally published in the United States.

• **U.S. copyrights registered before 1978** expire after 28 years. So if a photo, cartoon or poem was published 30 years ago, it may be fair game. Before you reprint, check to see if the copyright was renewed for another 28 years. Copyrights registered from 1978 on or in Canada last the owner's lifetime, plus 50 years.

• **Canada's loophole.** In Canada, you can reprint for "any fair dealing. . . for the purpose of private study, research, criticism, review or newspaper summary." That means you can quote 50 words or so from an article, especially if you then comment on the quote.

Sample release

### RELEASE

In consideration of my engagement as a model, upon the terms herein after stated, I hereby grant_____, his legal representatives and assigns, those for whom_____is acting, and those acting with his authority and permission, the absolute right and permission to copyright and use, reuse and publish, and republish photographic portraits or pictures of me or in which I may be included, in whole or in part, or composite or distorted in character or form, without restriction as to changes or alterations from time to time, in conjunction with my own or a fictitious name, or reproductions thereof in color or otherwise made through any media at his studio or elsewhere for art, advertising, trade, or any other purpose whatsoever.

I also consent to the use of any printed matter in conjunction therewith.

I hereby waive any right that I may have to inspect or approve the finished product or products or the advertising copy or printed matter that may be used in connection therewith or the use to which it may be applied.

I hereby release, discharge and agree to save harmless _____, his legal representatives or assigns, and all persons acting under his permission or authority or those for whom he is acting, from any liability by virture of any blurring, distortion, alteration, optical illusion, or use in composite form, whether intentional or otherwise, that may occur or be produced in the taking of said picture or in any subsequent processing thereof, as well as any publication thereof even though it may subject me to ridicule, scandal, reproach, scorn and indignity.

I hereby warrant that I am of full age and have every right to contract in my own name in the above regard. I state further that I have read the above authorization, release and agreement prior to its execution, and that I am fully familiar with the contents thereof.

Dated:

_____
(Legal signature)

_____
(Address)

_____
(Witness)

• **Ideas can be borrowed.** If you like a cartoon or article you can usually do something based on a similar idea; but don't copy the whole thing.

### The political context

Since U.S. law is vague about "fair use," whether you're safe reprinting something may also depend on your political context. If you borrow a cartoon from a national magazine for a non-profit newsletter handed to a group of neighbors, chances are the big-timers won't know about it and won't care.

The bigger your circulation, the more careful you should be. Many copyright owners worry only about commercial reprints. So if your paper's a money-maker, watch out. And don't sneak copyrighted cartoons into ads.

Think twice before "borrowing" from the local newspaper. If they're hostile to your goals and keep their eye on your activities, they're sure to holler when you reprint without permission.

Handing out literature on private property

# Your right to hand out literature

The law gives you the right to distribute papers and flyers on public property and to deliver door-to-door, so long as you don't put literature in people's mailboxes in the U.S. (Slip it behind the screen door instead.)

### How about the mall?

The trouble with that is, shopping centers aren't public property. You can stand on the public sidewalk begging motorists to roll down their windows and take the paper as they drive in, but wouldn't you rather hand it out in the parking lot or inside the building?

• **In 1980 the U.S. Supreme Court** gave states the right to stop mall owners from kicking you off their property. However, most haven't passed such laws. In a few states like Massachusetts, the courts ruled that free-speech rights in the state constitution give you the right to hand out literature on mall property. But courts in other states put shopping malls off-limits.

If the mall lets the Boy Scouts or any group pass out literature, however, they can't discriminate against your group.

• **In Canada**, the right of mall owners to keep people from handing out literature is being challenged in the courts. In the recent *Eaton Centre* case, the Supreme Court of Ontario ruled that unionists can distribute union information in public areas of the mall.

### Campaign handouts

Anything you give the public must clearly identify the name and address of the person or group paying for it and reveal whether it's authorized by a specific candidate or not.

### You can leaflet even when you can't picket

One of the most powerful union tools is the boycott – asking people not to buy or use products made by anti-union companies. Canadian and U.S. laws bar *secondary picketing* against related companies – you can't picket a store because it sells boycotted products, for example. However, a 1988 Supreme Court ruling now gives American unions the right to hand out *flyers* urging shoppers not to patronize a store, mall or bank doing business with a boycotted company.

### Can you hand out material at work?

The boss may say no, but if it's union literature, labor law and the U.S. Supreme Court say yes. In the U.S., a company must let you distribute leaflets or papers during non-working hours in non-working areas, such as the lunchroom or parking lot (*Eastex vs. NLRB*

The political context

and other rulings), so long as the literature involves workers' "mutual aid and protection." That includes discussing political issues that affect workers, and it includes organizing at non-union workplaces. The company can't censor your handouts. What's more, if the employer lets people pass around things like flyers for a church rummage sale at work during working hours, it has to give unions the same right.

However, management can probably ban union literature that's devoted almost entirely to candidates for public office. And if the boss can show that handouts in waiting rooms or other areas could hurt customer relations or endanger people, you may have to avoid those areas.

● **If you work for the government,** you probably get equal protection from state law, plus all handouts are covered by the First Amendment to the U.S. Constitution, which says the government can't limit "free speech." (Your literature is considered a form of speech.) Public employers can also ban distribution in work areas during working hours (but not break time).

● **Canada labour law** offers little protection, so unions often must win the right to distribute literature through negotiations.

# Legal limits on union papers

## U.S. union elections

In the U.S., union democracy is protected by a law saying you can't use union funds to boost the candidacy of one person over another. Even subtle electioneering, such as filling your paper with big photos of incumbent officers just before elections, is illegal.

● **At election time, scrutinize all articles,** especially those by or about officers, to make sure they discuss legitimate union affairs and aren't dumping on opponents or otherwise campaigning. If you design promotional literature for a candidate, do it on your own time and without using union funds or facilities in any way.

● **To help members make an informed decision** on election day, unions can print each candidate's picture with a short statement, so long as everyone running for the same office gets equal treatment. Send a registered letter to each one's home asking for a photo and specifying the maximum length for comments. Print their responses in a logical order.

● **Democracy doesn't mean a free-for-all.** Although U.S. law is very particular about elections, the courts understand that once officers are elected, members have a right to read about what they're doing and thinking in the union paper. So long as dissidents can speak at meetings and get union mailing lists, the courts avoid "unjustified judicial interference in internal union affairs." So although membership input is a good idea, the law does *not* say you must print every hairbrained or angry article members send in. By setting clear guidelines for all members (p. 22), you'll show that you're being fair.

## Public elections

● **Feel free to discuss political issues** and make pitches for get-out-the-vote drives. While a U.S. union paper can also urge members to vote for endorsed candidates, you must take your own pictures and write your own articles – don't just reprint candidate literature. Election-time papers that promote (or dump on) candidates must go only to members – with less than 5% sent to outsiders.

When an American paper asks people to donate money to a union political action committee, you must print a long disclaimer – get the exact wording from your union.

● **The Hatch Act and state laws partly muzzle** U.S. public workers. While a federal workers' union can argue for or against candidates for *partisan* (where they're identified by party) elections, individual federal workers can't. So avoid quoting a public worker speaking out on candidates for upcoming partisan elections.

● **Canadian unions** have the right to get involved in politics (but that's being challenged in court). Check provincial law for possible red tape. Canadian public workers are slowly winning more freedom to be politically active, too.

# 5. Type: your alternatives

What'll it be today? How about a little **Times Roman** or **Helvetica?**

Computers can create all kinds of type

Investigate typesetting possibilities even before you plan your paper's first issue or your first leaflet. Just about every word should be typed or typeset – and never hand-lettered. Handlettering rarely looks as snazzy, and is harder to read.

The typesetting method you pick will determine much of your style: how well headlines stand out, how many words fit on each page, how interesting each page looks, and how easy the paper is to read. Some methods save you work, while others can give you a permanent headache. You can set it all yourself, or send the whole kit and kaboodle to a professional typesetter. If you're strapped for cash, spiff up that old typewriter, and you're ready to go.

The information for a leaflet, brochure or article is called your *copy*. Here are ways to get it typeset:

## Doing it yourself: small type

You're likely to find something around the house or office that sets small type, but chances are it can't churn out the big, bold headlines needed to attract readers to each page. For big type, turn to p. 38.

### Typewriters

The typewriter can be a godsend for leaflet copy, since it would be a real pain to run back and forth to a typesetter to

Regular typewriter,
without proportional spacing

```
Excessive noise
widespread problem
try claims that quieting
cost more than it can
the entire cost of noise
```

Selectric type

```
tions. The AEC, notorious
lack of caution, estimated
inspection would require

      (Information from
       Service.)
```

Executive typewriter,
with proportional spacing

```
The Women's
are sponsoring the
YWCA to share skills
and information
```

This is elite type

```
And the lines for
been drawn in such a
voting groups. Again,
```

1 inch = 12 characters

This is pica type

```
trict lines for the
The situation is even
Representatives. Here
tricts, most of whose
```

1 inch = 10 characters

When type isn't
justified it comes
out flush left,
ragged right

---

get the few paragraphs you may need. Many typesetters slap a minimum charge on each job, making a single leaflet really expensive.

While older typewriters usually give you only one size type, most modern models offer three sizes: *pica* (10 pitch), *elite* (12 pitch), and *micro* (15 pitch). The numbers tell how many *characters* fit into each inch typed across the page. A *character* is anything you push a key for, whether it's a letter, a number, a comma or a space.

Micro type squeezes 15 characters into each inch. That means you can cram plenty of words onto a page – but only people who adore footnotes would enjoy reading them. Stick with pica or elite for article or leaflet copy, and save micro for tiny election information you have to print.

Typewriters can be anything from the old-fashioned model with sticky keys to fancy ones that save words with a built-in memory, so you can change them later and spit out a new version. You might find a good used typewriter for a song; but ask about service, repair contracts and warranties.

• **Plain old typewriter.** If you're buying a brand-new machine, you can do much better than this old standby, which stamps a letter onto the paper each time you push a key. If you push the wrong key, the wrong letter is stuck on the paper. It doesn't have *proportional spacing.* That means each letter, whether it's an "i" or an "m," must squeeze into the exact same size space.

For the best quality, use an electric model with a *carbon ribbon* – a ribbon you type through just once before throwing it away. And before you start, clean the keys. (More tips on p. 132.)

• *Varieties*: Some typewriters have built-in correction tapes to fix mistakes.

• *A selectric model* stamps letters from a little metal ball. To change the type size or style, slip out the metal ball and replace it with another. Most styles are so ugly and hard to read, however, that they shouldn't be used at all.

• *An executive* typewriter has *proportional* letter-spacing, so an "M" gets four times the room an "i" does. The type looks better, and is easier to read.

• **Advantages:** Cheap, easy to haul around. More important: If that's all you've got, that's all you've got.

• **Disadvantages:** If you write at the typewriter, you'll find yourself typing

one draft after another start-to-finish. If you're not a great typist, you'll spend hours coating your fingers with typing correction fluid and retyping.

You can't get big type or a good variety of styles. Nor can you *justify* type. While the left-hand edge of each column is straight as a board, the right side isn't. (The type in this column is *justified*: each line comes out the exact same width, so the column has a straight right-hand edge.)

Since the letter-spacing is crude, type is awkward and irritating to read in big doses. And be careful – type can smear when you paste it onto pages.

## Typewriters with memory

Get one of these babies and you can correct mistakes before they get printed on paper. As you type, the typewriter stores your words in its memory. It delays printing them, so you can see what you're doing on a little screen, and fix whatever needs fixing. The memory holds several pages, so you can alter a whole document and print it over again.

Type is created by a little plastic *printer wheel* that spins around in the machine, stopping to strike characters onto paper whenever the typewriter's computer tells it to. To get a different style or size of type, snap in a new printer wheel. Don't get too excited – the selection is limited. However, you can usually find **bold** (a darker version of each type style) and *italics* (letters slant forward at an angle).

Prices start at around $200.

• **Advantages:** Small, portable, cheap. No matter how crummy a typist you are, you can print out perfect type – if you keep your eye on the little screen. Most have attractive *proportional spacing* and can *justify* type (explained above) or *center* it in the middle of the column. You can save an article or two in the memory, change it later, and print it out again.

• **Disadvantages:** The machine saves only a few pages, and the screen shows only a few words at a time; if you must fix something that's no longer on the screen, you'll have to print out the article all over again. You can't see a whole page, can't quickly move from one section of the copy to another, can't move whole paragraphs, can't get much variety in type styles, and can't get big type. And setting the margins can be as easy as microsurgery.

Type can smear during paste-up.

## Word processors

This is a big advance. A word processor (not to be confused with a *word processing program* for a personal computer, coming up on p. 39) does everything a typewriter with memory does, plus more. Its computer is bigger, and so is the display screen. The word processor keeps long documents in its memory, and its screen shows you practically a whole page at a time. The machine stores the whole job while you work on it, and prints it all out when you're done.

That means you can:

• *write and rewrite* on the machine, making unlimited changes with no hassle;

• *move type around* to different parts of the article;

• *make several copies* of the same article, change some of them, and store them all on the machine;

• *"center" type* in the column, *justify* it (p. 36), or leave it *ragged right* like old-fashioned typewriter type;

• *change the printer wheel* (p. 36) to get different type styles. But the selection is about as exotic as macaroni and cheese, with sizes of 10, 12, or 15 pitch (p. 36). It won't make headline sizes. To get variations like **boldface** and *italics*, you have to buy a separate printer wheel for each.

• **The advanced versions** also stick columns of type next to each other, saving you plenty of paste-up work. How many pages a machine will store depends on the size of its memory.

If you get a *spell-checker*, it'll act like a built-in dictionary, searching out each misspelled word and suggesting how to spell it right.

If you need more storage space, equip the word processor to use a *floppy disk* – a thin sheet of magnetic plastic that stores pages of information. When you're done with one disk, take it out, put it aside, and insert another. This lets you save the type from every leaflet and newsletter you've ever done (if that's your bag).

Word processors with hefty computers can also handle mailing lists (p. 172), phone lists, and form letters. Since they're stored on the machine or disk, you can always get a copy, make changes, or sort items in a different order.

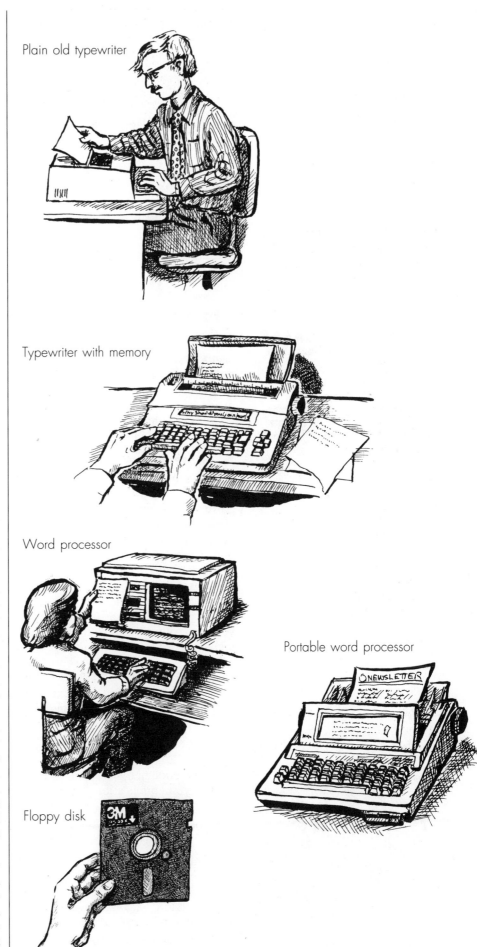

Plain old typewriter

Typewriter with memory

Word processor

Portable word processor

Floppy disk

Sheet of transfer lettering

Headline machine

- **Prices** of word processors range from $400 to $2,000. Your best bet is a mid-priced model – an ultra-cheap one might fall apart just as a crucial deadline approaches. If you're tempted to buy on the high end, then you probably can afford a full-fledged personal computer instead. Go for it – a computer can also make headlines, page layouts and more – see Chapter 6.

Unless you know the machine inside-out, don't get lured into buying a mail-order model. Instead, use a local dealer who can help you figure out how to work it and offer help when it doesn't work at all.

- **Advantages:** Isn't it obvious? No matter how poorly you type and spell, you can churn out great copy. You can correct, center and justify type and get a variety of styles.

- **Disadvantages:** A word processor won't help with headlines, page layout, or office tasks like accounting. What you see on the screen can be limited, and it can take you a while to move from one section of a story to another. Type can smear, and styles are somewhat crude and limited.

## Big headlines: to set them yourself

Every leaflet, newsletter, and paper needs big, bold headlines to attract readers. P. 68 explains why. Big type also comes in handy for subheads, topic heads, display quotes, and other special uses – see Chapter 8. Here are your options for making your own:

### Emergency headlines

If it's half past midnight and the leaflet *must* be printed in the morning, go through your stack of publications. (One of the first rules of publishing is to *never* throw anything away. If that makes your office look like a hamster nest, so be it.) If you find a headline that'll work, cut it out and use it – just this once.

Or type headlines as big and bold as you can (try typing twice over each letter), enlarge them on the nearest office copier (try a quick-copy shop), and paste them in place (p. 152 tells how). Then get prepared for the next emergency by lining up other options.

- **Advantages:** Cheap.
- **Disadvantages:** No matter how you slice it, typed headlines just won't stand out enough to call readers' attention to your publication. Chances are you can afford one of the following options, at least for the front page, to give headlines the pizzazz they need.

### Rub-off transfer lettering

With transfer lettering, you can make headlines yourself anywhere, at any time of day or night. Just stock up on plastic sheets of letters at a stationery, office supply or art store. Each sheet will make several headlines and costs around $10. Many stores carry several brands, with a free (or cheap) catalogue for each, showing the type styles and sizes you can buy.

Once you've picked out a simple, bold headline style, buy several sheets in various sizes, from at least 18 point to 36 point. (Type sizes are measured in *points* – p. 67 explains more.) Although that might set you back a pretty penny to start with, each sheet gives you months worth of headlines.

- **Advantages:** Easy and convenient, once you get the hang of it. (To get the best results, see p. 151.) Might be your cheapest alternative. Can look as good as the finest typesetting, and plenty of styles and sizes are available.

- **Disadvantages:** Rubbing off each letter isn't easy, especially for greenhorns. It can get expensive if you have more than a few headlines to set. For big headlines, you must buy separate sheets for capital and lower-case letters. Sheets may crack if left in the heat, or when they get old. Type is delicate and must be handled carefully.

### Headline machines

- **Lettering machine.** Consider this if you need a lot of headlining done quickly or at odd hours. It's easier than rubbing off letters and also can make labels for all-around office use. Since it's simple and sturdy, a cheap second-hand model should work fine.

Just turn a dial to the chosen character, press a button, and it comes out printed on a clear strip with its own adhesive. Do the same for each letter, and adjust the spacing if necessary. When you're ready to paste up, pull out the tape and peel off the backing.

A Kroy headliner costs around $500

new. It comes with only one size and style of type, but you can buy dials with other sizes and styles at $38 a pop. You'll occasionally need a refill cartridge strip, costing under $20. Kroy also offers a super-quick computerized version for over a thousand bucks, but for that money you'd do better to look into desktop publishing.

- **Desktop lettering system.** Kroy offers a portable, battery-powered unit with a keyboard, so it's easy to carry around and quicker than the standard headliner. What's more, it has a modest memory and 16-character display, so you can correct mistakes as you type. You can pick up one for under $500; tape cartridge refills cost $30 each.

The machine comes with one style of type in three sizes – one for little type and two for headlines. Each extra size and style costs $40.

- **Advantages:** Easy and cheap, if you get enough use out of it. If you make a mistake putting a headline on the page, peel it up and try again.

- **Disadvantages:** Type doesn't run bigger than 36 *point* (p. 40), which may not save a leaflet or newspaper from looking hopelessly dull. Styles aren't as attractive or varied as rub-off letters, and type can smear.

# Machines that set type of all sizes

## Word processing programs for computers

A personal computer equipped with a good *printer* (p. 52) can do practically everything but make ice cream. It depends on how you program it – and whether it has enough memory and storage space to work with fancy programs. See Chapter 6 for more.

If you want to do word processing on a computer, check out a special *program* – a set of instructions on a *floppy disk* (p. 50). A word processing program does everything a word processor does plus it can:

- *set big type.* It gives you a dazzling assortment of sizes and styles – as many as your computer can hold (or you can afford to buy);
- *set up simple pages* with columns of type next to each other;

Getting a headline for an emergency

Galley of type
from most typesetters

Page made by a
machine with layout
capabilites

Word processing program on
computer screen

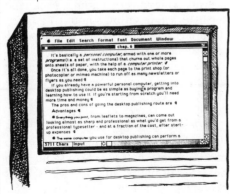

9 point type
This is 9 point Palatino type.

10 point type
This is 10 point Palatino type.

11 point type
This is 11 point Palatino type.

12 point type
This is 12 point Palatino type.

18 point type
# This is 18 point Palatino type.

20 point type
# This is 20 point Palatino type.

24 point type
# This is 24 point Palatino

36 point type
# This is 36 point

• *easily make some type italics,* **bold-face,** <u>underlined</u>, and more;

• *and check your spelling* with a spell-checker that's either part of the word-processing program or separate.

• **Make sure the program** you want can work on your machine. The "Mac" – Apple Macintosh – computers need programs made just for them. Most other computers are *IBM-compatible*, so they can use any program designed for IBM computers. The same goes for the *printer* (p. 52) – it has to be able to work with your computer and program.

• **Advantages:** If you're typing up articles yourself and have (or are willing to buy) a computer and printer, this is the way to go. Once you get the hang of it, a word processing program can be easier to use than a fancy typewriter. Add a page layout program, and you have a full desktop publishing system.

• **Disadvantages:** Buying a computer system and getting trained to use it takes time and money. If you need something portable, you must buy a separate *laptop* version to lug around. Unless you go the extra mile and get a *page layout program* (p. 50), you could be limited to simple page formats.

• **What program do you need?** Programs range from the simple to the sublime. But the more a program can do, the harder it is to get the hang of it, and you may not need every feature. Check with other groups, and see what programs they like best. Try program shopping at the store where you bought your computer.

• *Microsoft Word* and *WordPerfect* are two top-notch word processing programs that come in either IBM/compatible or Macintosh versions. They both do the basics described above, plus they have a *spell-checker* and *automatic hyphenation* to divide long words into two lines (p. 133). They can arrange type into columns or charts, and even do fancy things like wrap words around a picture (p. 145). These programs also work nicely with desktop publishing. With all their fancy features, they're on the high end of the price scale. Both cost $395 (or $219 to $265 at discount stores). They also gobble up more computer memory (p. 46) than simpler programs.

• *PFS: Professional Write* (for IBM/compatible machines) and *MacWrite* (for Macintosh) won't do the super stuff, but they may be all you need. They do basic word processing and can be used with most desktop publishing programs. PFS: Professional Write sells for $165 at discount stores. MacWrite's list price is $249, or $145 at discount stores.

## Desktop publishing does it all

With a desktop publishing program, you can put together almost any kind of page on a personal computer, including beautiful headlines. Chapter 6 gives the lowdown.

## Using a professional typesetter

Professional typesetting is more expensive than typing things yourself, and it usually involves running back and forth to a typesetting shop. You also need to know how to give the typesetter proper instructions (p. 134).

However, professional typesetting makes both small type and headlines that look really special – it's the Cadillac of type, as far as quality goes.

With typesetting, you have a large variety of sizes, styles and variations to choose from, so you can dress up each bit of information in whatever's most becoming. Each typesetter will offer *typefaces*, like Helvetica, Times Roman or Optima. Each comes in variations like *italics* (p. 36), **bold face**, and *light* (the opposite of bold face).

Sometimes you can also get *condensed* (squeezed-up, tall and skinny letters), *expanded* (a stretched-out version) or *extra-bold* (can make great headlines). Type sizes can range anywhere from 4 point (for tiny footnotes) to 96 or more point (for posters and huge headlines).

For generations, typesetting was based on a highly skilled industrial process called *hot type*.

But over the past 25 years, hundreds of new machines and systems were invented, revolutionizing the typesetting business many times over. Today's typesetter sits before a computer keyboard staring at a screen similar to what you see in offices. The old machines could only create *galleys* of type – with all the type strung into long columns that are then arranged onto each page by hand. But today's typesetting machines can also spit out whole pages, straight and neat as a pin.

Yet you still must make hard choices about where the type goes on each page. You could give the typesetter a layout when you hand over the copy, but then you must know exactly what fits where (*copyfitting*, p. 86). That's no easy trick.

Otherwise, you'll still ask for copies of type in long *galleys* and make rough layouts from them (p. 138). The typesetter uses those as a guide to put together pages. Or, if you don't want to pay the typesetter for layout, paste the galleys onto pages yourself. In that case, you'll have to straighten everything by hand – see Chapter 17.

● **Advantages:** You don't have to invest in your own machinery. And if you're a single-finger, hunt-and-peck sort of typist, professional typesetting can seem like manna from heaven, relieving you of all that typing.

All typesetters offer a wide selection of high-quality type.

Each job is stored on a disk, so it's easy to get corrections made. Changing the type style, spacing, or size of an entire newsletter or leaflet that's already set can be as easy as changing a few computer codes. (You won't need to have the job retyped, but you still have to pay to have a new copy made.) If you have a *modem* or *fax machine* (explained next), you can send everything to the typesetter, including corrections, over phone lines.

● **Disadvantages:** You may end up spending more to typeset every publication than it would cost to buy your own equipment. If all you need is a leaflet, professional typesetting may not be worth the time and money – especially since most typesetters slap a big minimum charge on each job.

You have less control over scheduling – if a big, rich client wants a job done fast, yours could be pushed aside.

You could end up running across town each time you need a little mistake corrected and waiting for it to be done. And if the copy's all typeset when you suddenly discover it doesn't make sense, plus the words are all misspelled and it's about twice as long as the space on the page, you're in big trouble. You must pay for each and every change you make.

It's getting mighty hard to find union-

Professional typesetter

ized typesetters. And if typesetters aren't highly skilled, you'll waste time correcting all their mistakes on top of your own.

## What to ask a typesetting shop

To get the best deal, shop around. Ask other groups to recommend their favorite typesetter or look in the phone book under Typesetting, Composition or Printers, and call several. Find an offset printer (p. 60) who also does typesetting, and it will save you plenty of legwork. Here are the questions to ask:

● **What are the rates** for both typesetting and putting together pages? Do they charge a minimum for each job?

● **How quickly will they finish the**

Optima type
ABCabcd

Optima italic
*ABCabcd*

Optima bold
**ABCabcd**

Optima bold italic
***ABCabcd***

Optima outline
ABCabcd

Optima shadow
ABCabcd

job? Do they work around the clock or just days? Can you arrange ahead of time to get a job done on a certain date?

• **Are they unionized?** Often quality union labor won't cost a penny extra.

• **What type styles, variations and sizes** do they offer? Most typesetters will give you a book illustrating what they can do.

• **Will the typesetter proof and correct mistakes,** or do you have to do all the *proofreading* (p. 135) yourself? Will you paste in minor corrections yourself or will the typesetter? Will you be charged for all corrections, even if they were the typesetter's errors?

• **How much will it cost to alter the type style or size** after the job is set? Will the typesetter store material so you can re-use part or all of it later?

• **Will it cost extra** for fancy moves like wrapping type around illustrations or tilting it at an angle? What else can they do? But don't get carried away looking for the fanciest machine around – you may not need these options.

• **Does the machine set special symbols** you may need, like boxes (❑) or arrows (➡)? Can it handle a foreign language, complete with accent marks?

• **Will a messenger pick up** and deliver type? Is that service free? Can you also deliver copy via a phone modem or fax machine? What's the cost?

• **Is there a printer** in the same shop, so you don't have to cart typeset pages around town to get them printed?

### Just gimme the fax, ma'am

Gone are the days when you had to run across town to bring the typesetter every little correction, or spend the whole day at the typesetting shop, laying out pages and proofing type. Instead, send your copy and page layouts to the typesetter via phone lines with a *fax machine*. They'll send you back *galleys* (p. 41) or complete pages on the same machine.

A *fax machine* is absurdly simple to operate. Put a page on the tray and dial a fax number on the attached phone, and the machine slowly copies the page, top to bottom, and sends it across phone lines. (The machine takes only flat sheets, so if you've cut and pasted things together, make a copy before faxing it.) The typesetter sends galleys or typeset pages back to you on the same machine. Proofread the faxed copy, mark your corrections (p. 136), and fax it all back.

The cheaper faxes cost in the $500 range. They make fuzzy copies that look like they have a bad case of shakes. That's fine for proofs, but find another way to transport pictures and other *graphics* (p. 157) and to send an actual page *mechanical* (p. 149) to the printer. (If the typesetter also does the printing that's no problem, because the page mechanical stays put.)

Get a fax equipped with a *laser printer* (p. 53), and you can send back and forth type, artwork and pages suitable for printing – *if* you aren't fussy. Fax machines break type (and everything else) into small dots, but the dots aren't as fine as those a laser printer makes on its own. You'll still see some shakiness in type and pictures. Fancy faxes also have built-in memories to save pages, and some even link up directly with personal computers.

If you don't have your own fax machine, chances are you can find one nearby – at a copy shop, hotel lobby or office. Faxing costs around $2 to $3 a page.

### Phone modems

If you type articles on a computer, consider sending them to the typesetter with a *phone modem*. Basically, that means your computer calls their computer, and then sends the job over phone lines. The advantage over a fax machine is that you don't get shaky type and typesetters don't have to retype the whole thing – they just add the proper codes and spiff it up. But make sure the typesetting shop can accept type from your computer and program(s). More on p. 55.

A fax machine

Use the "fine" adjustment to get good fax copies like this one.

# What next?

Once you've picked your typesetter, see Chapter 8 for tips on choosing type styles for newsletters and newspapers and p. 8 for setting up leaflet or brochure type. Chapter 15 tells how to talk to typesetters in language they understand and how to figure proper widths for each column of type.

# 6. What can desktop publishing do for you?

How will you access the input?.... Gimme RAM in my hard drive.... I wanna interface with a 300 dpi Laserjet.....

The computer industry has introduced literally thousands of machines and products that claim they'll help anyone produce almost anything with ease and pizazz. Is this the magic answer to your publishing needs? Maybe.

## What is desktop publishing?

It's basically a *personal computer*, armed with one or more *programs* (i.e., a set of instructions) that churns out whole pages onto sheets of paper, with the help of a *computer printer*.

Once it's all done, you take each page to the print shop (or photocopier or mimeo machine) to run off as many newsletters or flyers as you need.

If you already have a powerful personal computer, getting into desktop publishing could be as simple as buying a program and learning how to use it. If you're starting from scratch, you'll need more time and money.

The pros and cons of going the desktop publishing route are:

## Advantages

● **Everything you print**, from leaflets to magazines, can come out looking almost as sharp and professional as what you'd get from a professional typesetter – and at a fraction of the cost, after start-up expenses.

● **The same computer** you use for desktop publishing can perform a whole slew of other office tasks – such as bookkeeping, updating and printing mailing lists, and yes, those tricky form letters that seem written for you alone.

● **After you and the computer have been broken in**, you can get lovely publications ready for the printer quickly, in your own home or office.

● **Typing articles** onto the computer gives you all the advantages of *word processing* (p. 37). You can make corrections and move things around with-

"I'm afraid the computer is down."

out retyping over and over again, and the machine will check your spelling.

• As you put each page together on the machine, you can experiment with various layouts and find out exactly how well the articles fit.

• Special effects that used to take forever, such as wrapping type around a photo, can be done lickety-split.

• The machine puts whole pages together, and you can get away with doing very little paste-up by hand. If you've got a top-notch *scanner* (p. 55), you can avoid much of the typing too.

• You'll never have another crooked line or word.

• Almost every week someone invents something new and wonderful desktop publishing can do, and standard programs are constantly upgraded.

## Disadvantages

• The money you put up front to buy the system can run anywhere from $4,000 to $10,000. If you lease a machine instead, you could end up spending a small fortune for a system you'll never own. (If you "lease to buy," that can cost 40% more than buying the same machine outright.)

• On top of that, you'll have to shell out money and time to set up the system and learn how to operate it. It may take longer at first to get the job done.

• If you now use a printshop to typeset and lay out your newsletter, going to a desktop system can pile more work, not less, on your shoulders. You'll be taking that work from your friendly typesetter, and the type quality won't be quite as high.

• Repair service for computer equipment isn't cheap. You'll pay a premium for fast service, and you often have to troubleshoot simple problems yourself.

• Since only one person can operate the machine at a time, you may end up doing layout all by your lonesome.

• It will take time and money to keep up with the latest inventions – and those *upgrades* are hard to resist.

• Getting type styles (*fonts*, p. 52) beyond the few that come with the machine will cost you.

• Transferring information from one computer to another can drive you crazy, if both machines aren't alike.

• If the machine "crashes" and you can't revive it, the whole job may get stuck inside a machine that won't talk to you. It's a royal pain to get the machine up and running again.

# When you're computer shopping

A word of caution: Prices for the same equipment vary widely from store to store, and with mail order companies. Buying from the cheapest source is fine – if you can get savvy help to walk you through the rough spots once the equipment is yours. A store that offers classes or technical support may charge more for the set-up – and it could be worth the money.

Look into getting a special discount through a university or your union. If you're a college student, check with the campus bookstore. Zenith offers a special price to unions.

Two terms you'll hear early and often are computer *hardware* and *software*. Hardware simply means the basic stuff – the computer itself and equipment that helps the computer work and save things. *Software* are *programs* you add to the computer, to make it perform specific tasks. Think of a VCR – the VCR machine itself could be called the hardware. The tapes you play in the VCR could be thought of as software.

## Look for these features

Don't be fooled by products that only pretend to do desktop publishing. The real McCoys have these features:

• WYSIWYG screen display. WYSIWYG stands for "What You See Is What You Get." It means just that – what appears on the computer screen is close to what the printed page will look like. You can see columns of type next to each other and can experiment with different page layout ideas before any of them hits a sheet of paper.

• Several different sizes and styles of type for each page.

• Word processing techniques for typing, storing and revising articles. You can write and rewrite, saving one or both versions on the machine. Cutting and moving paragraphs around is a snap. Type is attractive and *proportionally spaced* (p. 36).

• **Straight or angled lines**, circles, squares and other shapes. Make them without touching a ruler or agonizing over getting them straight. Just tell the computer where they go and how they should look. The same tools will create simple graphs and charts, too.

## Avoid these pitfalls

While desktop publishing could be the answer to your dreams, the road to desktop-publishing heaven is paved with exasperating moments.

• **Don't believe the computer ads** saying you can produce beautiful documents in a flash with little or no experience. Desktop publishing involves sophisticated equipment that takes time to figure out. You'll need to wade through a sea of material before you buy a single thing. Talk with people who already have systems – find out what they like and don't like. Or hire a consultant to recommend a system tailored to your needs. A service bureau (p. 54) might offer this service.

After the equipment is in place, you'll need training – whether through classes or self-teaching. Expect some "down time," when neither you nor the computer can figure out what to do. Expect some screw-ups.

• **Avoid the "ugly newsletter" syndrome.** If you're inexperienced, all the choices available in type styles and page design could lure you into producing one ugly newsletter. See Chapter 8 for the ground rules of good design. Or find a publication you like, and model yours after it. Or ask a professional designer who knows desktop publishing to help set up the look of your paper.

Some companies sell standard page formats that you simply dump your articles into. Watch out. Such formats tend to be boring, and articles never fit the way they're supposed to.

## What about repairs?

Chances are, at some point your computer will act crazy or stubborn and you'll need to troubleshoot the problem.

• **The first place to turn** for help is the manual that comes with the equipment or program. Beware! Computer manuals are notorious for making otherwise sane people start mumbling about how all computer freaks should be shot.

This baby can write articles, fix your grammar, drive you to work, mend your socks, wash dirty dishes, and....

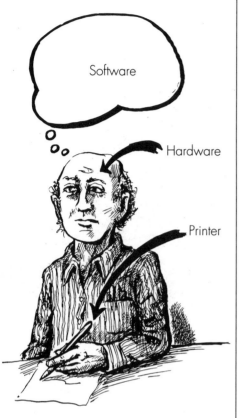

Software

Hardware

Printer

RAM memory stores the information you work with on the computer screen

Not enough RAM

Now- Where was I ??

• If the manual doesn't lead you to the solution, call the store where you bought the equipment and ask for advice. Or call the company that makes the equipment or program. They usually offer telephone consulting and will work through the problem by instructing you over the phone.

• Consider buying a service contract for repair and maintenance, either through the store that sold you the equipment or from another supplier. Many computers come with a one-year service warranty.

• Important questions to ask are: Will service be on-site, or do you have to bring the equipment to them? How quickly can you expect a service person to show up? Will they send someone out nights and on weekends? Most contracts cover normal wear and tear and "crash" repairs.

• Accidents are rarely covered by service contracts. For real peace of mind, buy computer insurance for repairs caused by accidents (like spilling coffee all over the computer).

Check the yellow pages under computer service and repair, or buy a computer magazine with a directory of services in it.

• A good bet for finding cheap help is to connect with a computer "user group." These self-help groups are a great swapping ground for all kinds of information. Authorized dealers for your brand of computer should be able to put you in touch with a user group in your area.

## A tale of two computers

The computer world is divided into two main types: IBM (and IBM-compatibles), and Macintosh. All Zenith machines, for example, are IBM-compatible. The technical differences between the two could fill a book, and the debate over which to buy can be hot and heavy. Both do excellent desktop publishing. The Macintosh has been favored by graphic designers because it relies more on pictures than computer-eze; but IBM/compatibles are quickly catching up.

Unions strongly urge people to buy Zenith, AT&T and NCR systems, which are all IBM-compatible, because they're union-made.

In practical terms, the distinction between IBM and Macintosh simply means that you must buy only equipment or programs that work on the type of computer you have. For example, some computer *printers* (see below) work best with IBM/compatibles, others with Macintosh. A few renegade systems – like NeXt – aren't compatible with either Macs or IBMs.

## The three basics of desktop publishing

• The computer has the power to process and store information, and shows you what it's doing on a VDT-type screen (like office word processors).

• The program (or *software*, p. 44) is a set of instructions your computer "reads" to learn how to do a given task – anything from accounting to setting up page layouts or word processing.

• A computer printer puts what you see on the computer screen onto a piece of paper.

• You'll find packages that sell all three parts as a whole system, or you can buy each separately. Here's how they work:

# The computer

Sometimes computer experts seem to be talking a foreign language. But if you learn these basics you'll know enough to get by:

## Computer memory & storage capacity

The price you pay for a computer is mostly based on the size of its memory and storage capacity. It comes in three varieties:

• RAM, short for Random Access Memory, is computer memory that temporarily holds information you type and work with on the screen. The newsletter article, letter, or other words you enter into the computer first sit in RAM. So does all or part of the *program* that lets you play around with that information. If you want to save this information, you must store it on a *hard* or *floppy disk* (p. 47), because once the computer is turned off, whatever was held by the computer's RAM disappears.

• **The hard disk.** To permanently save information inside your computer you need a *hard disk*. You don't see the disk – it's either built right into the computer, or sits inside a metal box placed near the computer. Don't buy a computer without one. If you already made that mistake, buy a hard disk and have it installed on your machine.

Think of the hard disk as a big filing cabinet that holds all your important papers. It keeps the programs, articles, page layouts, and other information you store on a computer at your fingertips in an orderly system. Everything you enter on the hard disk is stored in neat little files which you can call up and revise.

• **Floppy disks.** Another place to permanently store information is on a thin plastic *floppy disk*, which acts like a briefcase. Your computer will take either a 3½" or 5¼" disk (some take both sizes). It's like a hard disk, only it holds less and works slower. Just like a cassette tape, it can "record" and "play back" information, and you can carry it around with you.

This portability comes in handy when, for example, you want to use a compatible computer or printer in another building. Just put the programs and files you need on the floppy disk, and insert them into the other machine.

Floppy disks also give you great insurance against that most feared event – the computer crash. Computers sometimes just blank out – and lose everything you so carefully stored there. Making copies onto a floppy disk of what you're working on or what's stored on your hard disk can be a pain, but it means you always have a back-up in case something goes wrong.

### How much memory & storage do you need?

• **Bytes & kilobytes.** Whether it's RAM, the hard disk or a floppy disk, storage room is measured in *kilobytes* (abbreviated as k), and *megabytes* (meg). One kilobyte roughly equals one thousand *characters* (or letters). There are 1,000 kilobytes in 1 meg.

A 3½" floppy disk holds 800k (or 1.4 meg if your computer can handle a *high-density* disk). The 5¼" disk holds 360k (or 1.2 meg on the high-density disk).

A computer with 2 meg of RAM (memory) and a 40-meg hard disk (storage space) will get you started with

These computer systems aren't compatible

Mac

IBMs

A hard disk is like a filing cabinet

A floppy disk is like a briefcase

The mouse

Screen icons

DAAA

record 9/90

cpletter 7/30/90

Trash

desktop publishing. Get a larger hard disk (try an 80-meg) if you need to store lots of documents (e.g., union contracts or years of correspondence). *Fonts* (type styles) are sometimes stored on your hard disk – another reason to buy big. P. 52 explains more on fonts.

Keep in mind that the computer industry is constantly coming out with programs needing more RAM (memory) to work. If cost tips your decision in favor of a small-capacity computer, make sure it's one with slots you can insert *RAM chips* into later to beef up the memory. Then you won't need to scrap the computer for a new one.

If your computer is equipped with less memory and storage, you can still do desktop publishing; but you won't be able to run the biggest and best programs. A machine light on RAM works slower, too.

In the long run, buying a computer with enough memory and storage for future needs is better than adding on.

### Power & speed

The *microprocessor* gives your machine its power. It's like the engine of a car, with power similar to a V-8 or a 4-cylinder. The more powerful the computer is, the more efficient it will be.

The *megahertz* at which the microprocessor runs controls the speed of your machine.

How powerful and fast a computer do you need? Desktop publishing generally demands lots of power, because the computer holds and processes plenty of complicated instructions.

For IBM/compatibles, the 286, 386SX and 386 machines are best. For Macintosh, the Classic and LC models give you enough power. To double-check, ask around among people using the programs you want.

### What else you need

When you're computer shopping, make sure the salesperson knows you plan on doing desktop publishing.

● **The monitor (screen).** You'll need a *high resolution* monitor, meaning one that gives sharp, clear screen images. Reading small type or checking how a page looks is a royal pain without one.

For IBM/compatible machines, a *VGA monitor* gives good resolution. Some monitors come as VGA; others need to have a *VGA card* added on.

Color monitors that show all the colors of the rainbow look flashy, but they aren't necessary if you won't be doing *color separations* (p. 166). Spend your money on something else.

Most computer screens aren't big enough to display a full 8½"x11" page (the size of this page). To see the whole page, you must shrink it to fit in the screen. That can make the page so tiny that you have to squint and strain to read the type – if you can read it at all.

Buying a full-page or double-page computer screen isn't cheap ($500-$1,000 for a single-page screen). But if there's money to buy any fancy options, a full-page display is worth it. You'll spare yourself eyestrain, as well as the frustration of not being able to see the whole page at a legible size.

● **The mouse.** Eek! Don't worry, you won't need to chase this *mouse*. It's a small oblong box with one or two buttons on it. As you move the mouse around on a plastic pad on your desk, a little "cursor" on your computer screen moves in the same direction. You use the mouse to point the cursor wherever you want, click a button, and presto! You can then type in new words or instructions at that spot on the page. The Microsoft company sells its mouse for about $89 (discount store).

## The two basic computer families

### The Macintosh

The Macintosh, made by Apple, comes with everything you need for desktop publishing (except the *programs,* p. 50). Its monitor, mouse and *operating system* make the system ready to go with a minimum of fuss. The *operating system* is the structure, or rules,

that you, the program and the computer use to work together. Think of it as a language you all must know to get along.

The Macintosh was the first computer to use *screen icons*: cute little pictures that visually communicate what needs to be done, and where. For example, to call up an article you wrote earlier, simply aim the mouse at the icon that looks like a page with the article's title on it, and click. Or, to erase an

**48**

article you no longer need, look for the trashcan icon, and "throw it away." The computer language and codes you must learn are minimal. You simply see and respond.

The Macintosh can also run programs for business and office needs, including the popular ones originally made to work on IBM machines. But the number of programs available for the Mac doesn't hold a candle to the IBM/compatible world.

Choosing the right Macintosh model is mostly a question of how much memory, speed and storage you need. Some models, with the aid of special programs, can translate information from an IBM disk so you can work with it on your Mac. You might also want to buy an *extended keyboard* with extra keys that can be used to take shortcuts in some programs.

For entry-level desktop publishing the Macintosh Classic with a 40-meg hard drive will do fine (list price: $1,499). But if you want a big screen and a machine that works faster, check out the LC, equipped with a 12" monochrome monitor (list price: $2,700). If you want a fast machine that handles complex programs, look into the Macintosh II family.

• **Advantages:** The Mac's simplicity is its strongest asset – you don't need to buy much extra equipment, or learn much computer language.

• **Disadvantages:** The biggest drawback is that there simply are a lot more IBM/compatibles out there than Macs. To use an article someone wrote on an IBM, you have to either translate the disk information yourself using a special program, or send out the disk to a company that can translate it into a language your Mac can understand. There isn't the huge variety of programs that IBM has. You won't find any union-made Macs.

## IBM PCs & compatibles

IBM and compatible PCs (personal computers) fall into these categories – XT, 286, 386SX or 386. Stay away from the XT. If you already have one, you can buy an *accelerator board* to make it work faster; even so, the machine may never quite work up to snuff.

Recently, IBM/compatibles have progressed by leaps and bounds to become nearly as "user friendly" as the Mac.

Double-page monitor

The most common *operating system* (explained above) for IBM/compatible machines is MS-DOS. When you add a program (p. 50) called *Windows* to a machine with MS-DOS, it suddenly thinks, acts and looks (on the screen) like a Mac. Another alternative is to buy an IBM/compatible that uses the operating system called OS/2. In this case, you don't need to add Windows. OS/2 is already programmed to talk the desktop-publishing language.

Because MS-DOS machines have been around longer than OS/2 ones, you'll find more programs that work only on MS-DOS machines. But this is likely to change.

When shopping for an IBM/compatible, make sure you get the right monitor (a *VGA* type – p. 48) and buy a *mouse* (it's often an extra item). Then you should be ready to roll.

• **Advantages:** If you already have one of these popular machines, it may be relatively cheap to add on desktop publishing. And with the huge variety of programs that work on IBM/compatibles, you can pick and choose features to help manage your mailing list or keep track of dues, for example.

Monitor is too small

Since there are so many of these machines in use, you're likely to find other users to swap and share information with. You can find the union label on some models.

• **Disadvantages:** IBM/compatibles have definitely improved in the "user friendly" area, but you'll still find yourself spending more time learning "computer-eze" than on a Mac. The price tag may be smaller than prices for a Macintosh; but make sure the low price includes the right monitor and mouse. The average IBM/compatible system costs about $1,750.

## Other Computers

Some computers that fall into neither the IBM/compatible nor Macintosh world also offer good desktop systems. The NeXt computer, created by the same brains that invented Macintosh, is billed as the ultimate desktop publishing system. Take a long, hard look at such systems, and use the IBM or Macintosh as a yardstick of comparison.

A big drawback is that you won't get a wide selection of programs and equipment (printers, for example) that work with non-Mac, non-IBM/compatible machines. And you can't easily share information with other machines. Repair and troubleshooting help might be found only through authorized dealers, and if they go bust, you're out of luck in a big way.

# The program

*Programs* tell the computer how to act. When you buy a computer program (also called *software*), you get a floppy disk (or disks) the computer "reads" to learn how to do a given task. Then transfer the program onto your *hard disk* (p. 47); if you don't have a hard disk, you'll have to insert those floppy disks every time you use a program.

A *page layout program* tells how to lay out pages. An accounting program describes spreadsheets and mathematical formulas.

Sometimes you'll buy one program that does everything you need for desktop publishing. But there are really two separate jobs being done: *word processing* and *page layout*. If you don't plan on using word processing for other office tasks, such as writing letters, the word processing in the page layout program may be all you need.

## Word processing

You'll use a word processing program to write articles and other text. See p. 39 for the wonderful things you can do with word processing.

If you produce a very simple newsletter, you can get by with using a word processing program for the whole thing. Top-of-the-line programs like *Microsoft Word* or *WordPerfect* can put type into columns and make nice big headlines. The big drawback is that you can't see how the page looks on the screen, with columns next to each other, unless you switch to a *preview* setting. To make changes on the page, you must switch back to a simpler display. In other words, you don't have WYSIWYG (p. 44).

These word processing programs can also be used with a page layout program. Once you've used word processing to type your articles, store them as *files* on the hard disk or floppy disks until you're ready to move them into a page layout program. Now the fun begins.

## Page layout programs

These programs mimic the work of the typesetter and layout artist. On the screen you'll see familiar tools and terms you used back in the dark ages when you did all the layout by cutting and pasting. You work with an electronic "page" on the screen and add type and graphics by pointing and clicking the mouse at little *icons* (p. 48) displayed on the screen.

• **Set up the page.** To get started in a page layout program, you tell the machine the page size, margins, number of columns and other information for a page. Boxes and borders can be part of the page set-up, or added later. Then the screen shows you what looks like a blank piece of layout paper with all the specifications you just gave it.

• **After you set up a page** tell the machine to get the articles you wrote via a *word processing program* (p. 39), and put them right onto the computer "page" wherever you want. You can align type to the left or right or *justify* (p. 36) or center it, and choose any of several type styles and sizes.

You can add lines (to separate articles for example), boxes or circles (to

Blank computer screen

1. Open up this symbol to see what's in the hard disk

help an article stand out), shading (*screens* or tinting), or special borders.

• **The real beauty** of doing page layout on a computer is being able to change almost anything with ease. If you don't like the type size, push a button or two on the keyboard and mouse and poof! It's another size. Another button, and it's another type style.

If you're trying to decide whether to run a headline across one or two columns, no sweat – try each version and see how it looks. After a while, you'll wonder how you ever had the patience to do page layout the cut-and-paste way.

Once you set up the style of your paper (Chapter 8), you'll make *style tags* to automatically put text or headlines into the right size, typeface (p. 72) and placement your style calls for.

Take a good look at the page layout programs available, and pick the one that feels best. A popular choice is:

• **PageMaker**. Because this cornered the market early on, you'll find lots of people who know and use it. That could make it easier to find help, or to share information with others. There are two versions – one for the Macintosh, another for IBM/compatibles.

Word processing can be done with PageMaker – you don't need a separate program. It has other nice features too: It can wrap text around photos automatically (p. 134), turn type at an angle, expand or condense type to make it taller or thinner, and customize spacing between letters (called *kerning,* p. 134).

• *Advantages:* PageMaker is a simple, yet full-featured program. It's *PostScript* compatible (p. 53), which means you can print pages on a high-quality laser printer or even have a service bureau print them out (p. 54).

• *Disadvantages*: PageMaker isn't cheap. ($795 list, discount store $499). You'll need a powerful computer to use it. On a Mac, you can squeeze by with 1 meg of RAM, but you're better off having two. On IBM/compatibles, don't try it without at least a 286 computer with 1 meg of RAM.

• **If your computer is light on RAM** and your budget is tight, don't despair. There are page layout programs for you, so shop around. While small page layout programs handle the basics, the type *fonts* (p. 52) and printers they work with are limited.

*Publish It!* is a good program for IBM/compatibles and Macs.

2. Open up the hard disk and you'll see folders and documents like these

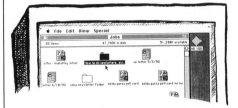

3. If you open up the "How to do newsletters, etc." folder, you'll find these documents listed

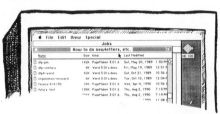

4. Open up the PageMaker folder and ask for a new file and you'll get pages that look like this

Tools you'll use to work on the page

5. Put column guides in PageMaker pages to set it up for your newsletter

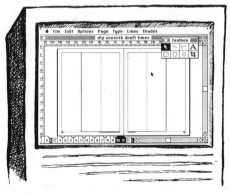

6. Dump chapter you wrote with word processing program into blank pages

7. Enlarge the type you're working on so you can see what you're doing

A *Publish It! Lite* version for IBMs is worth checking out if you're stuck with a dot matrix printer (see below). You won't break the bank buying this program ($50 list, $39 discount store), and it's simple to use; but you're limited to just a few type styles, and each file holds only four pages.

*Publish It! Easy* (for Macs) gives you similar plain-and-simple choices, so a beginner can get off to a flying start. But this program isn't just for beginners. You can switch around to different type sizes and column widths, and can even condense the type or shade it with special patterns. The program takes up 320K of RAM and can be used with nearly any printer (explained next). It includes its own word processing, all for $249 list, discount store $149.

• **If you have ambitious plans** for the design of your publication (Chapter 8) and use a Mac, look into *Quark XPress*. It costs a few dollars more than PageMaker, but makes it easier to do fancy things like starting paragraphs with oversized letters or making subtle changes in the width of letters. An IBM/compatible version will be out soon.

# Computer printers & fonts

The printer slaps onto paper what you see on the computer screen. You can create designs galore in your computer, but just how glorious those designs will look on paper depends on the quality of the printer and *type fonts*. If your printer is too crude to do justice to the subtle curves and flourishes of a type style, it won't look good.

A computer printer can print out several copies of each page; but to avoid unnecessary wear and tear, use a photocopier or a printing press for anything beyond a couple of copies.

### What's a type font?

In the desktop publishing world, a type *font* is one whole family of related type styles (p. 69). For example, when you buy Times, you not only get regular Times, you also get Times italic, Times bold, and Times bold italic; other variations may be thrown in too.

What kind of fonts you buy depends on your printer. Adding fonts can be as easy as plugging a cartridge into the printer, or buying a floppy disk with the font on it. Beware of bargain-priced fonts – they may be of inferior quality, and not worth the headaches.

Adobe and Bitstream make high-quality fonts for nearly every kind of printer. A floppy disk containing four fonts costs about $180 for the Mac, or $129 for IBM/compatibles. Fancy and hot-selling fonts will cost more. Font cartridges will run around $195 (list).

### Dots per inch

When evaluating any printer, find out how many *dots per inch* (called dpi) it makes. That's because printers make type out of teeny little dots. The more dots they can fit into one square inch, the finer the type will be. The standard *dot-matrix* printer can print only 72 dots per inch, making type much coarser and harder to read than type from a *laser printer* that prints 300 dots per inch.

### Dot-matrix printers

These are the bottom-of-the-line printers. Each letter is formed when a series of metal pins strikes out the dots in a matrix pattern.

In the worst cases, the dots are so big the letters look more like a bundle of spots than actual words. Apart from how awful that looks, you're sure to give your reader eyestrain. It can make a newsletter almost impossible to read.

The best dot-matrix printers – those called letter-quality – have more pins and strike out smaller dots to make the letters. They can make acceptable looking 10- or 12-point type (*point size*, p. 67), but the quality goes downhill for small sizes (9 point and under) and big sizes (over 18 point).

If you're stuck with a dot-matrix printer, you'll get better quality if you buy special computer software that helps it create sharper, clearer type. Check out *Type Manager* ($99 list, discount store $55) for fonts made by Adobe, and *Facelift* ($69) for fonts made by Bitstream.

Another way to make do with a dot-matrix printer is to use it to set articles and send out headlines to a typesetting shop – or set headlines yourself with a headline machine or rub-off transfer lettering (p. 38).

• **Advantages:** Favored for their low cost, these printers are improving

This is all *the type you* **get from buying** *one type font.*

Dot-matrix printed type
72 dpi

me-Warner had
ers, and other
the nation's
Gannett, the
owned 8 TV
Harris poll,

Laser printed type
300 dpi

·computer you use for
ng can perform a whole
ffice tasks – such as
pdating and printing
i yes, those tricky form
written for you alone.

Imagesetter printed type
1,270 dpi

i and the computer
ken in, you can get
ns ready for the printer
own home or office.

cles onto the computer
e advantages of *word*

bit by bit, and may become respectable.

- **Disadvantages:** Type quality leaves plenty to be desired. There's little point in buying many fonts, because they won't look very good.

- **Prices:** The Apple ImageWriter dot-matrix printer for Macs costs about $500. A higher quality choice for IBM/compatible owners is the Epson LQ-850 costing $749 ($500 discount store).

## Laser printers

For desktop publishing, this is by far the best choice. It churns out smooth, crisp, high-quality pages, including type, lines and pictures. The most common laser printers produce type and graphics at 300 dots per inch, and come with some fonts built in.

Here's how a laser printer works: The computer sends the image to the printer via a cable, using a special code language. The printer holds the job in its memory just long enough to receive the whole document. Next, the special code language is translated into characters, lines or whatever image you created, and a laser beam of light transfers the image onto the paper.

For everything to come out right on the printed page, it's essential that the computer, program and printer all understand the same language. Otherwise it'll be like English-speakers trying to understand Greek.

- **Bit-map laser printers.** The language code a *bit-map* laser printer uses is based on a grid pattern of dots turned on or off. That grid can't bend or curve, which doesn't affect the quality of the type much so long as you buy high-quality fonts. However, graphics can come out looking a little jaggedy.

Better models can reduce or enlarge type fonts to almost any size, but with cheaper bit-map laser printers, you can be stuck with a limited number of sizes.

- *Advantages:* Good type quality. Not as expensive as a *PostScript* printer (explained next).

- *Disadvantages:* Graphics may look choppy. Using this printer makes it near-impossible to hook up to fancy laser *imagesetters* (p. 54).

- *Prices*: The Hewlett-Packard LaserJet Series III are top-of-the-line bit-map models starting at $2,395. But decent printers start as low as $1,700.

- **PostScript laser printers** give you the best quality (that is, until something new takes their place). These printers

Dot-matrix printer

use an *object-oriented* method to create letters, lines, or any image by arranging teensy dots into an outline of the object. This outline is then filled in with little dots.

- *Advantages:* Type looks sharp and crisp, but you'll really notice the superior quality if you use clip art or *draw programs* (p. 54). Each outline can be enlarged or reduced, so letters can be anywhere from a microscopic 4 points tall to a huge 650 points, depending on the computer program. Using this printer makes it easy to print final pages with a fancy *imagesetter* (p. 54).

- *Disadvantages:* Quality doesn't come cheap. Printing complex pages can take forever.

- *Prices*: The Apple LaserWriter IINT is a PostScript printer that's a popular match for the Macintosh. Hewlett-Packard LaserJet Series III printers, a common mate for IBM/compatible computers, can have PostScript added on. Prices range from $2,500 on up.

Laser printer

Data-driven graphic

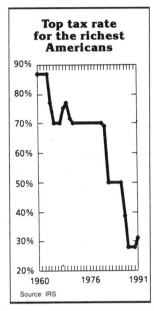

**Top tax rate for the richest Americans**

Source: IRS

Chart the above graphic came from

| Labels | A |
|--------|-------|
| 1960 | 87% |
| 1964 | 77% |
| 1965 | 70% |
| 1968 | 75.25% |
| 1969 | 77% |
| 1970 | 71.75% |
| 1971 | 70% |
| 1981 | 69.13% |
| 1982 | 50% |
| 1987 | 38.5% |
| 1988 | 28% |
| 1991 | 31% |

## What a basic desktop publishing system will cost you

*Prices range between:*

Computer ................. $1,500 – $3,000
(including standard monitor,
mouse and 40-meg. hard disk)

Full-page display ........... $500 – $1,000
(optional)

Laser printer ............. $1,700 – $3,000

Program ..................... $150 – $500
_____
Total ...................... $3,850 – $7,500

## Service bureaus

PostScript is also the language used by top-quality *imagesetting machines* – the newest generation of typesetting equipment. Linotronic imagesetters print anywhere from 1,270 to 2,540 dots per inch. That's quality.

You won't be buying one of these machines – prices start at over $20,000. Instead try a *service bureau* that has one.

For the very best quality, use your own printer for proofreading, and then put the whole job on a *floppy disk* (p. 47) and take it to a service bureau. Their imagesetter will "read" the disk and print out pages. It costs $8 - $10 a page. You don't even have to leave your office if you have a phone *modem* (p. 55).

If you don't need the best quality and don't have your own laser printer, many shops will also print out pages on a laser printer for about 50¢ to $1 per page.
- **What to ask a service bureau:**
- *Can they "read" the files from your computer?* Tell them what computer and program(s) you have, and ask which can be used. You must use a program that's PostScript-compatible, and you'll have fewer problems if your printer is PostScript too (p. 53).
- *How many dpi* (dots per inch) does their machine print? Usually 1,270 dpi looks great. Ask for samples.
- *How much does it cost?* You'll usually be charged by the page, but they'll also charge an hourly rate if they have to do extra things like fix your mistakes or change the typeface. Do they charge more for rush jobs?
- *How quickly can they guarantee they'll get the job done?* If you send the job over a phone *modem* (explained next), can you expect to pick it up in a few hours, or in a day or two?
- *Do they offer other services* like *scanning* (p. 55), translating files from IBM to Mac (and vice-versa), training or consulting?

# Beyond the bare-bones system

## Data-driven graphics

To help readers make sense of complex numbers and trends, this type of program is a must. Feed the figures into the machine and tell the computer what to make of them – a pie-chart, a bar graph, a line graph or two, you name it. Click, and it's done! (P. 157)

Check out *Cricket Graph* ($129) or *DeltaGraph* (for Macs only; list: $195, $109 discount store). You'll find some *spreadsheet programs* (used for accounting) also come with chart and graph-making tools. *Excel* is one such program.

## Computer clip art

Clip art, those little drawings you keep on hand for emergency use, also comes on computer disks. Instead of pasting in graphics, you put the clip art in the right spot on the computer page layout.

The advantage is that you can see how it looks before finishing the page, and can make it whatever size you want. But if you don't mind taking a few moments to paste pictures onto the finished page (p. 150), computer art isn't worth the bother.

Some computer clip art looks coarse and blotchy, while other kinds aren't half bad. The best stuff is created for PostScript laser printers.

Clip art must be compatible with your computer, programs and printer. Check the *file format* of clip art you're interested in to see if it'll run on your system. EPS and PICT, for example, are high-quality formats that work with a *PostScript laser printer* (p. 53). CGM is a high-quality format for *bit-map laser printers*. PNTG or PNT-formatted clip art won't look as good. P. 159 tells more.

## Draw programs

To draw your own pictures on the computer, give a *draw program* a whirl. You can draw shapes, reduce or enlarge them, tilt them, and do lots of other nifty things. The shapes can be filled with solid, tinted or textured patterns. For free-hand drawing, the mouse acts as your pencil or brush.

But unless you have a serious artist on staff, you may find these programs too expensive and awkward to be worth the bother.

*Adobe Illustrator* is a high-quality *object-oriented* draw program with versions for Macs or IBM/compatibles. *Freehand*, for Macintosh, and *Corel-Draw* for IBM/compatibles are other good choices. They also come with a hefty price tag (over $500, or $300 discount). For something simpler and cheaper, try lower-quality *bit-mapped* programs: MacPaint for the Mac ($125 list, discount store $92) or PC Paintbrush Plus for IBM/compatibles ($199 list, discount store $119).

## Phone modems

A phone *modem* connects your computer to other computers via telephone lines.

If you use a service bureau, you don't have to cart around the floppy disk. Just send the whole newsletter, page by page, over the phone. You're certain to run into a few snafus at first, but once you get it rolling, you'll love the convenience.

Whether you choose a plain or fancy model, get a reliable brand specifically made for your Mac or IBM/compatible. The *baud rate* measures how fast the phone modem sends and receives messages. A 2400-baud modem should do you fine. *Communications software* helps the computer understand phone line messages; it may come with the modem or be included in an "all-purpose" program you already have, or you may have to buy it separately.

Expect to pay $200 to $250 for a decent phone modem. Some computers come with built-in phone modems.

## Scanners

A scanner can "read" an image from a slip of paper in your hand, and copy it directly onto your computer screen. Once that image is on the screen, slip it into a page layout, and it'll show up on the finished page – without paste-up. While the image is on the screen you can fiddle with it, adding some lines and shapes and erasing others.

● **Scanning pictures.** Scanners have a lot of potential, but for now they mostly appeal to computer hackers who think it's a disgrace to do anything by hand. Most of the time it's faster to paste the original graphic on the page and touch it up by hand.

Scanners can "read" photos, but they must be broken into a pattern of grey shades (called a *grey scale*). Better scanners read more shades of grey, while the cheaper ones basically see black and white. Even the best still don't match the quality you get from giving photos to a printer and asking the printer to *halftone* them (p. 154).

● **You can also scan printed words** so they'll pop up on the computer screen. But since they come into the computer as an image, you can't edit the words you've scanned without an *OCR*

Phone modem

Scanner

Bit-mapped clip art

PostScript clip art

Proper ergonomics

(optical character recognition) *program* like OmniPage.

If you hate to type, a scanner can rescue you from much of it. But while improvements are steadily coming, there are still bugs in the system. Some scanners have trouble reading different styles of type, and you'll find weird characters pop up where words or punctuation marks should be.

Prices on scanners range from $100 for small hand-held types to over $4,000 for the fancy ones. You'll probably have to shell out $1,200 to $1,400 to get something worthwhile. The technology is quickly advancing, so cheaper, im-

proved models should keep coming out.

If you're just starting out in desktop publishing and can type, hold off on a scanner. Once you know the ropes, you can decide if it would be a time-saver or a toy.

## CD-ROM player & discs

One CD-ROM compact disc gives you 650 meg of information. You can buy one disk with, for example, a big dictionary, book of quotes, thesaurus and library reference book for $100. For now, you must also pay at least $600 for a drive to "play" your discs; but prices are falling.

## Preventive care to ward off disaster

Some glitches, like a surge of electric power, can destroy everything you're working on. By planning ahead, you can avoid such disasters.

• **First, buy a good surge protector.** It can cut the power supply, preventing any damage from too much juice hitting your machines. It ranges in price from $15 to over $100. A mid-priced one will do the trick.

• **Although the computer may seem** to be your best friend, don't ever trust it 100%. Make occasional *hard copies* (printed-out sheets) or floppy disks of what you're doing so that if the whole computer "crashes" you won't lose anything.

• **Ergonomics.** Working on a computer for most of the day can cause eyestrain, muscle aches and fatigue. The constant, repeating motion in the hands and wrists, especially if it's done at a bad angle, can cause "repetitive strain injury." It starts with tingling or numbness, and could lead to permanent damage.

Protect yourself by paying attention to *ergonomics* – the study of how to make the job fit the human being.

• *Get a fully adjustable chair*, desk and computer screen. Adjust them so that your hands rest comfortably at the keyboard, with the wrists slightly sloped down. Keep your elbows in close to your body, and plant your feet solidly on the floor.

• *Take breaks.* If you've got a pounding headache or your vision gets blurry, you've been working on the machine too long. The experts suggest a 15-minute break for every two hours at the keyboard – and every hour if you're typing non-stop.

• *Adjust the lighting.* When office lighting reflects onto your computer screen, the glare will hurt your eyes. Move lights or furniture around, or buy an *anti-glare shield* to fit over your screen.

• *Brightness.* Most computer screens have a dial that turns the brightness up or down. Set it so it's not so bright that it hurts your eyes.

• *Screen size.* To avoid eyestrain, it's worth investing in a big screen that shows whole pages at a time (p. 48).

• *For more tips,* union health-and-safety departments can help. The UAW, for example, publishes a "UAW Guide to Visual Display Units." Beyond that, what feels best to you is often your best bet.

A surge protector looks like a multi-outlet electrical plug

## Computers aren't the be-all & end-all

If you decide desktop publishing is more trouble than you're ready to take on, don't feel like you just crawled out of the cave. The bottom line is to produce a newsletter or leaflet that appeals to your readers; you don't need a desk-

top publishing system to do that. This technology will still be around when and if you're ready.

There are plenty of books and magazines on desktop publishing. Since the field changes practically overnight, get your hands on the most current material. Check out *Publish* magazine, 501 Second St., San Francisco, CA 94107; or visit your library.

# 7. Printing: What's right for you?

**P**rinting techniques are hard to imagine if you've never seen them at work. But this chapter should at least give you an idea what process fits your job, and how to work with it.

## Using a mimeo machine

Mimeograph is a do-it-yourself method that's cheap and easy to master. It's not hard to find second-hand equipment, and if you can't afford your own machine, many unions, schools and other groups have mimeos they'll share.

Mimeo prints by squeezing ink through holes in a *stencil*. Order stencils and other supplies from the company that makes the mimeo machine. Put the stencil into the mimeograph machine, ink it up, and away it'll roll, cranking out up to 15,000 copies from one stencil.

### Old-fashioned stencils

You can still find stencils you type the words directly into, but they have serious drawbacks. To correct major mistakes, you must start all over again with a new stencil. The only pictures and headlines you get are thin lines you must draw into the stencil with a *stylus*.

### Get a stencil-cutter

It's worth the trouble to instead find an *electrostencil* machine, or buy a mimeo machine with a built-in stencil-cutter. Then you can lay out and paste up pages as you would for other kinds of printing, complete with bold headlines, clipped art and other pictures. That'll give your publication the visual excitement it needs.

First make a *mechanical* by putting all the type and pictures together on a layout sheet (p. 149), and then slip the mechanical into the electrostencil machine. The machine scans each mechanical and copies it by cutting the image through a stencil at the same time. The stencil is stronger than the ones you type into, and prints more copies.

### Modern mimeo

The latest generation of mimeo machines, called *copier-printers*, is quite a step up. You don't need a separate stencil-cutter. Just place your page mechanical in the mimeo machine, press a few buttons, and it automatically cuts the stencil, loads it onto the roller, and starts printing the job. When it's done, it even spits the used stencil into the garbage. Some also print 11" x 17" sheets you can fold for a full-size newsletter.

The fanciest of these modern marvels can print a job directly from a personal computer (Chapter 6).

### Money

Fancy copier-printers start at $6,500, but you can pick up good, older equipment, including the stencil-cutter, for

Page mechanical

Leaflet mimeoed without electrostencil

Mimeoed with an electrostencil

Electrostencil machine
mechanical    stencil

Modern mimeo machine
called a *copier-printer*

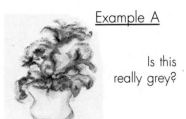

Example A

Is this
really grey?

$2,000 or less. Look in the yellow pages under duplicating machines and supplies. Get a service contract, if possible, and avoid machines so obsolete you can't find parts.

Even if you use someone else's machine, make sure you put money for supplies in your budget: for ink boxes ($15 each), paper, stencils (20¢ a page), stencil correction fluid, staples (if any), and needles for the stencil cutter. Paper comes in *reams* – bundles of 500 sheets – costing $4 - $8 for 8½"x11" and $8 - $12 for 11"x17" sheets.

## Tips for working with mimeo

Avoid messiness by cleaning the machine before each use and not over-inking it.

• **Anything but pure white** – even newsprint – could be cut through as black or a messy grey. And the edges of overlapping paper might show up as lines (*shadows*) on the stencil.

An experienced operator can adjust the stencil-cutter so it won't make a mess, and even if it does, you can patch up some messiness with *stencil correction fluid*. But your best bet is to xerox the mechanical before you put it into the stencil-cutter, turning it into pure black and white. If shadows or dirt appear on the copy, cover them with typing correction fluid made for copies.

• **What if you want photos** and other grey areas to show up? Neither mimeo machines nor printing presses actually print grey. They really print tiny black specks your eye mixes, so they look like grey – like example A.

To transform a photo into those tiny dots, get a print shop to make a *velox* print (at $5 to $8 a shot), and put that on the mechanical. The photo can be reduced or enlarged when you make the velox at no extra cost so it'll fit perfectly on the page (*sizing*, p. 162).

You don't have to go to all that trouble, though, if your electrostencil machine has a *photo* setting. When you press that, the stencil-cutter will break grey areas into tiny specks, leaving the

black areas pure black. P. 161 gives tips and tricks for mimeoed photos.

• **If the page has heavy black headlines** or pictures, the stencil could stick to the paper as it's being printed. Make that less likely by placing the mechanical in the electrostencil machine upside-down, so dark areas will fall at the bottom of the stencil.

• **Add colorful pizazz** to a mimeoed newsletter by pasting your front-page *banner* (p. 70) on a layout sheet. Print up several month's worth of front pages with the banner alone, using bright-colored ink. As you lay out each newsletter, leave a blank space on the front for the banner. Then mimeo each front page (with black ink) onto the papers with colored banners.

The mimeo itself can print with colored ink, if you replace the black *ink box* with a colored one. Expect to run several lousy copies, as the machine adjusts to the new color.

## Is this for you?

• **Advantages:** Although mimeo is taking a back seat to office copiers, it still makes sense for printing 100 or more copies of leaflets or newsletters on a regular basis. You can run off copies in your own office, whenever you need them. Older machines are bargain-priced, and all mimeos are dirt-cheap to operate. They're less likely to break down than copiers (coming up next), and can last forever. Quality is good enough for most purposes, and they can print on whatever paper your heart desires, even fancy stocks (p. 62).

• **Disadvantages:** Mimeo machines can be a real pain to operate. You could find yourself covered with ink, with stencils and paper flying everywhere. Mimeo can't print some tiny details, so quality won't match that of copiers and photo-offset printing (p. 60).

Older machines won't print paper larger than 8½"x14". (P. 66 discusses page sizes.) Newer ones print on 11"x17" sheets, but the print area is so small you'll have 1½" *margins* (p. 68) on the side of each page. You must fold, collate and/or staple newsletters by hand.

# Office copiers

You just can't beat the convenience of an office copy machine – until it

breaks down every week. The cheapest desk-top models are too slow to make more than a few copies at a time; but move up a notch or two, and you'll find machines that whip out hundreds of copies in a flash. Modern copiers do a good job with pictures and small details, and overall quality can be excellent.

If you don't have your own machine, you'll find quick-print shops with good copiers on almost every city corner.

## When should you use a copier?

This is the best choice for quickly running off a hundred or so copies. A sturdy machine is also fine for running off 500 leaflets now and then, but using a copier for all your printing needs is *not* the way to go – yet.

Any copier – even the most super-duper – gets expensive to run as the number of copies goes up. With every click of the copy button, copier parts wear out. You can count on replacing the drum and developer (sometimes called a copy cartridge) at least once a year – costing anywhere from $375 on up. The more expensive the copier, the more the drum costs. Then there are supplies. Every copier uses *toner*, a powder that acts like ink. Toner cartridge refills cost $40 to $60 a shot.

## Service

Copiers seem to enjoy breaking down. The machine itself tells you how to pull out all the pieces of paper it gobbles up. But normal wear and tear also require service. In offices with heavily-used copiers, the copier repairperson will seem like one of the gang.

Don't take a chance – get a service contract. It's expensive, especially if it covers parts like the drum; but that's better than getting socked with a repair bill you can't pay. You'll pay either a flat fee or a set amount for every copy made (around 1½¢ per copy) – or both.

## Tips for using copiers

Clean the copier glass often – smudges and dirt do show up. Sometimes copiers also pick up *shadows* (p. 58), giving you ugly black lines all over the place. Fiddle with the "light-dark" controls to get rid of those lines. If that doesn't work, "white out" the lines with *typing correction fluid* made for copies. Then run off that copy.

• **Colored originals.** Like mimeo machines, copiers divide the world into black and white – what's dark will come out black, what's light will be white, and what's in-between will be splotchy. Pastel images might not show up, and newsprint or colored backgrounds could look smudgy – or worse. Tinkering with

the machine's light-dark controls could solve the problem.

• **Photos.** If you have a copier with a photo setting, it'll pick up the grey shades in photos. To print a page with photos, you may have to make one copy without photos to get a "clean" copy. Paste the photo(s) in place, and run the whole job using the photo setting.

If you don't have a photo setting, make *velox* prints (p. 58) of photos you plan to use. Or buy a clear plastic *screen* of tiny dots at an office or artists' supply store. Letracopy HT, made by Letraset, costs around $5, and can be used again and again. Make a copy of the photo with the screen over it, put the "screened" photo on the page mechanical, and you're ready to run.

## Special options

• **Most new machines can reduce or enlarge** a printed area (down to 64% of original – see example B). That's an option worth having; it's great for making *graphics* fit a layout – p. 162.

• **Fancy models** will copy both front and back of each sheet of paper, then collate and staple the whole job. (But they only staple in the corner – p. 66 – and can't fold newsletters.) Just remember, the bells and whistles will cost you.

• **Paper sizes & weights.** Copiers print standard (8½"x11") and legal-size (8½"x14") paper. Most now also take 11"x17" sheets and can handle textured or heavy paper (p. 61) – within reason. Check it out.

• **Colored ink.** With some copiers, printing in red, brown, green or blue is as simple as replacing the black toner cartridge with a colored one. To get two or more colors on the same sheet, prepare two *mechanicals* (p. 57). Then run the paper through the machine twice, copying each mechanical with a different color cartridge installed.

## Should you buy one?

If you need a copier for other office tasks, it may be worth going upscale and buying one that can also print your newsletter or flyers. A good copier, such as Xerox's 5028Z, will reduce and enlarge and can handle photos, and it'll print pages as large as 11"x17". Its $5,325 price includes a three-year contract for service (but not expensive parts like the copy cartridge).

• **Advantages:** Having the machine in your office means you can fiddle

Try printing banner separately with colored ink

Modern office copier

What copiers can do to photos

Photo printed on copier with photo setting

Example B
Art reduced to 64%

High contrast

Halftone

<u>Chart H</u>

## Leaflet printing costs
### Spring 1991

Printed on one side only with black ink on 8½"x11"plain 60-lb. (or equivalent) paper.

| | *Number of copies:* | | |
|---|---|---|---|
| | 250 | 1000 | 5000 |
| Copier at quick-copy shop | $15 | $60 | * |
| **Offset** | | | |
| plastic or paper plate | $18 | $35 | $127 |
| metal plate | $40 | $55 | $155 |
| printed on fancy paper | $43 | $66 | $210 |
| with colored ink instead of black | $45 | $60 | $160 |
| with colored ink plus black | $75 | $95 | $225 |

Extra cost for each halftone (metal plate only): $15      Each velox: $7

\* ridiculously expensive

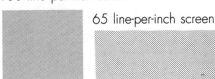

100 line–per-inch screen

65 line-per-inch screen

around with quality and quickly get copies at any time of day or night – as long as the copier behaves. You don't have to mess with ink, stencils and adjusting rollers. Copiers reduce or enlarge graphics (p. 59) for pennies a shot, and some do a fine job with photos. Every year copiers get faster and more economical for small jobs.

- **Disadvantages:** Expensive to buy and expensive to keep. You can't do without a service contract, and the more you print, the more it costs. Fancy "extras" cost extra. Makes sense only if you're printing 100 copies or less of each job – and can't get easy access to someone *else's* office copier.

### Quick-copy shops

Commercial shops will copy each 8½"x11" page for 6¢–10¢, and charge $15–$20 for 250 copies. Most also have paper-plate or plastic-plate printing equipment (explained next), which will probably be cheaper for 500 or more copies. You may have to wait a couple of hours or overnight to get your copies, but that probably beats the time a full-scale print shop would take (p. 64). For larger jobs, however, the savings in time and money quickly disappear.

- **Advantages:** Cheap and fast for small quantities, and it's easy to get graphics reduced or enlarged.
- **Disadvantages:** Most shops are non-union and staffed by exploited part-timers, so quality varies from shop to shop. Since speed is often their middle name, you may have trouble getting people to fool around with the controls to get photos and details printed right, or to fix *shadows* (p. 58). To get fancy stock (p. 62), you may have to bring your own paper.

# Offset printing

Offset covers a range of processes, from the simple printing machines in the local quick-copy shop to the huge *web press* used by newspapers. Offset usually means *photo offset lithography*. Each word describes part of the process.

In a nutshell, photo offset printing involves the four steps in example C.

### Photo

The finished mechanical is called *camera-ready*. The printer shoots that with a camera to get a *film negative*. There are only two colors to the negative – black and transparent. Black type, lines, etc. become transparent on the negative. Dark greys and dark colors become clear too, and white or light colors come out black. Some colors are hard to predict. To the camera, red looks like black and a pure, *non-repro* shade of *blue* looks like white.

Usually more shows up on the negative than you'd like – spots of dirt, *shadows* (p. 58), etc. A printer fills in the transparent areas made by dirt and shadows with a fine brush and liquid.

- **Halftones.** With only black and transparent on the negative, how do photos end up printed in shades of grey? If you look at any printed grey carefully, you'll find that it's really made up of tiny black and white dots. How does it get that way? It's *halftoned*.

Each photo is shot separately, with a dotted *screen* between the lens and the negative film. The screen could have from 65 to 200 or so "lines" per inch, and this determines how visible the dots will be. As the light goes through the screen it's broken into fat and skinny dots, depending on how light or dark the grey is.

Meanwhile, either you or the printer puts black or red paper, the exact size and shape the photo should be, on the mechanical. Called a *silhouette* or *knockout*, this black or red shape appears as a clear *window* on the film negative when the page is shot. (Sometimes printers don't bother with knockouts. You put lines (a *keyline*, p. 154) on the mechanical and they use it as a guide to cut a window for each photo directly into the negative with a blade.)

Once the photo is halftoned separately, the printer just slaps the halftone negative into the window, and presto! The halftone is integrated into the page.

- **Fancy moves.** The halftone negative can be reduced or enlarged as it's shot, so the photo will turn out the right size (*sizing*, p. 162). Or plan to have the photo's edges cut or partly covered by the black of the page negative by *cropping* (p. 160).

A printer can put *screens* into negative windows to give you flat grey areas on the printed page. Other techniques on p. 164 are also done with negatives.

## Lithography

Lithography is based on the simple principle that oil and water won't mix. The film negative, complete with halftones, is placed over a thin metal plate coated with light-sensitive chemicals. A strong light is beamed onto both. The light shines through the transparent area (type and lines, etc.) of the negative, where it hardens the chemicals on the plate into a greasy lacquer surface. But the light gets blocked by the black areas of the negative. In those areas, the chemicals are washed off.

Then the plate is fastened around a cylinder on the press and doused with water. The water settles only on the metal, and not on the greasy hardened chemicals. When an oil-based ink is rolled on, it's repulsed by the water and settles on the greasy areas. If it were unrolled, the "inked plate" now would look exactly as the page mechanical looked, except the greys are dotted, paper edges have disappeared, and there are no colors except the ink.

This metal plate is covered alternately with water and ink as it prints.

## Offset

If you printed paper directly against this plate, the paper would be soaking wet – and the image would be printed backwards. By *offset* this is avoided. The wet plate prints a mirror image onto a rubber-coated "blanket" cylinder. When the rubber-coated cylinder then prints onto the paper, the image becomes frontwards again, and drier.

## Sheet-fed presses

Most offset presses are *sheet-fed*, which mean large sheets of paper are printed one at a time. There may be one page or 32 pages on each sheet, depending on the size of the press. A small press can only print one side of the paper. To print both sides, the whole job is sent through the press a second time, with the paper flipped over. That doubles all your costs except paper.

After the paper's printed, an automatic *folding machine* folds each sheet into pages and a *cutter* slices the pages to size. A *collator* puts pages in the right order, while a *binder* or *saddle stitcher* staples them together.

## The paper

Plain paper is called 60-lb. offset, with a white wove or vellum finish. To make your newsletter or leaflet look

special, consider a colored, textured and/or heavy paper stock.

Most paper comes in huge packages, and prices vary widely. Printers will stock several choices, plus they might have fancy leftovers from someone else's job which you could pick up for a song. Or try a paper dealer. If you don't find what you want, consider special-ordering the paper. However, you might get billed for a full package you don't use up, and delivery could take a couple of weeks. Ask the printer to show you samples, feel the papers, and nail down the delivery date and price.

Here are the variables:

• **The weight.** This measures how heavy a standard bundle of *text* paper is. (*Cover* stock is weighed differently – 65-lb. cover stock is similar to 119-lb. text.) Try 60-lb. text for most jobs. (That's about the same as 20-lb. mimeo or copier paper.) Consider 55-lb. paper for one-sided leaflets only; it's so thin the ink might show through on the back. To make leaflets or brochures nice and sturdy, look into 70- or 80-lb. stock. But the heavier the paper, the more it costs.

• **The color.** Each paper comes in a variety of colors. Don't get carried away with using color, though. If your paper or leaflet has photographs, stick to white or an off-white ivory; pastels and dark papers wash out and ruin photos. Photos printed on green paper will have

Example C

Four steps of photo offset printing: Camera-ready mechanical

knockout
non-repro blue lines
Photo

2. The negative is *burned* into a *plate* with the image on it.

1. The *mechanical* (the laid-out page) is photographed to create a *film negative*.

film negative
window
opaquing
Halftone negative

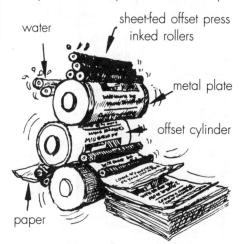

3. The plate is fastened around a cylinder on the press, and inked up.

water
sheet-fed offset press inked rollers
metal plate
offset cylinder
paper

4. The plate rolls around, transferring (i.e. *offsetting*) the image onto a roller and then onto paper.

Printed leaflet

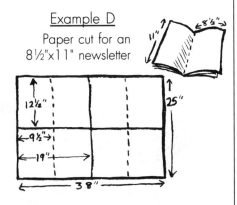

Example D

Paper cut for an
8½"x11" newsletter

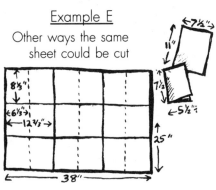

Example E

Other ways the same
sheet could be cut

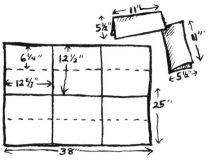

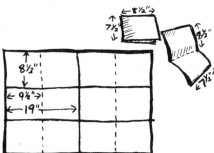

Example F

Paper is recycled

Example G

Paper *can be* recycled

people with green faces.

Avoid loud colors like pink or chartreuse – they'd give anyone reading fine type a headache.

Since printers' inks are transparent, the paper's color will blend with the color of the ink, changing it. Look for samples of various ink colors printed on the paper you want, so you'll know what you're getting.

• **The texture.** Although textured papers will cost you, many look and feel wonderful. Each paper company offers a variety, from a pebbly surface to subtle lines (*laid*), to a smooth *velvet* or *satin* finish. Photos come out best on slick *coated* stock; but choose a *matte* or non-glossy version if you've also got small type. With shinier types, the glare interferes with reading.

• **The size.** Papers come in standard sizes, usually 23"x35" or twice that big (35"x45"), or 25"x38". As example D shows, those big sheets are easily cut into an 8½"x11" leaflet or newsletter.

If you'd like an unusual-size brochure or newsletter, example E shows different ways standard 25"x38" paper can be sliced. Always figure an inch or so of each dimension will be wasted, *trimmed* off as the paper is cut to size.

• **Recycled paper** is available only in limited weights and colors. You're saving forests only when you buy paper made of *post-consumer* waste. The recycled paper this book is printed on is 10% post-consumer waste. (Pre-consumer waste refers to paper-mill rejects that would've been thrown back into the paper-making vat anyway.) True recycled paper comes in packages with one of the recycling symbols in example F. The symbol with hollow triangles that aren't in a dark circle (example G) means the paper *can* be recycled, *not* that it's *made* of recycled fibers.

• **Newsprint.** This is best used for throw-away items like the daily paper. It comes in rolls and can only be printed on a *web press* (p. 63). Don't settle for the very cheapest grade of paper – it looks grey, ruins the photos, turns yellow within weeks, tears easily, and makes your paper look like a puppy rest stop. Instead, try 35-lb. *bright*, or better yet, use the 50-lb. white offset paper that comes in rolls.

## The ink

You needn't stick to black ink. Ask to see the printer's chart (p. 146) showing the colors you can get. Colored inks cost slightly more than black, plus the cost of washing the press (around $15).

Printing with a color *in addition* to black on the same side of paper is more expensive. To prepare a mechanical for that, consult p. 166. The printer has to make two sets of negatives and plates. One plate is covered with black ink, and the second is rolled with colored ink – whatever shade you chose. To print two colors on a small press with one plate, the whole job runs through the press twice. That's time-consuming and can double all your costs but the paper.

Each ink is semi-transparent, so printing one color on top of another gives you a third color, just like mixing two different colors of paint. P. 146 gives tips on choosing ink colors.

Some inks have to dry overnight before the paper can be folded.

### Printing in full color

A whole rainbow of colors can be made from four *primary* shades – red, blue, yellow and black. Look carefully at full-color pictures in the newspaper, and you'll notice that they're made from tiny dots. (In magazines, the dots are so eensy you can see them only with a magnifying glass.) Just as your eye mixes black dots to see grey, it mixes those basic colors to get all the other shades. In the old days, no group with less than a million members or a readership of stockbrokers could afford full-color publications. But that's changing.

By using four colors, you can carry full-color photos. But there's a hitch: How do you separate photos into dots of primary colors? Printers make *color separations*: When shooting the negative for each plate they use *screens* (p. 60) and *filters* to block all but one of the basic four colors each time. That gives them four plates, and they roll the right color ink on the right plate. Separations now cost $85 to $125 a photo.

But if the ink is too strong on the red plate, the photo will come out with a red tinge. If you're printing in color, ask for a *color key* proof that shows the colors on sheets of clear acetate laid over each other. Or for a few dollars more, get a more accurate *chromalin* or *match print*, showing the color mix on paper.

Remember: With freedom comes responsibility. The more color you have, the more decisions you must make about where and when to use it (p. 147). That's fun – if you've got the time.

## Services printers offer

• Some offset print shops will type-set and set up pages as well as print them. But don't just hand them a bunch of articles and expect them to put together a whole paper. That's your job – p. 138 explains why.

• The mailing services some printers offer can save you both time and money. See p. 173.

• For folks with money to burn, there's no limit to what a printer can do to fix up photos. Fancy machines can even change the earrings your photo subject is wearing.

## Choosing standard photo offset

The basic process described above is a sheet-fed photo offset method using a negative and a *metal plate* (as opposed to a paper or plastic plate). Here's why such a press may – or may not – suit your job:

• **Advantages:** The best quality, especially for photos. You can play around with all sorts of papers, ink and special techniques (Chapter 18).

All big presses use metal plates, and if you're printing several thousand copies, a photo offset press is economical. Each metal plate can print 100,000 copies or more. The negatives are expensive, but the printer normally saves them, so you won't have to pay for new ones if you reprint the job later.

Many shops are unionized.

• **Disadvantages:** May be too ex-pensive and slow for small jobs, and the right printer might be miles away from you. Not all shops are unionized.

## Variations on the basic offset press

Dozens of presses have been designed for specialty needs, and more variations come out each year. Here are features you might look for:

• A **perfecting press** prints between two and six plates at a time. A press with two plates can print both sides of the paper at once. Or you could instead adjust the rollers to print two colors on one side, with the other blank. A four-plate press gives you even more options, including two colors on both sides. Each added plate you use costs just $50–$75.

• From **computer disk to film negative.** If you use a desktop publishing system, it's now possible to give the printer a floppy *disk* (p. 47) with the whole page on it, complete with photos. The printer transfers the disk information directly to the film negative, with no messy paper *mechanical* (p. 149) at all. However, you need a mighty sophisticated desktop system to get computerized photos to look half-decent.

• **Halftone screens.** If you're heart-set on having photos printed perfectly, find out what kind of halftone screen the printer uses (p. 60). An 85-line screen makes big dots like those in the daily paper. Some magazines have dots invisible to the naked eye, made with 200-line screens. The finer the screen, the finer the picture.

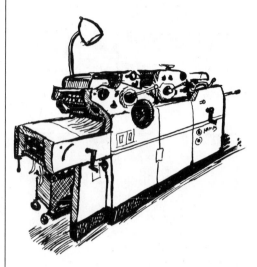

Small two-color offset press

# Web offset printing

Most large newspapers are printed with a huge *web press*. It prints some 4,500 *tabloid* (11" wide) newspaper pages each minute.

A web press has between two and eight cylinders that carry plates. It prints on *newsprint* (p. 62) or paper that comes in huge rolls instead of separate sheets. The roll of paper is threaded through the press, which prints both sides at once and one color right after another at breakneck speed.

Shop around for a press that's the right size for your job. Adding a second color to highlight the front, back and *centerfold* (p. 76) of your paper costs around $200.

Most webs are offset presses. Others are *flexographic*, and print inked plates with raised letters directly onto paper, with no *offset* cylinder. Their water-based inks are brighter and won't smudge. Both kinds of plates are made from negatives, so you prepare the exact same kind of *mechanical* (p. 149) for both.

## When a web is practical

Since the web press is huge and delicate to set up, the basic fixed costs are stiffer than for a sheet-fed press. But the cost of printing each copy is much less. The bigger the quantity, the cheaper the cost per newspaper.

• **Advantages:** The web press runs so quickly you can sometimes get the whole paper printed, folded and bun-

Chart 1

---

### Brochure printing costs
#### Spring 1991

Printed on both sides of an 8½" x11" sheet of 60-lb. offset paper, black ink, folded into thirds.

| | Quantity | | |
|---|---|---|---|
| | 250 | 1000 | 5000 |
| Offset: | | | |
| paper or plastic plate | $44 | $65 | $176 |
| metal plate | $74 | $95 | $206 |
| w/fancy paper | $80 | $107 | $266 |
| w/ colored ink (other than black) | $89 | $110 | $221 |
| w/ black & 2nd color ink | $119 | $157 | $307 |
| Extra cost for each halftoned photo (metal plate only): $15 | | | |

Web press

## Newspaper printing costs

### Spring 1991

A 12-page newspaper, with 11"x14½" pages, printed on a web press with 50-lb. offset paper.

*Black ink only:*
2500 copies: $1,153
5000 copies: $1,447
10,000 copies: $1,971

*Using half-decent newsprint instead:*
2500 copies: $1,042
5000 copies: $1,266
10,000 copies: $1,555

*Colored ink* in addition to black on eight pages:
2500 copies: $1,353
5000 copies: $1,647
10,000 copies: $2,171

Hafltones usually cost around $15 each

## Newsletter printing costs

### Spring, 1991

An 8-page 8½" x11" newsletter, printed in black ink on two 11"x17" 60-lb. (or equivalent) sheets folded together.

| | Quantity | | |
|---|---|---|---|
| | 500 | 1000 | 5000 |
| Copier at quick-copy shop | $145 | $268 | $931 |
| Offset: | | | |
| plastic plate | $175 | $255 | $715 |
| metal plate | $300 | $355 | $815 |
| w/fancy paper | $315 | $440 | $1,062 |
| w/2nd color on all pages | $575 | $635 | $1,110 |

Halftones usually cost $15 each

dled overnight. When you print at least 2,500 copies, this can be your cheapest option. Many shops are unionized.

- **Disadvantages:** The press is so speedy you may not get top-notch reproductions, especially if you use poor-quality paper. A slight maladjustment, and for several hundred copies the color will be in the wrong place; or ink will be so watered down it looks ghostly grey.

You could be limited to just standard sizes for papers and newsletters (p. 66). Ink colors could also be limited.

# Paper or plastic plate offset

Quick-copy shops often use paper (*electrostatic*) or plastic plates instead of metal ones. The plate costs from $1 to $7, with the more expensive plastic ones yielding better quality.

When your page *mechanical* (p. 149) is photographed, the image is developed directly onto the plate. This process, called *photo-direct*, takes less time. There's no costly negative, but all type and graphics (including photos) must be pasted onto the mechanical.

If your job is mostly type with a few simple drawings, you may not notice a big difference in quality; but photos and special effects are another story.

To use a photo, you must get a *velox* print (p. 58) made ahead of time, and paste that onto the mechanical. But it won't look as sharp as a *halftone* made with a film negative (p. 60). Special effects, such as inserting type into a photo (*doubleburns*, p. 164) simply can't be done, because they involve a negative.

If you find a full-service print shop that works with plastic plates, you might get skilled union labor, a good variety of paper stocks, and presses that print two colors at a time. But most paper and plastic plates live instead in quick-copy shops (p. 60).

## Pros & cons

- **Advantages:** Quick, cheap, and may be convenient. The printer can usually touch up the plate to get rid of *shadows* (p. 58) and other mess. Plastic plates print up to 20,000 copies.

Some shops can make paper plates directly from a computer via floppy disks (p. 47), which clears up many quality problems.

- **Disadvantages:** If you want nice-looking photos and special effects, stay away from paper and plastic plates. Paper-plate quality can rival mimeo at its *worst*, and most shops are non-union. The plate wears out after 1,000 - 2,000 copies. Colored or off-white backgrounds might become messy blotches, and sometimes even non-repro blue (p. 60) will reproduce. To minimize such problems, make a xerox copy of the mechanical, and touch it up as you would for a copier (p. 59).

# Shopping for an offset printer

Look up printers in the yellow pages and call several; prices can vary radically from one to the next.

## Get a quote

Ask for a written price estimate, called a *quote*, by describing your paper or leaflet in detail.

Include: the page size, the number of pages, how many ink colors you want on each page (including black), the kind of paper, whether you'll use photos or special techniques (p. 163), if pages should be folded and/or stapled together, whether you'll prepare a camera-ready *mechanical* (p. 149) or instead ask the printer to typeset pages, and how many copies you need. Ask how long the job will take, and if they charge extra for rush jobs.

For a special brochure, will they show you a *blue-line, dylux* or *silverprint*, made from the film negatives? That'll help you check the quality.

Before you decide on a printer, ask to see how jobs similar to yours came out. When you visit the shop, keep your eyes open, checking to see if the normal print job is carefully done. Pay special attention to the photos.

Is the shop unionized? Ask a union printer to put the *bug*, a little symbol identifying the union, right on finished copies, so readers will know you support union work.

## Comparing costs

Use charts H-K to weight comparative costs, not for precise estimates.

# 8. How to have style

A well-designed paper, newsletter or leaflet campaign has its own "look." Rather than coming across as a hodge-podge of clippings from here and there, everything in the paper seems to belong. Your paper's style identifies it immediately, month after month, so people will recognize it as a "friend" at first glance and pick it up.

Setting up a consistent style means most articles will look similar. Any changes happen for a *reason*, to signal readers that this isn't a regular story. Instead, it may be a photo caption, head-line or listing of services. By changing the type style and placement only occasionally, you minimize confusion; those special areas really stand apart as different. But if you're constantly switching everything around, nothing stands out and everything looks confusing.

With style, you set up a visual language people respond to, often without knowing it. For example, you might always box a list of feature articles in a specific place (such as the front page bottom) in similar type every issue. People quickly learn just where to look and what to look for, so it's easy to find what interests them.

# Your image

Some people are afraid that a neat and consistent publication will look too "professional" and not like the grassroots effort that it is. "Professional" takes many forms. It can mean extravagant "showing off," or it can mean useful techniques that make your publication easy and fun to read.

Good design makes you look competent. If you're a grassroots group, people may have little information about whether to take you seriously and believe what you say. A good design indicates you're careful and know what you're doing.

Having your own style helps you, the editor(s), even more than it helps the reader. Once you figure out the type style and column width for one article, you've figured it out for almost all articles, and don't have to make a new decision every time. Only if you discover new needs, or realize that something's confusing or hard to read, should you alter that style.

At times you'll get bored using the same headline type over and over again. Just keep in mind that a page that takes you hours to plan, typeset and lay out will take the reader only a few moments to read. And when readers consciously notice the style ("What weird – or nice – type that is!"), it may mean they aren't reading the words. Getting across your message is, after all, the whole point of publishing. In a way, good style is invisible.

Legal-sized mimeoed paper, ready to be folded

# Page & paper size

The size page you choose determines much of your format. Unless you've got money to burn, you're limited to a few standard sizes for a newsletter or newspaper, depending on available paper and printing machines. (See Chapter 7.)

## Mimeoed & copier-printed papers

● **Legal size: 8½" wide by 14" tall.** This is the biggest size paper you can fit on many mimeograph machines and some copiers. It works well if you can sandwich all your information on both sides of just one sheet, but it gets awkward to read once you have to staple pages together.

● **7" wide by 8½" tall.** Fold legal-size sheets of paper, and you get a handy little book-style newsletter. This is a convenient size for up to 24 pages or so (6 sheets of 8½"x14" paper folded gives you 24 pages). You'll arrange type sideways on each sheet, then fold it. That's extra trouble, but it makes a mimeoed paper seem special – and much easier to read.

● **Standard-size paper: 8½" wide by 11" tall.** The clue to using this size paper is the stapling. It's tempting to just staple each page in the corner, especially since many copiers automatically do the stapling, but you'll end up with an awkward-reading, haphazard paper that'll fall apart in no time. You

Mimeoed paper with one staple

Folded paper is easier to read

could instead staple neatly two or three times along the left-hand side; but your best bet is to find a machine that prints larger sheets of paper you then fold into a magazine-style newsletter.

## Copier-printed & printed papers

● **Standard-size folded newsletter: 8½" wide by 11" tall.** Most printing presses and office copiers can print 11" by 17" sheets, which you can fold to get a standard-size newsletter.

Web presses can usually print a newsletter this size on cheap paper, saving you money if the quantity's right (p. 63).

To make sure the paper doesn't fall apart, consider asking your printer to *saddle-stitch* it – in other words, put staples in the fold.

For most publications this is an ideal size; pages are big enough to keep articles from being cramped, while they're small enough for convenient reading. However, if your paper normally runs to 24 pages or more, such a bulky paper could scare off potential readers and become too strung out. Then it's time to move to a bigger paper size.

## Printed papers only

● **Odd sizes:** Some printers can cheaply print unusual-size pages, such as 7"x11", or 9½"x11½". Check with your printer – and compare prices. See p. 62 on paper sizes.

● **Tabloid: 11" wide by 14" to 17" tall.** This is the maximum size you should consider. Tabloid-size pages are often printed on a *web* press (p. 63).

If the paper will be just four to eight pages long, however, don't go to a tabloid size – unless you want a fragile, unwieldy paper that encourages people to skim rather than read thoroughly.

# The basic style

If you publish a short newsletter and don't have time to get fancy, design your pages like examples A or B. They involve just a few simple decisions.

## Article type

This is the typeface for all your stories. In the first example, it's just typed on a normal typewriter. In the second, it's typed on a word processor or computer.

• **Ragged or justified?** With an old-fashioned typewriter, you get *flush left, ragged right* type whether you want it or not. It's lined up along the left-hand margin and uneven on the right-hand side, like example A.

With advanced typewriters, word processors and computers, you can also *justify* type (p. 36), along the right-hand side, like example B.

Justified columns make pages look neat and orderly, and they're easier to paste up. Many designers prefer the look of ragged-right type, however, because it can be easier to read and looks interesting. If that's what you want, make it your style for *all* articles. Warning: If your pictures and headlines aren't strong, that jagged column edge can be distracting.

• **Make it easy to read.** With advanced typewriters and word processing, you sometimes get a dazzling choice of type styles and sizes. But don't get carried away with that lovely variety. Choose one simple, easy-to-read typeface for the bulk of your stories.

## What size is the type?

All type is measured by *point size*. Although a point is a mere 1/72 of an inch, every change in point size is significant. A 10-point typeface is exactly 10 points tall, from the top of the "T" to the bottom of the "y." But because the widths of letters vary with the type style, one 10-point typeface may look bigger than another, and may be so fat it takes up more room.

Standard-size newsletter
Tabloid newspaper

Example A

Example B

10-point typefaces

This is 10-point Palatino

This is 10-point Bookman

This is 10-point Franklin Gothic

11-point typefaces

This is 11-point Palatino

This is 11-point Bookman

This is 11-point Franklin Gothic

ALL-CAPITAL LETTERS GET
REAL HARD TO READ IF
THEY'RE USED FOR MORE
THAN A WORD OR TWO

10-point type
with two points leading
is easy to read

10-point type
with no leading
can be annoying to read
and looks crowded

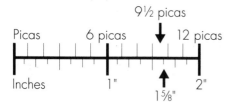

**Stodgy, conservative type style**

Tall, elegant type style

A type style with flair

---

Article type should be 10 or 11 point in size. (The type you're reading is 10 point.) Anything smaller can look as inviting as a legal contract or IRS form. And remember: Older people are often farsighted and prefer to read large type.

Type also needs *leading* – 1 or 2 points space between each line so the tops and bottoms of letters don't touch. P. 133 explains more.

## Why use columns?

Plan to divide pages into columns of type rather than typing each article straight across the page. Here's why it's well worth the trouble:

• **The page is easier to read.** People read faster when they see words in groups and don't have to read straight across, word by word. Narrow column widths encourage people to read word-groups. Around six words per line is ideal.

Even more important, when people have to read across one wide column, they constantly lose their places from one line to the next. That's frustrating. The extra trouble it takes you to type into columns saves countless readers from an annoying experience. Otherwise, many will think of something they'd rather do, and put the paper aside.

• **It gives you flexibility.** It's hard to fit a tall, skinny picture into a newsletter that's typed straight across the page. But when you have two or more columns, you can fit some pictures nicely into one column, without wasting space. Spread wider pictures across two or more columns.

No matter how many columns you put per page, each should end up the same width as the column(s) next to it. Switching around column widths is a time-proven way to disrupt the orderly image the paper needs.

P. 131 explains how to set up column widths when you type articles.

## Try using picas

You may find it easier to measure things like column widths in *picas*, the standard measure used by typesetters. Since there are six picas to an inch, that means you won't have to fool around with many fractions – a 4½-inch wide column, for example, is 27 picas wide. At an office or art supply store, pick up a ruler that marks picas as well as inches.

## Margins & gutters

An even *margin* of space around the page keeps it neat-looking and makes printing easier. Margins usually measure ½" (3 picas) on each side, top and bottom. But the *gutter*, the space between type columns, should *never* be more than ¼" (1½ picas) wide (unless you plan to insert *lines* between columns – p. 75). If you place columns too far apart, you create a gaping, disruptive canyon in the middle of articles.

## Headlines

No one is attracted to a page full of small print. A good headline jumps out at people and makes them start reading the page before they know what they're doing. (See p. 118 for headline wording.)

• **Example A: Typeset or computer-made** headlines. Pick a type style that's big and bold enough to stand out; simple enough to be read quickly; and interesting without being so fancy that readers are struck by the letters instead of the words. It should go nicely with the article type and have the right personality. See p. 69 for more.

Resist any temptation to hand-letter headlines. No one can draw type that's as bold, consistent and functional as typeset headlines. P. 151 shows how you can make beautiful headlines yourself with rub-off transfer lettering.

Pick one consistent style for all headlines. Plan to use several sizes of that style, from 18-point to 48-point, so you can adjust headline size to the length and importance of each article.

If you can't typeset every headline, aim to at least put a big, bold headline on the front page and above key articles.

With a computer, what you get depends on what you have – the styles and sizes loaded into your machine (p. 52).

• **Example B: Headlines from a typewriter or word processor** (p. 37). Resort to these only if you're really strapped for time and money. They're too small to really draw readers to articles. Even typed headlines can stand out a bit, however, if you underline them, surround them with empty space (p. 142), and/or enlarge them on a copying machine before pasting them on the page.

• **Headline size.** Headlines should *not* fit comfortably into the page. They should jump out and call to readers: "Look at me! Over here!" (A little headline instead whispers, "Um, by the way, if you have a chance, you *might* look over here . . . Oh, never mind.")

You'll need bold type as big as 48-point for newsletters, and up to 60-point for tabloid newspaper headlines.

● **Headline placement.** Decide whether all headlines will be *flush left* or *centered*. If you're pasting up headlines by hand, *flush left* (example A on p. 67) is the easiest. To *center,* you'd have to measure the space alongside each headline, to make sure it's smack in the middle. But if headlines are set on a computer, centering them over one or more columns (example B) is as simple as pushing a button.

Plan to leave lots of space above and beside each headline. Headlines will stand out better, and the page will look relaxed rather than crowded. (More on p. 142.)

### Pick your type style(s)

Once you've chosen a typesetter or decided what computer, typewriter or other set-up you'll use (Chapter 5), get samples of all the type styles available. Most typesetting shops will give you a little book showing the styles they offer.

Each type style has its own personality: Some are stodgy and conservative, some are tall and elegant, some demand to be taken seriously, and some have a rakish flair. The number-one rule of picking type styles is: Be practical. Find one that has variations you may need, such as italics or boldface, and that's easy to read. The number two rule: Make sure the article type goes well with the headline style.

Number three – and the most fun: Pick a type that fits the image your group wants.

Type comes in two basic families: serif and sans serif. *Serif* type has little thingamajigs called serifs at the ends of every straight line. But *sans serif* doesn't. (*Sans* means without in French.) A sans-serif "T" is simply two straight lines (example C). The words you're reading are in serif type. So is the classic typewriter used in example A.

● **Article type.** Serif type is faster and more relaxing to read at long sittings than sans serif. (But sans serif stands out better in small quantities.) Choose a serif style for all article type. Sans serif can be used for calendar listings, photo captions, or other tidbits.

Resist all temptation to use *italics* or **boldface** for anything longer than a

photo caption. Both are fine for emphasizing a word or two, but are hard to take in large quantities. And please outlaw setting sections in all-capital letters – they're nearly impossible to read.

● **Headline style.** Either pick a bold headline type style that's *real* different from article type (a sans serif style for the headline, for example) or stick to one that's simply a big, extra-bold version of the article type. Anything in between will look funny. The chapter headline on p. 65, for example, is Times Roman Bold, a bold version of the Times Roman used for the words you're reading.

Will headlines be *all-caps* – meaning that all the letters are capitalized? *Warning*: If it's a serif type style, don't do it. All-capital letters look alike, since they're all the same height. When they're *serif* to boot, the serifs on the tops and bottoms of letters seem to run together, so each letter is harder to read. It's annoying.

The norm these days is example B on p. 67 – to capitalize the first letter of a headline, and that's it (except for proper names, etc. in the headline). An old-fashioned alternative is to capitalize first

Grey screen sets off banner from the rest of the page

4-column tabloid paper

Margins
Gutters

Example C
Serif T's

T T T

Sans serif T's

T T T

**Typeface too fancy**

Too light for headline type
No big news

Serif all-cap headline
SERIFS RUN TOG
This is better

Sans-serif all-cap headline
BIG NEWS TODAY

Initial cap for each word
Big News Today

Initial cap for entire headline
Big news today

Too many type changes

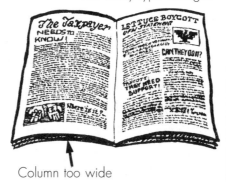

Column too wide

Example D

Style sheet for paper mock-up on p. 71

## Our style

| Function | Type style | Variation | Size | Placement | Space above | Space below | Width | Lines |
|---|---|---|---|---|---|---|---|---|
| Article type | Times Roman | Med. | 10/12 pt. | Justified | — | — | Y14 picas | 1/32" under each article |
| Headlines | Times Roman | Bold, Initial Caps | 18pt. to 42pt. | Flush Left | At least 2 picas | None | 1 or 2 columns | — |
| Subheads | Times Roman | Bold Initial caps | 1/2 headline size | Flush Left | 1 pica | none | 1 or 2 columns | — |
| Kickers | Times Roman | Light Italics | 14pts. | Flush Left | At least 2 picas | 1 pica | 1 Column | Hairline under each |
| Banner | Neil Bold | Bold Screened 40% | 24pt. | Centered | — | At least 2 picas | Full page | Bold lines Above & Below |
| Topic heads | Neil Bold | Bold All caps | 14pt. | top outside of Page | None | 1 pica | 3 columns | 1/16" line up to type |
| Paragraph breaks | Times Roman | Bold | 12/13 pt. | Center | 1/2 pica | 1/2 pica | 1 column | Light Underline |
| Captions | Helvetica | Light | 10 pts. | Flush left under graphic | 6 pts. | 1 1/2 picas | 1 or 2 columns | Hairline below |
| Bylines | Helvetica | Med. | 10 pts. | End of article Flush right | 2pts. | | 1 column | none |

Margins: 1/2" all around    Gutters: 1/4" between

| Special: | | | | | | | | |
|---|---|---|---|---|---|---|---|---|
| Staff box | Helvetica | light & med. | 9 pts. | Flush left | lower right-hand corner, p.2 | | 2 columns | 1/32" box all around |
| "What's Inside" box | Helvetica | Extra Bold | 10/12 pts. | Bottom of Front Page. Heads flush left, numbers flush right, dots in between | | | 2 columns Set type + 27 picas | 1/32" all around |
| Centerfold | Same - Times Roman | Med. | 10/12 | Justified | — | — | Set article type + 14 1/2 picas | 1/32" under each article |
| Boxes | Same - Times Roman | Med. | 10/12 | bottom when possible | 1 pi. | 1 pi. | Set type 12 1/2 pi. | 1/32" line all around |
| Calendar listings | Helvetica | Light | 9/10 pts. | Flush left ragged right | 1 pi. | — | Y13 picas | Thin line between columns |
| Page setup | Helvetica | numbers Bold, rest med. | 14 pt. page nos. | Bottom page numbers Flush Right | — | — | Full 3 columns | 1/16" line up to numbers |

Other: Little circle at end of articles. Keep articles complete on same page. Mostly photos & headlines on front page & mailing space on back. Page guideline: no more than 2/3 full of article type.

letters (*initial cap*) of *each* word, like the example A headline – but that up-and-down jerkiness can interfere with the flow of the words.

## The banner

No matter how simple your paper, you need a special front-page *banner* (also known as *nameplate, masthead* or *flag*) announcing, with flair, the name of the paper. It's one of the few areas that works as a symbol, not as something people read each time. So feel free to design it with fancy type or even draw it by hand. Go out of your way to make the banner look different from headlines, so people won't confuse the two. Make the banner fill the whole width of the paper, margin to margin.

A newsletter banner should never run more than 2" tall; otherwise it gobbles up too much valuable front-page space, getting in the way of big pictures and headlines. If the banner dominates the front page, its sameness overwhelms the news that makes each issue special.

Banners should show the name of your publication, nice and big, and then in little print the date, volume and number of this particular issue, the name of your group, probably its phone number, and possibly its address. (Vol. 2, No. 7 means this is your second year of publication and the seventh issue you've published this year.)

Save all other information, such as the names of the people on the editorial committee, to put in a *masthead* box inside the paper – usually at the bottom of page 2.

## Amount of article type

If you don't enforce strict limits on article type, your paper will be overcrowded. Set a *page guideline* for the whole paper, which you stick to for each issue. (More on *copyfitting*, p. 85.)

The ideal is to fill only *half* of each page with article type, leaving the other half for big headlines, pictures, and just plain space. Use that as an average. Some pages, like the front page, will have less type, while a page full of listings could have slightly more type.

Devoting two-thirds of a page to article type should be the absolute maximum – unless you've limited readership to a loyal band of professors who just love to read. Today's generation of TV viewers expects to be entertained and informed with pictures, etc., and will be put off by pages chock full of type.

# Beyond the basic style

Whether your paper's big or small, begin designing it with the same simple categories as the p. 69 samples. Design a more distinctive style by varying them, and then adding new elements. When you go beyond imitating the basic style, take time to design the whole paper *before* you write articles for the first issue. You'll need to fiddle around with various ideas without being rushed with down-to-the-wire deadline pressure.

## Make a mock-up

Even the experts can't invent a successful visual style all in their heads. You have to see various type styles, sizes and spacing together to know how well they'll work and to troubleshoot for possible problems.

Type up sample columns of articles, headlines, etc. in the style you want. Or, if you're using a typesetter, ask for typeset samples in your chosen style. (Either give them an article to typeset, or ask for samples from other jobs done in that same style.)

Then start playing around with the type samples, cutting and pasting them into columns of various widths and seeing what placement works best.

When you're done you have a *mock-up*: a sample page that may read like gobbledy-gook, but has the "look" you're aiming at. This mock-up is your typesetting and layout guide. Try to anticipate all your paper's needs, and design a way to deal with each one, following the guidelines below.

Make a *style sheet* (example D) based on the mock-up. It'll spell out exact type styles and spacing for each style category.

If you're working on a computer, set up a sample page on the machine, and see what you think. To check out other options, it's easy to change column widths, type styles and headline sizes. To experiment with a typestyle that's not in your system, ask a computer *service bureau* (p. 54) to loan you the *screen fonts* for the styles you're interested in. Load them into your computer, and they'll show up on the screen. To print a sample onto paper, however, you must use a *modem* (p. 55) or transfer the page to a *floppy disk* (p. 47) and pay the bureau to print a *hard copy* of it.

## Desktop publishing formats

Are you tempted to buy a set of *templates* – ready-made designed pages for desktop publishing? Don't. Most offer conservative corporate design, meaning that the name of the paper is huge and overwhelms everything else. The hidden message is that the organization is the be-all and end-all, and dominates everything and everyone discussed in articles. Headlines and stories meekly follow, without creating a fuss.

## Keep it simple

As you consider varying type for different uses, don't get carried away with all the wonderful varieties you can order. Good design focuses the casual observer's attention on the real attention-getters – the headlines and pictures. Everything else is carefully designed to stay out of the way.

Mock-up

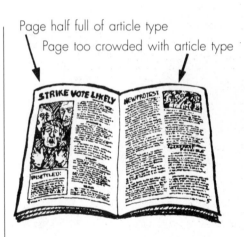
Page half full of article type
Page too crowded with article type

Conservative corporate design
Banner overwhelms headlines

# Varying basic style categories

Some kinds of information deserve a change from the basic style, cluing readers in that they're neither regular parts of articles nor headlines.

This is 10-point Futura light

Futura book

Futura

**Futura bold**

Futura heavy

**Futura extra-bold**

Range of headline type
for one newsletter

# Aab

# Aa

# Aa

# Aa

# Aabc

# Aa

# Aabc

Subheads & kickers

# Aabc

Aabc

Aabcd

 Display quote

Limit all changes to variations of two basic *typefaces*, such as Century and Helvetica, so your paper will look simple and uncluttered. When it looks simple, it looks easy to read and understand. This book, for example, is set entirely with variations of Times and Futura – that's all.

The challenge for a good designer is to see how small a change you can make in the basic style and still signal the reader that an area of type, such as a photo caption, is different.

Vary typefaces for each category by using a different *weight* (light, medium, bold, heavy or extra-bold), a different size or placement (*flush left* or centered), variations like *italics* (slanted forward so it looks rushed), or adding more space, or underlining (for one-line tidbits only).

Use the *style sheet* on p. 70 to help you pick type and spacing rules for each category your paper needs. Fill in all the variables, from how much space goes above type, to when you capitalize letters, and you'll have a clear, absolutely consistent style for nearly every purpose.

## Varying article type

Decide how far paragraphs should be indented – usually 1 *em* (the amount of space an "M" takes up) for narrow columns and otherwise, 2 ems. This paragraph is indented 1 em. (Some styles don't indent the first line of each paragraph; they just leave space between paragraphs.) Also, specify the *leading* – the spacing between lines (p. 133).

Don't vary basic article type, or you'll just confuse and annoy readers. But, you cry, how can I keep long articles from looking deadly-dull and hard to approach? Try these tricks:

## An enlarged letter

How about drawing readers into each article by setting the first letter in big, bold type? The big letter is the same style as either the headline or article type, and could be underlined – or even put in a box. Should the letter pop up above the article type, or will you indent a few lines at the start of each article to make room for it? That's called a *drop cap*. How many lines are indented?

If you do this once, do it the same way for *every* article. This book, for example, opens each section with a slightly enlarged letter.

## Introductions

Or lure readers into long articles with a paragraph that's bigger and bolder than the rest, possibly set across more than one column, possibly set off by lines. If that's what you want, don't *also* use display quotes (see below) –- it'll be too confusing.

## Paragraph breaks

To break up long articles and give readers a chance to pause without losing their places, try one of these:

- **Leave a touch of space** between each paragraph – just two or three points extra will keep articles from looking dense. Or:

- **Paragraph subheadings.** Every three or four paragraphs, throw in a little subheading – like example E. The nice thing about subheadings is that they give readers intriguing little hints about the article, before they dig in.

Make sure subheadings don't look anything like headlines – or they'll confuse people. How so? Keep them small. In fact, subheadings can be the *same* size as article type, if they're bold and centered within a column, with extra space above them. Make rules for exactly how much extra space they get: Four to 12 points space above each subheading and zero to six points below should be plenty.

For articles set on a plain typewriter, type each subheading in the middle of the column (centered), underlined, with a blank line of space above it.

- **More enlarged letters.** Don't stick a giant "Scarlet A" smack in the middle of the story – that only works for long magazine articles. Be subtle. Every three or four paragraphs insert extra space – up to 12 points – and then make the first letter of the next paragraph big and bold. Try indenting a couple of lines to make room for it.

## Display (or pull) quotes

Chances are, your favorite magazine takes nifty little sentences or quotes out of a long article every so often, and repeats the words in a nice big *display (or pull-out) quote*, to draw readers in. Why not do the same? Plan a standard type style, size, and spacing for display quotes. Will they be set off from the article with heavy lines or double-lines above and below the quote? If so, how heavy? (See p. 75 for measuring line widths.) Or will you put each quote in a box? What kind? Will it have shadows along the bottom and side?

## Bullets & symbols

Encourage writers to slip visual breaks into the writing itself as much as possible – like a "Q & A" format for an interview, for example, or dividing a list of ideas into separate points (1., 2., 3., etc.) See p. 117 for more. Or even better, use *bullets* instead of numbers for each idea or point. A *bullet* is a big black dot (or rectangle) signalling the start of each point – like those used on p. 72.

Decide what style type you'll use for the Q's & A's and what kind of bullets you want. Will the bullets (or Q's and A's) be *flush left* (p. 67) or indented? How much extra space will you put above them?

If some articles will run more than a page long or you expect to carry several short items, consider signing off at the end of each article with a little box, circle or other symbol.

## Column widths

For newsletters printed on folded legal-size paper (p. 66), choose a one- or two-column format. For a regular newsletter (pages 8½" wide), choose two to three columns. For a tabloid newspaper (11" wide), choose three to five columns per page.

The smaller the type, the narrower the columns should be. Never plan columns of 10-point type wider than 24 picas (4") or 12-point type wider than 30 picas (5"). With *justified* type (p. 67), the gutter between columns can be as narrow as one pica. Don't ever make the gutter more than ¼" (1½ picas) wide, unless you plan to put a thin line between each column. Lines work well with *ragged right* type (p. 67).

*Warning*: If you plan to type articles

Example E

Page without paragraph breaks

Page with paragraph subheadings

on a word processor or computer with a simple program (p. 39), you may be limited in how many columns the machine will put on a page.

## Special pages

Will you carry items that aren't really articles, like a monthly calendar, classified ads, or a list of services? To signal that this is a different kind of information, design a model page (or part of a page) that looks different. For little items that'll be skimmed rather than read start-to-finish, a *san serif* type (p. 69) is fine – like the captions in the outside margin of this page. While *serif* type makes reading flow smoothly over the long haul, *sans serif* styles help make little items stand out on their own. If each item is short, try extra-thin columns of type. Use boxes, lines and other visual clues to separate this info from the rest of the paper.

Special type

Enlarged letters

## Headline variations

The best way to ruin a good headline is to crowd it, so it blends into everything else. Give it room to breathe by making rules for how much space – at the least – must be left above and below each headline. (The space *below* a headline is usually kept to a minimum, so readers will plunge right into the article as soon as they've read the headline.)

Consider dividing all but the very shortest headlines into several lines of type, with space next to them. A reader's eye can't read at a glance a headline stretched across the page. But a headline split into several lines will be seen all at once. Or try other variations, like dropping headlines down into the first column of type (example F). Whatever you do, make it consistent.

Some styles even set up a special column of space to the left of each article, and only headlines are allowed to jut out into that space. Some leave a big

Example F
Dropped headline style

Subhead

Headline split across two lines stands out better

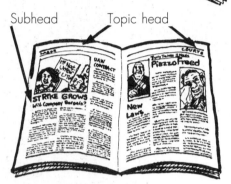

Subhead    Topic head

Topic head serves as headline

Topic headline

Space between paragraphs

Slumlord Flees!

Fearful Slumlords Lower Rents

Kicker

band of space above all columns, and make rules for how headlines are placed within that space (example L on p. 148).

## Subheads

Use *subheads* when you want to keep the headline short and catchy, but need more information to lead people into the article. Subhead type should be around half the size of headlines, and set in the same typeface (or a not-so-bold variation of the headline type).

## Kickers

Do you want to add a little background information to headlines? Then try *kickers*. Conventionally, a kicker stands above the headline, flush left italics and/or underlined, and set in a light, smaller variety of the headline typeface. Size can be linked to the headline, like half the headline size. Some style sheets demand that a kicker go with every headline, to keep headlines short.

## Topic headlines

Topping the "President's Report" with the same old headline every month is duller than a doornail (p. 82). To make room for a real headline, which tells readers what's interesting about this particular report, make "President's Report" into a *topic headline.*

A topic headline (also called a *stand-ing head*) is set in smaller type, and usually stands above the headline, off to the side. If you put topic headlines on the outside of every page (to the left on even-numbered pages and the right on odd-numbered pages), the reader will spot them while casually flipping through the paper.

Since each topic head reads the same every month, it could become a symbol like the banner, and be set in a fancy typeface. Topic headlines are often enclosed in a box or surrounded by lines. Some have big spaces between each letter, or dots between each word. Just make sure they're set aside and aren't big or bold enough to interfere with the headlines.

Sometimes you'll instead make a topic headline so big it dominates a whole page full of short articles, such as "News from the Neighborhoods." In that case, the headlines above each article function more like subheads.

Consider using topic headlines for regular features like sports, news from the health committee, letters to the editor, or bargaining updates. *Always* put a big headline or subheads beneath the topic head. If the "President's Report" rambles, pick the most exciting information for a big headline, with small subheadings cluing readers in every time the report switches to a new subject.

# Other style categories

## Photo captions (*cutlines*)

Use a special type style, size and/or weight so *captions* won't get confused with article type. A sans-serif style (p. 69) might work well. Do captions go above, below or next to photos? Consider putting a line under each caption. How thick is each line (p. 75)?

Will you put *credits* alongside photos or cartoons to identify the photographer or artist? If so, make them small – 6 pt. is fine.

## Bylines

Will you give credit to the author of each article (p. 22)? If so, does the name go above or below the article? How should it be typeset and placed?

## Special type

Is there a "What's Inside" box on the front and/or back page, enticing readers to open up, with selected headlines?

Where does that go? And what kind of type should you use? Does it include little pictures from various articles?

Using special type for other purposes is tricky; be careful not to overdo it. Things like charts and tables, letters to the editor, or the editor's reply might also deserve special type. And although you should avoid continuing most articles from one page to another, front page articles are an exception (p. 76). How should those few *continuation headlines* be typeset? And what do they say? Do you just steal a word from the real headline before adding "continued from p. 1" or will you repeat the whole head?

## Page set-up

Most publications put the page number, name of publication, and date on every page. Sticking the page number into the margin space on the outside of each page makes it easy to find. But should it go on the top, bottom or side? And if you include the name of publication and date, where do they go? Is there a line separating them from the rest of the page?

### Banner

If you want to get fancy, design a little "What's Inside" box or announcement of the next meeting as part of the banner. Even with that, don't let the banner get taller than 2" or so.

Some large papers place a headline or article above the banner, but that's dangerous; the banner then breaks up the flow of the page. People expect to see the banner at the top of the front page, and that's where it belongs.

### Staff box or masthead

Here you give credit to everyone who worked on the paper. You might also list officers and their phone numbers, the paper's phone number and address, how to subscribe, your editorial policy and other basic information. People may expect to find the staff box in the lower right-hand corner of p. 2. Since it's standard information that doesn't vary much, keep it small and out of the way.

### Advertising

No community or labor paper should look like an ad rag. Keep advertising under control by making rules to place ads out of the way. Then people won't get the ads confused with the articles, which could be a disaster.

Put all ads at the bottoms of pages, with a line separating them from articles. Or reserve the inside column or selected left-hand pages for advertising. Don't put ads at the tops of pages or on the outside, where they'll overpower the articles (unless the page has no articles). And keep them off special pages like the back page or centerfold. Advertisers may complain about being pushed aside; but if you've got the readers they need to reach, they'll get used to it.

Enforce guidelines specifying, for example, that no more than 40% of the paper's space can be taken by ads (p. 26). When you carry advertising, it's more important than ever to use big headlines, space and pictures for articles. Otherwise, the ads will look more appealing than articles.

### Lines

Lines (or *rules*, p. 144) can never make up for a badly organized page. However, they're great for emphasizing an order that's already there. One caution: If you do your own paste-up, put-

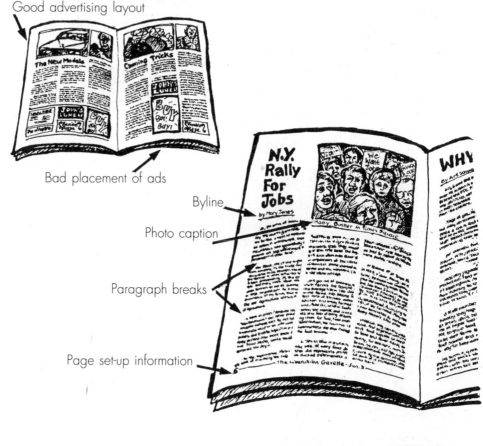

Good advertising layout

Bad placement of ads

Byline

Photo caption

Paragraph breaks

Page set-up information

Hairline _____

1/64" line _____

1/32" line ▬▬▬▬▬

Fancy line ∿∿∿∿∿∿

Dotted line ●●●●●●●●●●●●

ting lines all over the place and getting them straight can drive you crazy.

Lines come in many weights: the thinnest is a *hairline* rule. Next is a 1/64" wide line, roughly equal to a 1-point rule used by many typesetters. Then there's the 1/32" line or the 2-point rule. These are usually all you'll need. Don't use squiggly, dotted or other fancy lines; they just attract attention to themselves – and away from the words.

The same can happen with big bold lines. Although they can be powerful eye-catchers, keep them out of the way – maybe just a bold border at the very top of the page. Or keep heavy lines short, such as a little, fat bold line above or beneath (but not both) a display quote. When in doubt, forget it.

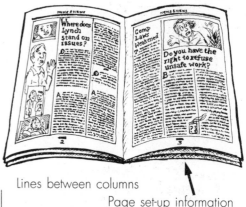

Lines between columns

Page set-up information

Lines

Continued articles

Margins

Symbols

Tabloid front page folded

Consider putting thin lines across the top and/or bottom of pages, above or below topic headlines and display quotes, between columns of ragged type, around photos or around the whole page. Putting thin lines under captions will separate them clearly from articles.

## Boxes

Will you occasionally set off charts and other information related to the main article in a box? If so, you'll have to set type within the boxes narrower than the norm (p. 133). What kind of line should be used? Will you shade the boxes with a screen (p. 164)?

Back page

Mailing space

Centerfold

Letters page

# Those special pages

Pages with a special function deserve special treatment.

## The front page

With a quick glance at the front page, many people will decide whether to pick up the paper or walk on by. To hook them, make front-page headlines and pictures especially big. Some papers even set front-page articles in type that's larger than normal. Others don't have any article type on the front page at all, just headlines, pictures and a "What's Inside" listing to give readers a hint of the scope the paper covers.

If your paper is tabloid size (11" wide), it'll be folded when people first see it. To grab them with that initial glance, plan to always fit at least one big headline and picture above the fold.

Some tabloid papers are designed to have two front pages: the folded paper looks like a magazine, with striking front and back covers. Unfold it, and you find a bigger front page, newspaper-style. Consider this format when you plan to mail the paper to people's homes.

## The back page

• The mailing space. If you mail the paper, design a space for the reader's address right on the back page. Then you won't need to stuff the paper into envelopes or mess up the front page. If you want the mailing space on the front page, put it along the bottom edge and *screen* it (p. 164) so it doesn't stand out too much.

The mailing space should be in the lower right-hand corner, around 3" tall and 5" wide. Put non-profit mailing info (p. 168) in the upper right corner of the space. Once it's designed, check with the post office to make sure you've met their requirements. If you put the mailing space on the back of a tabloid paper (11" wide), tell the printer to fold the paper backwards. (But to get some mailing discounts you must fold the paper again – p. 170.)

• Design that back page to look irresistible when the paper's folded, so people will be attracted even if the paper arrives in the mailbox upside-down. Even if you don't mail your paper, give back pages special treatment; many people flip the paper over with a glance at the back before they decide whether to open it. Others never look at the back at all. If you've got a regular feature that's fun to look at, like a "bulletin board," cartoons, or service listing, why not put it on the back?

## The centerfold

In the middle of the paper is this big, two-page stretch of paper, ideal for special long features, photo essays, a calendar, or information you'd like people to post on the wall.

Since the centerfold doesn't need to have full margins in the middle (a little *gutter* (p. 68) is fine), plan to set columns of type a bit wider than normal.

## Others

How about carrying letters from your readers, the calendar, or retiree news in a special place every month? Where? P. 140 gives tips to help you decide.

# 9. Planning & scheduling each issue

**B**efore planning a specific issue, recruit a committee (p. 4), hammer out the paper's goals and policy (pp. 13 and 22), and think about your readership (Chapter 1).

Design the paper with Chapter 8's assistance. Know where and how it'll be printed and typeset (Chapter 5, 6 and 7) and get a firm commitment from both printer and typesetter (if any) on how long they need to do the job.

Now it's time to let loose on the first issue.

## Stick to a schedule

Set a regular publication date and stick to it. If the paper or newsletter could come out anytime between now and next Christmas, readers won't know when (or whether) to expect it. They'll be less inclined to take it seriously. If you miss your deadline, you may also have to revise distribution plans, subscriptions, ad commitments (if any), and beginning the new issue.

If you get off schedule before publication, the quality of the paper, not to mention your working relationships, suffer. You'll be rushed; paragraphs will be left out; the wrong picture will end up with the wrong story; facts won't be accurate; spelling mistakes will be everywhere. All this makes you look incompetent.

## Meet after each issue is printed

Don't rest too long on your laurels when the paper comes out. Instead, start working on the next issue right away by calling the newspaper committee together.

Consider inviting to this first meeting officers and other leaders who aren't full-fledged staff members, as well as your reporters and people who distribute the paper; their feedback and ideas could prove valuable.

Before the meeting, poll officers, committee heads and reporters who can't make it in person and find out if anything's coming up that the paper should cover.

## Evaluate the last issue

While it's fresh in people's minds, discuss various problems that cropped up. Did the schedule run smoothly? Did all the papers get out on time? Did policy questions come up that the committee should discuss? Do you need more ads to break even financially? Did personalities clash over editing decisions? Plan how you'll iron out such difficulties in the future.

How did readers react to the paper? What bombed? What got rave reviews? Ask reporters and distributors to tell all. Did any mail come in?

### Plan the next issue

Even though you know there'll be changes, get a head start and assign articles now. By being on top of things, the committee can make sure the paper covers key news. Advance planning also helps you reach out to grassroots members, asking them to write or talk about projects or news they're involved in. It gives the inexperienced writer time to think about an idea, without feeling too pressured.

If you don't plan and just wait to see what articles surface, you'll find that a small clique – or you – writes most of them. Some articles will repeat each other, while you'll suddenly discover that no one covered big events like the annual picnic, and no one took pictures.

Finally, without a plan you'll likely panic at all those pages you have to fill, and you'll end up with a paper that's impossibly crowded.

### Make a list of ideas

Plan a variety of articles (p. 82), with something for everyone in your audience. Think of important news that'll break soon, and key events.

As you brainstorm, remember that your goal is to reflect many aspects of the group – from what terrific people

your members are to why bankers favor higher interest rates – not just what happened last month. P. 19 discusses the paper's goals.

• **Some of the best ideas** come from informal chats. Some groups hold open meetings or sponsor educational speakers and discussions. These give you an idea what's on readers' minds. So does recruiting lots of reporters who keep their ears open.

• **Your group's officers** should keep you posted on problems they run into and the day-to-day work your group is doing. If it's a community paper, you might appoint a committee of local leaders to consult with the newspaper committee and give you ideas.

• **Invite readers to write** the paper or call the office about whatever bugs them. Many papers carry a "Q and A" feature responding to readers' questions and gripes.

• **Other ideas come from reading** other papers, magazines and newsletters, and watching the news. You can pick up a lot by clipping information and reading between the lines (p. 92). Often they'll briefly report on something you can do a better job with.

• **Staff discussions can help.** If two people each know a little bit about something, they may have enough facts and hunches together to explore it.

• **Throw in standard features,** such as the "roving reporter" (p. 99), an activities calendar, legislative update, a letters page, meeting notices, ads for your group (with a form for new members to fill out and send in), and a little blurb asking for volunteers.

The dummy

# Organize the ideas

Pick the best ideas and rate them in order of importance (and variety). Think who might write each article, and how long it should probably be – a half page, quarter page or whatever.

Once you've decided on priorities, some people – your officers, reporters and distributors – can cut out, while the core committee gets to work.

### Make a dummy

Fold over sheets of plain paper to make a miniature booklet, the same number of pages as you expect your

newsletter or paper to be. This is a *dummy,* where you roughly decide what goes on which page, and what doesn't fit at all. Start with "must" features and the most important articles, and plan where they go. If you carry ads, block out space for probable advertising.

Since people browse through a paper by turning left-hand pages and glancing to the right first, put your most exciting articles on right-hand pages. (And some people browse backwards, so that next-to-last page is important.) Bury a bureaucratic bomb you're told to include on a left-hand page. For more tips on what goes where, see pp. 76 and 140.

Don't worry about exactly how articles will look on each page. You'll adjust the dummy as the paper progresses and lay out pages later (p. 139). Now you're just mapping out how much information will fit.

When you run out of room, you're done. If that forces you to leave out items that absolutely must be printed this issue, slice the size of other articles so everything will fit. Or, if you can afford it, add four more pages.

Think of picture ideas for each page. If you can't dream up a good cartoon or photo idea for a particular story, leave space anyhow. You've got a whole month to come up with something. Chapters 12 and 18 should help.

## How long should each article be?

Once you've decided what goes in the paper, how much room it gets, and who should write each piece, tell each writer how many typed pages to make the article. To do that you need to *copyfit*. P. 86 explains how.

Brainstorming for article ideas

Example A

Check off each step as you go. You'll be aware of problems before they get too serious.

| Article subject | Length (pages) | Writer (name) | Photographer or cartoonist (if any) | Assign article, graphics | Check-up | First draft due | Editing copy (Who's editing?) | Final copy & graphics | Article to typesetter (or typist) | Article proofed and corrected | Pages laid out, pasted up | To printer | Appearance date | Distribution deadline | Next planning meeting |
|---|---|---|---|---|---|---|---|---|---|---|---|---|---|---|---|
| | | | | 10/2 | 10/6 | 10/9 | 10/10 | 10/13 | 10/13 | 10/14 | 10/17 | 10/18 | 10/22 | 10/24 | 10/26 |
| Convention Story | 2 | Len | Sandy | ✓ | ✓ | | Ed | | | | | | | | |
| Sandie Brudman profile | 1 | David | Sandy | ✓ | ✓ | ✓ | Ed | | | | | | | | |
| Earth Day | 1 | Lucy | Yolanda | ✓ | ✓ | | Ed | | | | | | | | |
| Did you know facts | ½ | Shawn | | ✓ | | | Ed | | | | | | | | |
| Imports Up | ½ | Chris | chart | ✓ | ✓ | ✓ | Ed + Lydia | | | | | | | | |

# Plan the whole issue's schedule

At this planning meeting, plot the responsibilities and timetable for the whole month. Since most of us are only human, plan a human schedule people can live up to, without nervous breakdowns. After you've worked out the bugs on a relaxed timetable, you can tighten up future schedules. After all, the longer it takes to produce the paper, the older the news will be.

- **Work backwards.** Start with the date the paper must appear and then allow enough time for each process, from the printing through the paste-up, layout, typesetting, editing, writing and research or interviewing.

- **Make a chart** showing each deadline, using example A on p. 79 as a model. Xerox several copies and fill in exact dates and articles as each issue of the paper rolls around.

If you have an office, post the schedule on the wall. Use a chalkboard, or cover the basic chart with clear plastic and invest in a grease pencil (p. 160) so you can use the same chart over and over for each issue.

- **As you clear each deadline,** check the proper space in the chart, as example A on p. 79 does. Then you'll know at a glance if there are bottlenecks, and whether to panic.

Here are dates your schedule should include:

### The planning meeting

This is the meeting you're at. It should happen about a month before the paper or newsletter comes out. To make sure it does, schedule the next planning meeting now.

### The assignment deadline

Each member of the committee should oversee one or more articles, from finding an author to making sure the article's coming along, to helping green writers figure out what they're doing. By the assignment deadline, scheduled just a couple of days after the planning meeting, committee members are in touch with everyone working on articles, graphics, layout, typesetting and/or printing. Give people a good

week or two to finish articles. Never assign an article you won't have room to print; you'll create bad feelings and lose writers fast.

For important articles or less experienced writers, work together to plan the article. Then problems and disagreements can be ironed out right away. Make helpful suggestions, like who to interview.

### Check-up deadline

At this point committee members get back in touch with article writers. Sometimes you're just reminding people to get started. But you're also finding out if there's trouble.

Find out if the article is developing differently from what you expected. You may have given it too much or too little space in the dummy (p. 78). It may not even be worth writing, as it turns out.

If a writer says the length you assigned won't work, then you know ahead of time you must come up with a less ambitious idea or fiddle with the rest of the pages, so the article gets the room it needs. Or maybe it should be the first installment of a series.

Schedule a meeting of the newspaper committee now, so you can adjust to such problems early in the game, and update your dummy. If a key article needs more room, or there's late-breaking news that must be covered, ask someone to hold up another article until the next issue. If an article won't be done on time, expand something else, or assign a new article to someone who works fast. Or plan to fill the area with pictures.

### First draft deadline

Be very strict about enforcing this one. All articles should be finished on time, except those covering an event that hasn't yet happened. If articles are late, the schedule falls apart. Ask that articles be typed, double-spaced, on one side only of each sheet of paper. That'll make editing easier. If they're typed on a computer, ask for the *disk* (p. 47).

Get in touch with authors of late articles immediately. Sometimes you can finish the piece together.

As soon as the article is in, check the length against what you assigned. If by any chance it isn't typed, type it out. Don't worry if it's just a few lines long or short. If it's off by more than that, it has to be cut or expanded.

Meeting the deadline

How-to information

## Editing deadline

Some groups plan an editing meeting, while others don't – see p. 122. By this date you've got each article in hand, and are discussing with its author, by phone or in person, what the problems are. Nothing should ever go into or out of the article without the author's knowledge. If the author won't allow essential editing, see p. 124.

## Last copy & graphic deadline

At this point, articles are edited, checked with the author, and marked up for the typist or typesetter (p. 134). Make sure this deadline leaves enough time for typesetting or typing, printing, layout, paste-up and emergencies.

By this date, graphics (p. 157) also should be ready. Plan to have several extra photos on hand, so people doing layout will have leeway deciding which fit best on each page. If a cartoon doesn't quite do the trick, you have time to ask the cartoonist to make a few changes.

## Layout & paste-up time

Now all the articles are typed or typeset and graphics are done, ready to be put into pages. Schedule plenty of time for layout, so you can have fun and get the right "look" through trial and error (Chapter 16). If you hire someone to do layout, don't do a disappearing act; exchange ideas back and forth, so the layout fits your goals.

If you're doing layout and paste-up by hand (not on a computer), collect as many people as you can collar, and schedule several days for layout – hopefully including the weekend.

Working on a computer is faster – but lonelier. Have a couple of people work together to share ideas, check for layout mistakes (p. 146), proof the pages, fit in graphics – and keep your computer operator from getting too crazed or burned out.

## Press date

On this date you deliver the paper, at last, to the printer, copier or mimeo machine. If it's a printer, check out the date well ahead of time.

## Appearance date

Some printers take several days, while web presses often do the job overnight (p. 63). Get a firm delivery promise from your printer.

Personal experiences

Example B

## When you're out of work

If you've ever been laid off, or if you ever worried about being fired, you know what those words can do to a person.

In this country, when you're out of work you suddenly feel less of a person. Everyone has a place to go, you don't. The poorest job looks beautiful and fulfilling because it's there, it's a place to go, a place to be, it makes you part of something.

It's not right, but in this country we judge people first by their work. "What does he (or she) do?" is usually the first question we ask about someone.

The work ethic we've heard so much about is so ingrained in us that when we're out of work we feel guilty, inferior. It may be no fault of ours when they close down a plant or move an office, and suddenly you have no job.

Suddenly men and women who worked and were proud all their lives are standing on unemployment lines, feeling second-class, hating the forms they have to fill out, angry at the clerks who make them go through this degrading experience.

You know it's not your fault, but it doesn't help. Millions of other people are still working and you wonder where you made your mistake, why you're not working.

Unemployment is like a hot fire that runs through a family. A man and his wife can never put it out of their minds. Unreasonably, guilt and a sense of failure flow through every thought, intrude on every conversation, as they self-consciously pick their words carefully, anxious not to hurt or to seem too critical.

Kids who are old enough to understand are old enough to become frightened. The parents they trusted, took all their security from, are now frightened themselves, helpless.

Unemployment checks, less food on the table, saying "no" to movies and fifty cents for ice cream. Because suddenly you don't have another fifty cents for carfare or to help buy a quart of milk.

Out-of-work is a terrible, demeaning, frightening situation for Americans today.

When the President coldly calculates more unemployment to "cool" the economy, he doesn't really know what out-of-work means. He doesn't know anyone who's out of work. He doesn't know anyone who's worried about being out of work.

Exposé

Example C

## Recipe for a strong union

Take one medium-sized plant, carefully separating company from union and throwing company part away. To the union add several local members, thoroughly mixed for equality.

Sift democracy, participation and education and blend with union-member mixture.

Season with pride-in-unionism and let rise on-the-job until thoroughly strong.

When done, you will find this union capable of anything!

– UAW Local 469 "Target"

Example D

## The missing character

Xvxn though my typxwritxr is an old modxl, it works quitx wxll xxcxpt for onx of thx kxys. It is trux that all thx othxr kxys work wxll xnough, but just onx kxy not working makxs thx diffxrxncx. Somxtimxs it sxxms likx a committxx is somxwhat likx my typxwritxr – not all thx kxy pxoplx arx working. You may say to yoursxlf, "Wxll, I am only onx pxrson. I won't makx or brxak it." But it doxs makx a diffxrxncx bxcausx a comittxx, to bx xffxctivx, nxxds thx activx participation of xvxryonx. So thx nxxt timx you think your xfforts will not bx missxd, rxmxmbxr my typxwritxr.

In short – come on out to your union meetings each month.

---

Alert your distribution crew to pick up the paper on this date and get it on the streets as soon as it rolls off the presses (p. 167).

# Kinds of articles to carry in your paper

Suppose local government pleads poverty and plans to drastically cut social services. If you didn't think much about it, you'd just write about what's happening and how terrible it is. Yet there are as many exciting angles to each story as there are members in your group. Each approach pursues your group's goals in a different way. To make your paper effective and interesting, aim for a variety of approaches (p. 117).

## Make articles, not columns

Whatever you do, don't publish lots of vague "columns" written by various officers, topped by dishwater-dull headlines like "President's Report" or "Education Committee Report."

Organizing information that way is asking people to read a long article just because the president wrote it or the education committee submitted it, even though many readers don't know beans about the president or education committee. Many won't bother.

And when you string all the president has to say into one long column, vital information could get lost at the end. If the column starts slowly, few people will stick with it long enough to find the last tidbit. Readers won't even know what they missed.

Convince your officers and committees that their columns will be more popular if they're organized as *articles*.

Ask officers like the president what's going on this month. If the president just came back from a safety conference or wants to encourage people to complain about lax garbage pick-up, plan an article about just that. Either the president writes it, or you quote the president to get his or her views. Top the article with an exciting headline that makes readers realize it discusses their own welfare (p. 118). They'll then eagerly read it because they *want* to, not because they feel they *should*.

There'll be months when the president or education committee doesn't have a thing to say. If they have to write

columns anyhow, they'll ramble on about the weather and how fast time flies. It'll waste readers' valuable time, and make them less likely to read the rest of the paper or future columns.

When the president says nothing's going on, give him or her the month off, to save energy for the next month. Next time the president might write (or contribute to) several articles.

## How-to information

These articles give people valuable technical knowledge, plus practical experience. Explain union grievance procedures, people's legal or contract rights, what child-care services are available, how to repair a leaky faucet, or how to recycle your garbage.

Translate all technical information into everyday language. And leave people with a good idea how they can and cannot actually *use* their rights, not just the letter of the law or regulation on paper.

When government cuts key services, for example, explain how people can still get emergency help. Show how to file protests if you're denied unemployment pay or food stamps, or how to qualify under new rules. Explain how to write legislators to oppose the cuts.

## Personal experiences

People's real experiences can prove ideas as well as a notebook full of facts and figures, and they're bound to be more interesting. What happened to the writer or the people interviewed can breathe life into abstract ideas. Their experiences with banks, companies, agencies and schools show directly how those institutions operate.

Example B was written by a worker who'd been through an extremely painful experience. But instead of taking it as a personal failure, he knew most people would feel the same way if they were denied work. The story then makes a political point, bridging the gap that too often divorces people from politics in the commercial media (p. 20).

When the state cuts services, interview decent people who don't know how they'll survive without assistance, or whose children will have to quit school because of tuition hikes. Talk to oldsters who can no longer afford the bus fare or the heating bill. Interview state workers who'll get laid off or be so swamped with work they can't do a good job. Show they're caring public servants, not faceless bureaucrats.

Be on the lookout for upbeat personal experiences too, such as the unionist who successfully filed a grievance when told to perform an unsafe job, or the woman who went after the company that installed a buckling kitchen floor and got her money refunded. Telling how real, live people fight against injustice will give them credit for blowing the whistle, and it'll encourage others to realize they can win by fighting back. And print candid interviews with group leaders, so others can identify with their experiences, their aims and their frustrations.

### Exposés

That mythical "power of the press" becomes real power when you investigate and publicize wrongdoing. When you expose behind-the-scenes maneuvers and get to the root of a crisis, your publication becomes an invaluable organizing tool.

If a block-busting real-estate company opens an office in your neighborhood, expose who they really are and how they operated in other communities. If the company blames workers for the poor quality of the widgets you make, investigate their buck-passing and reveal the real problem, such as orders of bad parts.

Show how a politician you oppose gets his money. Show how a private university isn't paying its fair share for the public services it gets. Get behind appearances with the hard facts.

Exposés make people take notice of your paper and are fun, both to read and to work on. Once you've earned a reputation for exposing and getting action on injustice, whistle-blowers will call you first with juicy information.

When the government pleads poverty, demand they open the books. Dig into public records to uncover waste and blatant subsidies to the rich. Chapter 10 on fact-finding suggests how to find the dirt. P. 29 reads you your legal rights.

### Analysis

The economy is going to the dogs and few of your readers understand why, or what they can do about it. Most people are thirsty for economic information, written in everyday language.

Typed copy

Typeset article

People will see how their problems can be solved by group action only after they have a grasp on where those problems come from, and why. Why is management really cutting down production, and can you expect an upturn? Why does business need to be regulated? Why is the city subsidizing big developers with scarce tax dollars, and what should it do to strengthen the community instead?

Explain why your group believes in certain principles, supports this or that issue, and lobbies for a particular bill. Print the voting records of political candidates.

When local government goes broke, dig into what triggered the crisis and how government could make do without abandoning social needs.

### Group activities

The commercial media follow around high-placed individuals, and often ignore or distort group action. Make sure people getting together in your group don't feel it's never been done before.

Show how other groups have reacted to problems similar to those your readers face. And go out of your way to build support for like-minded groups.

When you're faced with state service cutbacks, publicize protest activities in

This paper has too much article type

other states, or remind readers of your victory over earlier cutbacks.

Even the idea of group responsibility must be explained over and over again with a new twist each time, as examples C and D on p. 82 show.

Strengthen your own group by publicizing its activities. Make an exciting photo essay (p. 145) of your annual picnic, interview people at your educational meetings or on the picket line, and give a lively account (please don't just publish those boring minutes!) of your meetings, showing how they tackle important issues. Then preview highlights of the next meeting.

### Feedback from readers & fun features

Reach out to members and invite their contributions. When you make the paper a forum, where members gain a better appreciation for each other and discuss the group's goals, you're building solidarity.

Some members volunteer for Big Brother or Sister; they might write a few words about it. Some are willing to share treasured recipes handed down from Grandma. Some draw cartoons or write poems. Some were cheated by a door-to-door salesperson and want to warn everyone else. Some just got married, had a baby, or retired after 30 long years. Some build cabinets, sell homemade pottery or hold garage sales; offer to advertise their skills and special events free in your paper.

Welcome letters to your paper, and reserve room to print them. Get the ball rolling by asking your reporters to hunt up member talents and good story possibilities.

Ask people to fill out a survey and send it in – then print the results. Invite a reader debate over an issue your group hasn't yet decided. Ask several members the same provocative question and print the answers along with a photo of each member asked (p. 99).

But watch out. When government is cut back, for example, people's first reaction might be that government's too big anyhow. So when you invite reader comments, you might get socked with an attack on government that echoes the commercial media's bias. That doesn't educate anyone.

Get readers to think beyond their first impulses. Instead of surveying them on what they think of government cutbacks in general, ask about specific services like buses, highway repairs, monitoring pollution or assistance to the elderly, and whether those should be cut or expanded. Or write a few articles explaining why your group opposes cutbacks before you invite debate from readers. When a reader sends in an argument based on false facts, print it and write a response that politely corrects errors; or better yet, ask another reader to respond.

### Speeches & conferences

Talk to people *before* they go, so they'll know what you need for the paper. If they just hand you a rousing minute-by-minute agenda of everything that happened from 8:30 a.m. on – starting with the flag salute – they'll put readers to sleep. Worse yet, they may come back with nothing – just a vague thanks to the members for having such a great time at their expense. What you really need is a story that shows readers what's in it for them – why it was worth their money to send someone on a "junket."

A report doesn't mean dutifully noting everything that happened. It means picking the highlights – the most exciting and meaningful happenings – and giving readers a feel for why they're important. Ask people to take notes on rousing speeches and classes, including facts and ideas that particularly impressed them. Ask them to take down a few quotes, word-for-word, of clever statements that really hit the nail on the head, or that made the entire audience stand up and applaud.

Ask them to take pictures of people busily discussing the world's problems or hard at work – not sunbathing or staring at the camera as they're shot. Ask them to bring back a program with speakers' names spelled right plus other handouts – many can be turned into great articles.

Ask people to think about how this experience will make them better activists and help them better serve the group, or how it applies to local problems.

Will the staff write such articles, or do you expect delegates to write their own? If it's the delegates' job, give them pointers on writing. Suggest they liven up the report by interviewing leaders and other delegates – Chapter 11 shows how. If the staff does the write-up, tell delegates you'll interview them when they return.

# How to plan article lengths

What we have here is a failure to copyfit

## Why copyfit?

Copyfitting gives you a way to assign exact lengths to each article during your first planning meeting (p. 80). Then the writer knows what's expected, and if people write articles longer than what's assigned, they're forewarned that editing may be necessary.

Without copyfitting, people will write articles too long to fit in the paper. Then you're left with tough choices: mercilessly chop down articles so they'll fit; leave out an article someone wasted precious time and energy writing; or print a crowded page. The first two alternatives will poison your relations with volunteer writers. The last will damage your paper's popularity with readers.

Once you know how to *copyfit,* however, you can tell a writer exactly how long the article should be.

## Start with style

To copyfit you must know the paper's *style* (Chapter 8): the typeface and type size for articles, the number of columns per page, and the page size.

Remember, no page will be filled to the brim with article type. Plan to reserve half to a third of each page for graphics, headlines and space. That's your *page guideline,* explained on p. 70. The page guideline is a rough average for the whole paper. Some pages might end up more crowded than the norm while others, like the front page, will be much airier.

## Choose your method

Sometimes writers will know about how long to make a half-page article simply by being familiar with the paper – especially if you give writers an idea by showing them a half-page article that's already printed. But it's safer to be more precise.

You could copyfit by counting how many words will fit nicely on a page – but that takes time and patience. Instead, try this:

## How many pages of typed copy can you fit?

Ask everyone writing for your paper to type articles double-spaced on regular-size 8½" by 11" paper. At this stage, the article is called the *copy.* If you're publishing a newsletter with standard (8½"x11") size pages, between a page and a page-and-a-third of copy is plenty for each newsletter page. That will leave room for pictures, headlines and space.

If the type on the printed newsletter page is smaller than the typed words on the copy, you can fit more – up to two pages of copy – on each printed page. If you're printing a *tabloid*-size newspaper (p. 66) with pages 11" wide and 14" to 17" tall, plan two to four pages of copy for each newspaper page.

That's a general yardstick, and the specifics vary for each paper, depending on its style. Each type style takes up a different amount of room. And if your pages aren't standard sizes, what do you do?

If you've already published a paper in the style you want, dig up a typed, double-spaced page of copy that went into it, and use that as a guide, comparing it with the typeset version in the paper. How much room does it take up? Measure the total height of the column (or more) of type your one page of copy was set into, and write it down. (If the page of copy extended into more than one column of type, measure its height in each column separately; then add them together.) Then skip to Step 3 of the copyfitting exercise on p. 86.

Typical conference report

1. One full page copy . . .

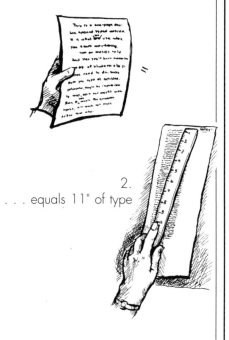

. . . equals 11" of type

2.

3. Columns are 10" tall

4. Column-inches per page

10"
× 3 columns
──────────
30 column-inches

1 column-inch

5. Page half-full of article type
   Page full of article type

$30 × \frac{1}{2} = 15$ column-inches

7. In this style, ⅔ page copy makes a half-page article.

6. Pages of copy per typeset page

$$\frac{15 \text{ column-inches}}{11" \text{ per page}} = 1.36 \text{ pages copy}$$

## Precise copyfitting for your paper

**1.** Type one full page of copy, double-spaced on an 8½" by 11" sheet.

**2.** Typeset that same copy into one column of type in your paper's style, and measure its height. Suppose the type is 11" tall.

**3.** What's the maximum height for a column of type in the printed paper? Measure the total height of the printed page, minus both top and bottom *margins* (p. 68). If each newsletter page is 11" tall and there's a half-inch margin at both the top and bottom, for example, columns are 10" tall.

**4.** How many *column-inches* are there on a printed page? No matter how wide your type columns are, a *column-inch* is one column wide in your style, and one-inch tall. So multiply the maximum height of your type columns (step 3) times how many columns there are per page.

If your style calls for three columns of type per page, the total is 30 column-inches per page (3 columns times 10" each). That's how much type you could fit if you didn't have a single headline or picture. But you wouldn't do that, would you?

**5.** How many column-inches of type fit nicely into a page? Multiply total column-inches per page (step 4) times your page guideline (p. 70) – saying how much of the page should be filled with type. Suppose just half the paper will be solid type (with the rest headlines, pictures and space). Multiply one-half (½) times 30 column-inches to get 15 column-inches of type per page. That's what you're aiming for.

**6.** Find out how many pages of copy fit comfortably on a page by dividing the number of desired column inches per page (step 5) by the number of column-inches one page of typed copy yields (step 2). Round it off to something easy to talk about. For example, if you divide 15 column-inches (step 5) by 11" (step 2), you get 1.36 – or just about 1⅓. So for this style paper, plan to write 1⅓ pages of copy for each typeset page.

**7.** To plan a half-page article, divide the answer from step 6 in half. For a one-third page article, multiply it by one-third, and so on. In the example, half of 1⅓ is ⅔. So for a half-page article in the paper, write around two-thirds of a page of typed copy.

## So not everyone will type articles?

Then there's the real world. Not everyone can type, and you know someone will give you a nice story scribbled up and down little sheets of note paper, with half the writing scratched out. Well, if that person's going to be a regular contributor, you could copyfit for Moira Kennedy's handwriting the same way you did for typed copy, finding out how many pages of her scribbled copy are needed for a one-page article.

Ask regular contributors who don't type to please use standard-size pads of lined paper, and to leave every other line blank (double-spacing). Once Moira's written an article that way and it's typeset, follow the steps above, substituting a sheet of handwritten copy for the typed sheet in step one. Now you know exactly how many pages of scribbled copy you need for each article.

For new contributors, do a *word count* – count the number of words in a half-page article, and ask writers of half-page articles to stick to that length.

# 10. The facts: finding & using them

**P**eople want – and need – to learn something new from your publication. As Chapter 3 explains, it's mighty hard to get some kinds of news from the commercial media. And if you just rehash gripes without investigating what's really happening and why, readers will stop taking you seriously.

Look over the first draft or outline of each article. Do you state things you don't prove? Do you tackle issues you don't know enough about? Are there important questions you can't answer?

## Where to find the evidence

### Be on the lookout

Once you get past the fluff and bias (p. 18), you can pick up plenty of useful facts from newspapers and TV. If an article buried on the back pages of the *Daily Planet* includes juicy information, tear it out, noting the date and page. If a TV report reveals interesting facts, write them down. File those notes and clippings; many will come in handy for future articles.

### Meetings & conferences

Chances are, every time people go to a meeting or conference, they bring back flyers and pamphlets chock full of facts. Encourage delegates to drop off copies in your office.

## International unions

Most unions have research and public relations departments, plus experts in health and safety, labor law, politics (including voting records), health care, and benefits. Most publish a monthly newspaper or magazine, plus pamphlets and fact sheets. To find out what's available, call each union's public relations or education department. And ask to be put on the mailing list to get *news releases*.

The AFL-CIO in Washington (815 16th Street N.W., D.C. 20006) has its own research staff and paper (*AFL-CIO News*), plus departments that publish newsletters and pamphlets around specific areas. Ask the Union Label and Service Trades Dept. to put you on the mailing list for the *Labeletter*, so you'll know about boycotts and product news.

## Union news & graphics

Try these services:
- Press Associates, Inc., 806 15th St. N.W., Suite 632, Washington D.C. 20005. Weekly articles on labor and politics.
- Union Communication Service, 1633 Connecticut Ave. N.W., Suite 200, Washington D.C. 20009. Monthly packet of short articles and cartoons.
- Labour News & Graphics, from the Canadian Association of Labour Media, 130 Union Street, W. Fergus, Ont. N1M 1V1. Monthly articles and cartoons, plus a newsletter full of tips.
- UAW-LUPA Newsline, 8000 E. Jefferson, Detroit, MI 48214. Almost-monthly short articles and graphics on politics, economics, etc.

## Community & grassroots groups

Is a local group organizing to improve the schools or fight electric rate hikes? Chances are, they've had to research the issues and can give you facts, plus put you in touch with sympathetic experts. Try fact-finding consumer and civic groups like Public Interest Research Groups or the League of Women Voters. They also keep up on politicians' voting records.

What other groups are out there? Go to the library and thumb through the *Encyclopedia of Associations*.

## Alternative publications

- *Dollars & Sense.* This gives a monthly diet of easy-to-read articles on how the economy operates, for $19.50 a year. Write *Dollars & Sense* at One Summer St., Somerville, MA 02143.
- *In These Times* is a good, almost-weekly national paper costing $34.95 a year. Articles are long, but packed with information. Contact them at 2040 N. Milwaukee Ave., Chicago, IL 60647.
- *Garbage: The Practical Journal for the Environment.* To get six issues a year for $21 ($29 in Canada), write: Old House Journal Corp., 435 Ninth St., Brooklyn, NY 11215.
- *Annual Directory of Alternative and Radical Publications.* This lists a wealth of papers and magazines put out by environmentalists, feminists and others. It costs $3 from the Alternative Press Center, Inc., P.O. Box 33109, Baltimore, MD 21218.

## What's Business up to?

To find out, plus get inside political scoops and facts like executive salaries – with some critical analysis – try *Business Week* and *The Wall Street Journal.* Pick up copies at the newsstand. (But if you have a blood pressure problem, don't read the *Journal* editorials.)

A computer "search"

# To help you dig further

- *Manual of Corporate Investigation.* This handy guide lists helpful publications and agencies, and even defines a few economic and legal terms. Send $10 to the Food and Beverage Trades Dept. of the AFL-CIO at: 815 16th St. N.W., Washington, D.C. 20006.
- *Raising Hell.* This little gem by Dan Noyes tells you how to research government, individuals, corporations and property, and defines some financial terms. It's available from *Mother Jones* Magazine, 1663 Mission St., San Francisco, CA 94103 for $3.75.

## Computer "on-line" services

Once you have a computer hooked up to phone lines via a *modem* (p. 55), a wealth of information is at your fingertips – for a price. Every second of computer time you waste will cost you, so before you do a "search" on your own, go to a public or university library and ask for help. Also, if your computer modem is a bit slow (1,200 bauds), the same search can cost you twice what it would with a fast, 2,400-baud modem.

For most searches, you string together words (or phrases), and the machine hunts through thousands of sources, pulling up those that link the same word groups. (If you aren't specific enough, you'll spend a fortune getting bizarre articles on, for example, birth labor instead of labor unions.) "Download" those you want onto your machine.

If you work evenings or weekends, services like Dow Jones and Dialog offer special low "after dark" rates.

For the most sources try:

● Vu/Text. Here you'll find all major newspapers, wire services like AP, and business journals. A search could cost less than $10, with the average running around $15.

● Nexis. This is the Cadillac of computer files and has everything, including corporate financial records, government facts and popular magazines. Look into discounts offered to unions and other groups. But even with the discount, a typical search can cost $40.

## Electronic bulletin boards & networks

Bulletin boards give you current, specialized facts for little or no money. For example, the Economic Bulletin Board offers the latest releases around the clock from the Census Bureau and other federal fact-gatherers. Contact the U.S. Department of Commerce, Office of Business Analysis and Economic Affairs, Washington D.C. 20230.

●*Computer Readable Databases,* edited by Kathleen Marcaccio. Look for this handy directory in the library. It lists computer bulletin boards, on-line services, CD-ROM discs (p. 56), etc.

● *PeaceNet, EcoNet* and *Conflict-Net.* These non-profit networks link labor, environmental, peace and other groups around the world. They can put you in touch with "data bases" full of information, or help your computer talk to other people's computers via *con-*

*ferencing* and electronic mail (*e-mail*).

To subscribe, contact The Institute for Global Communications at 3228 Sacramento St., San Francisco, CA 94115. The basic charge is a one-time $10 sign-up fee plus $10 a month for an hour of evening or weekend time, and more time for $5-$10 an hour.

● *Laborline* and *SoliNet.* These give unions valuable facts on grievances, women's wages, health and safety, executive salaries, retirement plans, and so on. Both offer conferencing, e-mail, news and support services.

*SoliNet* is bilingual (English and French), and features a popular weekly round-up of labour news, plus lobbying info. Contact Marc Belanger, Canadian Union of Public Employees, 21 rue Florence St., Ottawa, Ontario K2P 0W6.

*Laborline* comes out of the George Meany Center for Labor Studies (10000 New Hampshire Ave., Silver Spring, MD 20903), which also publishes a newsletter and does computer training.

Doing research

# The public library

This is a good place to look if you're not sure what else to do. Just tell the librarians what you want; it's their job to help you find it. Try thumbing through these books: (The first three are also in paperback at the bookstore.)

● *The Statistical Abstract of the*

*U.S.* This gives a generous smattering of figures the government collects, from the month-by-month humidity of Kansas City to how much we spend on schools for the deaf, how many people wear contact lenses, foreign exchange rates, or bills President Truman vetoed.

- **The World Almanac and Book of Facts.** It has pictures, too.
- *The Handbook of Labor Statistics.* It tells how many people have a job, how long an average job lasts, what people do, how much they make, plus benefits. It includes facts on strikes, prices, foreign industry, and the Gross National Product.
- *The Congressional Directory* and other government records. These keep track of congressional staff and committees, lobbyists, bills, resolutions and speeches. The Secretary of State's office may keep similar state records.
- *The Almanac of American Politics,* by Michael Barone and Grant Ujifusa. This tells who's who, plus a short history of their districts, campaign contributions, their ratings with various groups, coalitions and trends, etc.
- *Canadian Almanac and Directory.* Get the latest lowdown on topics ranging from trade unions, AM radio stations, the Queen, and child welfare agencies, to the population of Maidstone Township, price changes, or major awards granted to chemists.
- **CD discs for computers.** See p. 56.

# Government fact-finders

Nine times out of ten, a government agency regulates, taxes, collects facts on or is in charge of the institution or activities you're wondering about. Government departments both gather "raw" statistics and prepare special reports. The Freedom of Information Act guarantees you access to all unclassified records – federal, state and local. So don't let busy bureaucrats discourage you from seeing what they've got.

## Tax assessor's office

Tax assessors keep records on the assessed values of buildings and land, and the tax bills and abatements (tax refunds) on all property, big and small. They're legally required to help you sift through the records.

## The periodicals room

Here local libraries keep old, new and very old issues of local papers and national ones like *The New York Times*. The periodicals room is also filled with a myriad of magazines, both popular and specialized, past and present. Some magazines publish an index each year, so you can look things up by topic. And libraries have other indexes, listing all the articles written on a given subject.

## Special services

Big libraries may offer *InfoTrack*, a group of compact discs showing what newspaper and magazine articles have been written on each topic. A *microfiche* system like *NewsBank* will look up – and pull out – whole newspaper articles on your subject, plus facts like recent changes in labor or civil rights law. If your public library is a "depository," it keeps all government documents.

## Business libraries

If the local university has a business school, chances are it has a business library. Some big city libraries have a business branch, too. This is the best place to find out about corporations. They carry SEC reports (p. 91), plus the annual reports companies give stockholders, and a whole slew of magazines. Both the *Business Periodicals Index* and *Funk and Scott's* will show you what's been written on specific companies or industries, and where to find it.

## State & federal

State and federal governments keep track of banks and loans, campaign contributions, food and nutrition, pollution, industrial accidents, housing, labor-management relations, crime, schools, health, consumer rights, employment and civil rights, not to mention their own handling of welfare, urban renewal, public works, prisons (they call it corrections) or planning.

To pick their brains, sift through a guide to state and federal government in the library or get hold of a phone book covering the state capital (the library should have one) and look up the state or U.S. government. Pick the most likely office, and give them a call. You might get what you need right on the phone.

Some states have a separate Citizen Information Service, and Uncle Sam might have a federal information center in your area.

- **Securities & Exchange Commission (SEC).** Corporations that sell stock publicly must report to the SEC their financial condition, mergers, court cases, executive salaries, and how much stock their directors own. You'll find these reports in the regional SEC office, in business school libraries, or by writing the SEC in Washington.

- **Bureau of Labor Statistics (BLS).** The U.S. Department of Labor will send you the Monthly Labor Report for $20 a year. It also has BLS offices in a dozen regional centers. Write or call the regional office or the bureau in Washington D.C. for a catalogue listing hundreds of reports on wages, working conditions, job trends, and so on.

### Congress & politicians

Congress has its own fact-finders – the Congressional Budget Office (CBO) and General Accounting Office (GAO) publish ground-breaking studies. Call the local or Washington D.C. office of senators and representatives from your area. Their staffs also do useful research. And they often offer fact sheets showing their platforms and records (in the best light possible) on specific issues.

Facts are everywhere

# Make sure it's true

If there's one thing that makes people mistrust you and your whole publication, it's finding out that you printed something untrue. Don't print anything you're unsure of. And find another source to confirm controversial statistics or to explain what they mean.

### Who can you believe?

You can trust a source for some facts more than for others. Do the facts jibe with its normal bias? A commercial paper must cater to advertisers and accept "business as usual." When it gives the business scene a rosy glow, be suspicious. Examine the facts and look for other opinions. After all, they're printing what they *want* to believe. But when that same paper exposes business wrongdoing or failure, that's more credible because it contradicts the paper's normal bias.

### Ask the experts

After you dig up the statistics, look for an expert to test your conclusions on. You may see changes in the numbers from one year to the next without knowing why. Or you'll get hold of a financial statement without being able to wade through it.

The best analysis may come from community and labor activists involved in the day-to-day effects of the statistics. When you have questions, give known activists a call. If you've done the research to pinpoint what you don't know, you'll get the most from such interviews (more on p. 96).

Want to see our first draft of the sentences to the far left? Then turn to p. 110.

# Don't let the facts fool you

Some facts are hard to find, others are hard to understand, while others are deliberately distorted. Look at examples A through J on pp. 92-93. Can you sniff out what's fishy about those figures? Then check the guidelines below.

### What do the numbers measure?

Example A's official unemployment

"Forget the statistics – I'll give you the facts."
–Archie Bunker

## Example A

After steadily rising several months in a row, unemployment dropped in June, reports the Bureau of Labor Statistics. It appears the recession is finally ending.

## Example B

Americans are better off then ever, the government reported in 1986. Personal per-capita income was 37% higher than in 1973, even after adjusting for inflation.

## Example C

General Ecstasy insists it can't afford the wage and benefit hikes the union is demanding. "Our profits are only 5% of sales," explains Chairman Foghorn.

## Example D

The average income in Fat City is now $45,000. Mayor Smiley is proud that his small town has achieved such extraordinary prosperity.

## Example E

The nation's poor are better off today than in the past – the poorest fifth of our citizens have seen their family incomes rise 8 percent from 1982 to 1987.

## Example F

Police Chief Frank Joyce reports that crime in the central city has dramatically dropped over the past ten years.

## Example G

During the New York City blackout, looters made off with millions of dollars in merchandise. Yet a survey of arrested looters proves that it wasn't poverty that triggered the crime wave, reveals the district attorney. Forty-six percent of those arrested had jobs.

## Example H

"Nearly three out of four respondents said they expect the nation's economy to stay the same or improve this year," reported The Detroit News in early 1990. "Few in state fear '90 recession," blared the headline.

figures don't tell how many people are out of work. They count only those actively looking for jobs. When the job situation seems hopeless, homemakers and teenagers temporarily give up looking. People who can't find full-time work retire early, take part-time jobs or go back to school. They aren't counted as unemployed because most are "out of the labor force." That's why official *unemployment* can fall even when fewer people have jobs.

In example B, *personal income* doesn't tell you what workers make. It lumps dividends, rents, and interest income together with wages and salaries.

Yes, personal income was 37% higher in 1986. But workers' wages had dropped a painful 10% from 1973 levels. Things like buying and selling real estate and executive bonuses had pushed the incomes of the rich through the roof. And *per capita* (per person) incomes also rose because young mothers had been pushed into the workforce as dad's wages fell. Much of that second wage went to pay higher child-care and other expenses.

To get exact definitions for other official figures, consult The Statistical Abstract of the U.S. (p. 89).

## Is a meaningful measure being used?

If you got hold of General Ecstasy's annual report to stockholders, you might see a very different picture from the publicly touted figures in example C. The profits stockholders value are figured as a percent of *equity* (the money invested in the company), no matter what the sales figures are.

## Watch out for averages

Averages mask big inequities. To get an *average* income, you just add up everyone's income and divide that by the number of people.

In example D, Mayor Smiley and 29 of his friends may rake in $1 million a year each, while Fat City's 1,000 other workers eke out a living on $16,350 apiece. Because some are very rich, the average income will be $45,000.

The *median* gives you a better picture of how Fat City residents are faring. Pick the person in the middle, one who makes more money than half the population, but less than the other half. The *median* is that person's income. Since everyone in Fat City except 30 rich peo-

ple makes $16,350 a year, the median income is $16,350.

## Don't compare apples with oranges

Example E compares 1987 with 1982, the lowest year of a terrible recession, when the poor hit rock-bottom. To find real trends, compare 1987 with another non-crisis year – 1979. You'll find that the standard of living for the poorest fifth of the population dropped by 9 percent, even while the richest fifth enjoyed hefty 19-percent (after-inflation) income gains.

Likewise, don't compare family income with individual income. When looking at wages from one year to the next, subtract the effects of inflation (using Uncle Sam's *Consumer Price Index*) and you'll get *real* wages.

In example F, the police chief is talking about *reported* crime only. If insurance companies have stopped writing policies for the central city, chances are many crimes now go unreported.

## Do the figures justify the conclusion?

The exact same numbers can tell a different story, depending on who uses them. Read example G carefully, and you'll find that looters had a 54% unemployment rate. If you consider that a bit steep, you'll draw opposite conclusions from the same survey.

If you look at the actual poll behind the upbeat article in example H, you'll see that most people expected no change. The number who thought things would get worse (24%) was actually higher than those who expected things to get better (18%). So if you add the percentages differently, you could stress the opposite: More than three out of four respondents expected the economy to stay the same or get worse.

## Avoid projections

Example I is absurd. People should not extend past trends blindly into the future.

There was a similar problem with the 1984 Rand Corp. study that pooh-poohed census figures showing that women made 59¢ for every dollar men got. Women actually made 64¢, announced Rand. It invented that figure by adding in the *potential* wages of women homemakers, based on their education and work experience. Then it concluded that this proves we don't need affirmative action. One big hitch: It's well documented that women don't make what they deserve, based on education and work experience. That's one reason they may need affirmative action.

### Don't get confused by rates of change

What's fishy about example J? A typical union member was paid $101 more to start with – $389 a week, compared to $288 for non-union workers. If you make $389, a 4.1% raise is worth $1 more than a 5.2% raise based on $228. What's more, the figures didn't count hefty union benefits and bonuses.

### Beware of polls & unscientific surveys

For all you know about example K, maybe just 2% of the executives who got Maxi-Management's survey bothered to fill it out. And no one checked their claims with the secretaries.

# Polls are tricky

The shakiest statistics of all are public opinion polls. Here are questions to ask about polls:

### What's the source?

Who paid for the poll, and how reputable is the polling company? Well-known national pollsters like Gallup, Harris, and CBS use reliable methods, but many local TV or newspaper polls don't. Politicians running against each other often come out with opposing polls, and lobbying groups can usually find a "hack" pollster to tell them what they want us to hear.

### How was it conducted?

Don't trust postcard, magazine or phone-in polls. A good pollster makes sure people can't answer twice, and that they get an accurate cross-section of the general population. At least half should be women, for example.

How big was the sample? If fewer than 400 people are questioned locally, or fewer than 1,000 nationally, don't hang your hat on the poll results – especially if it's broken into smaller subgroups, like people under 24.

Was it adjusted for various factors? Pre-election polls, for example, don't bother with Americans who don't usually vote – and today, that means the

## Example I
Over the past ten years, the number of households hooked up to cable TV in Mediamart, Md. grew by 5,000%. If those rates continue over the next ten years, each family will have 20 cable-connected TV sets.

## Example J
"Pay hikes for unions at 17-year low point," screamed newspaper headlines in 1985. Over the last year, union pay and benefits rose only 4.1%, compared to non-union gains of 5.2%.

## Example K
Eighty-eight percent of the American and Canadian executives responding to Maxi-Management's questionnaire reported that their secretaries enjoyed four coffee breaks each day.

## Example L
With these class differences in schooling, rich students are three times more likely to go to college than working-class kids with the *same* academic ability. (Jencks & Reisman, *The Academic Revolution*)

The facts: finding & using them

<u>Example M</u>

On February 10, 1991, a union member from Plasticso went into the Travers City General Hospital and had surgery performed on his eye by Doctor Hilda Fuerste. He was released from the hospital on February 12, and told to report to the doctor on February 20, 1991. On February 20 the doctor told the employee the eye would take time to heal, and that he should come back on March 12, 1991. Meanwhile Fred Glynn (Plasticso insurance dept.) called the doctor on March 8 and asked the doctor if the employee was given a release for February 20. Doctor Fuerste said she assumed her secretary gave him one. On March 12 Fred Glynn called Doctor Fuerste and asked her to make out a release for the employee and backdate it for February 23, 1991. The employee never received his release from Dr. Fuerste. He was called by Plasticso, who told him Plasticso had the release and to report to work.

<u>Example N</u>

The average American labors more than two-and-a-half hours of every workday just to pay federal, state and local taxes. If you begin work at 7:30 a.m., you won't earn a penny for your family until 10:05. Or look at it this way: You'll have to work every workday until April 28 just to pay your taxes for the year!

majority of us are being left out.

## Don't trust polls that neglect the undecided

If the definite answers add up to 100%, those who "don't know" or can't decide are left out. Yet people straddling the fence may be the key factor. And what does the *majority* think? If an opinion gets less than 50% support, it may not matter that it's 10% higher than another position.

Also, don't expect any poll to be accurate down to the last percentage point. A well-done poll could still be about 3% off.

## Were people asked loaded questions?

When the Business Roundtable paid Opinion Research Corp. to poll people's attitudes on creating a federal consumer protection agency, business got the answer it wanted. The poll said 75% of Americans opposed such an agency.

But the key question wasn't that simple. It asked: "Do you favor setting up a Consumer Protection Agency over all the others, or do you favor doing what is necessary to make the agencies we have now more effective in protecting the consumer's interests?"

# How to use the facts

Once you've gathered the facts and have managed to understand them, how will you present them?

## Reveal the source

When you print startling facts, quote the source you got them from, so your reader won't suspect you made it up. Putting the source in parentheses, as example L does, keeps it from interfering with the flow of the writing.

## Don't get carried away

Don't try to get people's respect by overloading your article with trivial facts, as example M does.

The exact dates sound too official and dry. They actually make it harder to figure out what's going on. You may have to write grievances and legal papers that way; but for an article, use phrases like "two weeks earlier" and "the next day." Facts *don't* speak for themselves. It's their impact on us, not the number of them, that makes the article meaningful.

If you've knocked yourself out doing a lot of research, you'll be tempted to write a 16-page treatise, crammed full of every single fact you discovered. But no one will read it.

To uncover a few priceless gems, you'll dig up countless other interesting facts that aren't as important. No matter how painful it is, put those aside so you can make the gems shine.

## Show what the numbers mean

Most of us can't picture plain numbers. You might get confused between

an accident rate that grew *to* 110% its former level and one that grew *by* 110%. (The one growing *to* 110% is 10% larger, while the one that grew *by* 110% is over twice as big.)

If an article states that the U.S. is spending $1 billion for a new weapons system, it doesn't excite people much more than if it were $1 million. Your job is to give facts life, to compare them to things we understand, like example N.

If the government gave me $1,000 *every day*, it wouldn't equal $1 billion until 2,739 years or about 100 generations later, when I'm long dead. That helps me realize what an incredible waste it is to throw $1 billion away on a weapons system, if we really don't need it.

Here's another mind-boggler: If Uncle Sam gave $1,000 to every man, woman and child in St. Louis, Mo., Providence, R.I., and Albany, N.Y., it still wouldn't cost $1 billion! We calculated that with population figures from *The Statistical Abstract of the U.S.* (p. 89).

## Don't overdo percentages

Stay away from figures like "76% of our members" or "35% of American voters." Few people think comfortably in percentages. Substitute fractions like "three out of four members" and "one out of three American voters." That's not as exact, but it's close enough – and much easier to picture.

## Don't stretch the truth

Exaggerating is no better than lying. If one witness says several hundred people showed up and another just as reliable saw a thousand, pick the smaller estimate just to be safe.

# 11. The successful interview

## Why bother to interview people?

What's the best way to keep your paper or newsletter from looking like the diary of a small clique? Invite readers to join in, so the paper becomes an exciting forum where they meet all kinds of people.

Printing letters to the editor and being on the lookout for new people to write articles will help. But what about the many readers who just won't sit down to write an article or letter?

Get in the habit of interviewing everyone, from the member too shy to write to the stranger with interesting know-how to share. Interviews give readers a fresh perspective, plus they show your group's interested in what the average person has to say.

For example, if someone got hurt by a faulty product, only that person can tell it like it was. Or if management gives the union a hard time, quote in the paper exactly what was said. Then readers will realize what you're up against and will get mad at the source of the problem, not the union.

Every time you print someone's words, you give readers a new person-

ality to talk with – whether it's a good guy they identify with or a bad guy who makes them angry.

## Who can you interview?

### The average person

It's impossible to exaggerate the value of personal experiences. More than anything else, they make readers feel that your paper or newsletter is theirs, too.

Use personal interviews as a regular source of information. Interview a witness to an event, or someone familiar with a job or whatever situation you're looking at.

Whether you're covering a picnic or a hearing, show readers what it's all about by asking people why they're there, and what they think of it. Instead of just reporting resolutions and speeches at a convention, talk to a typical delegate attending for the first time, or collar several delegates.

After all, who doesn't get tired of hearing officers praise their own organization? Readers will be more impressed when the person down the street or on the next machine speaks in favor of your group's work. And the mystery of not knowing who might appear in the paper

Big shot trying to fool reporter

next will lure people into reading each issue.

For example, suppose you win a big grievance, and Sandi Polaski gets the promotion she deserves plus a bundle of back pay. Interview Sandi. If she's excited about her victory, a quote will make the story exciting. (Even if she's lukewarm about it, she'll probably say something worth quoting, if you ask the right questions.) Sandi's experience gives living proof that the union is worthwhile, that it helps someone readers can identify with.

And you can bet that once Sandi's gotten the royal treatment in your paper, she and her friends will read the paper with more trust and interest – so long as you didn't distort what she said.

At first you might feel funny interviewing people; they might feel up-tight too. But rest assured that once the article is done, people love to see themselves taken seriously in print.

### Interview leaders

To find out how contract priorities are shaping up this year, interview the bargaining chair. To clarify your group's position on tax giveaways, interview your staff expert on taxes. To find out how your local block council will respond to city cutbacks, interview its activists.

Interviewing someone in the know can be a fun, easy way to research an article on almost anything.

### Interview big shots

Suppose you want to know why potholes aren't getting fixed in your neighborhood. Or you want clear answers on whether new engines will be built at your plant. Interview government or company brass, and write a hard-hitting article based on that interview.

And who knows? If you interview the right person at the right time, you might find out something you aren't supposed to. Or you might catch someone lying or using twisted logic, so your paper can make a mockery of official rationalizations.

Or suppose Steve Babson is running for office using vague campaign literature that only tells you how pretty his children are and how much he loves his wife, family and country. With an interview, pin him down on issues that affect your members. If he doesn't give you clear answers, tell your readers just that.

### Getting big shots to talk

You can get interviews with high officials more easily than you'd expect. Just politely but firmly call the office, ask to speak with the top dog, and tell who you are and what you want to talk about. Most officials don't like to see in print that they refused to talk to a reporter; they also may be anxious to give you their side of the story. Be persistent – keep calling back if they don't return the call.

Some, however, are wary of reporters. Feel out the situation. If they refuse to talk to you as a reporter, you or a friend can pose as a student, job applicant or curious consumer. Appearing harmless can get suspicious officials to talk more openly.

After that, it's catch as catch can. Some big shots will talk on and on when coaxed by a little flattery. Others reveal things they didn't mean to say if you challenge them. Only experience can help you psych them out.

Be on your guard when interviewing people experienced at slipping out of reporters' questions. Did they really answer the questions, or change the subject? Are they subtly putting you down, flustering or embarrassing you to get you off their backs? You can expose such underhanded treatment in the article; so remember it, be brave, and continue.

If you're looking into government or politics, old politicians or appointees may tell you a lot, as long as it doesn't directly concern them. Try to find someone who's bitter about being fired.

# How to get a good interview

### The basics

• Don't go into an interview cold. Even if you're just talking to someone over the phone, be well prepared. If the person's friendly, you'll show you're trying to do a good job. If the person's trying to fool you, being well prepared will tip you off. Start every interview armed with background information and a list of questions you want answered.

Before you pop the questions, find out enough about the subject to discuss it intelligently. A good interview will fill in the holes on a topic you've already looked into through reading and other discussions. If you're talking to more than one person, save your "star witness" for the last interview, where you can ask the most informed questions.

- **What will readers want to know?** What information will further your group's goals? Even before the interview starts, think about the article you want to end up with. Then you'll know what to ask to get that article.

- **Where's the person coming from?** Do a background check to see what that person's done that would be worth discussing. Is he or she likely to be sympathetic to your inquiry or tight-lipped? What is she or he likely to know that your readers won't find out any other way? Does your subject have an ax to grind? Ask friends in the know.

- **Always make a list of questions** you want answered. Write clearly, so you won't find yourself awkwardly scrambling through your scribblings at the interview.

As you find out more during the interview, you'll think of new questions. Write them down – or a word or phrase to remind you – so you won't forget. Before you leave, make sure that all the questions are taken care of. If not, think of new questions to get at the same information, and ask again.

- **Begin by putting the person at ease.** You might mention mutual acquaintances, throw out a compliment, or joke around. If the person gets uptight during the interview, lighten things up with occasional banter and swapping stories. Just don't lose track of time.

Get the ball rolling by first asking non-controversial questions, making it clear that you're familiar with the topic.

When someone is unaccustomed to the limelight, hold the interview wherever he or she feels comfortable. And unless you're doing a quick "roving reporter" interview, spend a little time chatting while your subject gets used to your tape recorder or note pad.

When you interview a government official or other big shot, you may need to appear more sympathetic than you really are. Ask a question or two you already know the answer to so you can get an idea of how honest the official's being. But don't act too dumb, or you won't be taken seriously.

- **Don't let any interview get way off the track** for more than a minute or two. People will want to tell you fascinating and moving stories, and you won't want to interrupt them. Politicians will try to "wow" you with their latest accomplishments; you could be so impressed by their knowledge and power that you let them get completely off the subject.

Sidetracks can be interesting, even more interesting than the article you plan to write. You may have a good time chatting about this and that, but when you emerge from the interview you could find yourself empty-handed, with no article. Don't let that happen. Come with a clear idea of what you need to know, and stick with it. An interview is not a normal conversation.

- **Listen carefully.** Every so often you'll hear hints you should follow up on, going beyond your prepared questions.

## The fine points

- **Ask open questions.** If you ask a loaded question like, "This hospital's notorious for treating workers badly. What do *you* hate about it?" you'll hear only what people think you want to hear. But if you ask, "What's it like working here? How are workers treated?" you'll get a more honest answer.

- **Ask questions that require a good answer.** If you ask, "Did such-and-such happen?" or "Are you happy here?" you'll get a yes or a no. "What did you see happen here yesterday?" would be better. Stick to "how," "what," "when," "why" or "what kind of" questions, to start the person talking. The exception is when an official's evading your questions and you need a straight yes or no.

- **Ask one question at a time.** Don't let a period of silence fluster you. The person may need time to think, so sit back and relax, or work on your notes.

- **Ask brief questions.** Don't give speeches to show off what you know.

- **A slightly negative question** can be more stimulating than a positive one. If you praise Senator Paskal and then ask what the person you're interviewing thinks, you may just get a nod or a shrug. But if you say, "I hear Senator Paskal didn't really represent the minorities in his district. What do you think?" or "Is it true that your group is hurt badly by this decision?" you'll get a lively answer, whether in agreement or defense.

Trouble using a tape recorder

• **Sift out what the person actually saw,** experienced, or can back up with facts. Take that more seriously than second-hand stories, assumptions and guesses. If a second-hand story is important, line up an interview with the person who first told it.

On the other hand, don't come across as not trusting the people you interview, as you ask what they saw firsthand or how they know this or that.

• **Look 'em right in the eyes** whenever you can. That way you seem more genuinely interested and you make people feel they're taking with a person, not just a newspaper.

# Record the information

## Try a tape recorder

If you can get a tape recorder, take it to your first interviews, especially if you want exact quotes. But keep in mind that using a tape recorder is more work, because once you get home you have to copy down what's on the tape. It's probably best to start out both taking notes and tape-recording the conversation, so you can use the tape to double-check your notes. Or bring someone to the interview to help take notes (although that will make the interview less intimate).

## Taking notes

You can't write down everything – and you don't want to hold up the interview while you're scribbling away. Jot down just enough phrases to help you remember things. And speed things up by developing your own abbreviations for common words. For example, when you hear someone say, "We went to see the supervisor and complained about favoritism," you might write, "To sup, compl re favor."

But take special care to get down precise facts and juicy direct quotes you could use in your article. And make sure you have the whole facts (p. 91).

Fill in your notes as soon as you get home, before you forget what they mean.

When you're interviewing at an office or home, take a good look around before you leave. Do you see anything worthy of comment? Do the books on the shelf or the people coming in and out tell you anything about the situation? What about the gestures, sincerity and emotional style of the person you interviewed?

Example A

## Assessing Cambridge

Rudolph Russo is chief assessor for the City of Cambridge. In that capacity, he assesses property within the city, and grants abatements to those who make a good case that they've been overassessed.

Rudolph – better known as "Rudy" – summoned one of our reporters into his office last week and gave her the third degree.

"You want to know so much, now let me ask YOU a few questions," he menaced. He proceeded to demand name, address, school attended ("MY daughter goes to Harvard," he gloated), place of origin – all of which he threateningly wrote down – and concluded the session by demanding of our researcher if she was "one of those crazy people who lives in a commune."

Rudy Russo has good reason to be edgy...

# When the interview's over

How do you turn an interview into an article?

## Should you fiddle with direct quotes?

Few people speak perfect English. Some expressions that sound fine in a conversation look funny when written. Someone might tell you, for example, that "I would kinda think, well, he don't like that and um – I don't think, he ain't gonna take it lyin' down, you know." Save that person from being embarrassed in print for collecting her thoughts out loud. Rewrite the quote so it sounds right to readers. "He doesn't like that, and I don't think he'll take it lying down," is better.

Improve other interviews by putting ideas in a logical order and leaving out repetitions or sidetracks.

Be careful, however. When you spiff up a friendly interview, don't destroy the individual style that makes each person's speech and thoughts unique. How much you should change is a judgment call only experience and circumstances can dictate.

## Make sure it's right

For friendly interviews, call back the people you talked to and read them their quotes to make sure you didn't misunderstand or go overboard with editing. If anyone's embarrassed by the final version, explain why it's important, or brainstorm then and there on how to fix it. Or volunteer to withhold the name. In any case, get the person's approval before it's printed.

If you're nailing a big shot who definitely wouldn't approve, you don't have much leeway with direct quotes. Leaving out whole questions and answers is fine. But don't make changes the person can catch you with, damaging your credibility. Carefully repeat the exact words and put "..." when you leave out part of an answer. If the person's words sound ridiculous, so much the better.

### The "Q & A" format

Write an article based on your interview in question-and-answer style, and it'll be fun to read. However, this format only works when you conduct one interview, whether with a person or a group, and when the personality and ideas of that one person or group form the core of the article.

### A personal story

If your questions don't add much to the article, leave them out. Instead, write the article from the point of view of the person interviewed, as if he or she were telling it. Introduce it with something like: "When Foreman Smith tried to slip a little extra work into the Gear Dept. without hiring anyone new to do it, Shelly Cziezler and her co-workers had a surprise for him. In Shelly's own words, here's what happened:"

### When it's one of several sources

Most of the time you'll use the information from interviews to write an article in your own words, adding insights from your research and other experiences.

Always include direct quotes. Pick the cleverest, funniest, most revealing, most touching or shocking sentences that make the points you plan to emphasize. Use these quotes to launch or sign off your article, or to dramatize an idea or two within it.

# For example

In the margins you'll find articles based on interviews.

### Making good from bad

Even if your interview is a bomb, you might turn it to good use when you write the article, as example A illustrates.

The reporter was trying to get the goods for an article on city corruption by interviewing the chief assessor. Instead, she came out of the interview redfaced and empty-handed, feeling like a fool. But after another reporter got the facts through other sources, they used this unsuccessful interview to dramatically launch the first article.

Example B

## Opinion: Is management serious about quality?

**Don McGovern, KTP** – I don't know. Quality means more profit. So why do they cut out jobs and increase the work load? Why not give a person time and good equipment to do it right the first time? Then everybody profits.

**John Wheeler, KTP** – Yes, I think the company would like to have quality, but they're not going to sacrifice quantity to get quality – period.

**Leon Cissell, KTP** – I feel that my foreman Mr. C.B. Herrod does make a serious effort to put quality into the units.

**Vicki Staggs, LAP** – I believe the company could have better quality if they took into consideration the feelings and our input about our jobs. They say they want to hear what we have to say but they usually don't listen.

**Jim Jeffries, LAP** – If it's convenient to run quality, then they will run quality. Personally, I think that quality should be like a door you put on that fixture. It should be built into every job and not just when it's convenient to put it in.

UAW Local 862 On line

### Roving reporter

Don't wait for news to come to you. Create exciting feature stories for your paper simply by becoming a "roving reporter" (example B).

If you're a typical reader, you'll turn to the roving reporter feature as soon as you get the paper. After all, you're never sure who'll show up there – it

Example C

## Learning can make your job safer

"I felt the school was very rewarding since it touched on a lot of our problems locally," said Janice Purtee.

Janice and LeRoy Smith of Hillsboro Mfg. attended the UAW annual health-and-safety seminar during the week of April 9 through 12. This was the biggest class they have ever had.

The instructors pointed out that in a welding department overhead ventilation was of no use, since it only pulled the fumes past workers' faces. Ventilation should be down near the machine where it is needed.

Different types of safety on machines were demonstrated, such as guards over foot pedals, or mesh guards over fans or belts. Unionists learned that anytime you can get your finger through the mesh or wire, it's not sufficient protection for the worker.

Janice said, "The industrial hygienist noted that in medical schools in Ohio only 11 hours of Occupational Health are required for each student. So most doctors cannot diagnose our problems."

"On record keeping," LeRoy said, "I have a copy of a form that the company has to complete and post in the plant by Feb. 1."

The instructors stressed that safety and health should be negotiated in each contract.

## A four-year-old speaks out

Audrey is an almost-four-year-old who spent one year in Head Start and will return in September. I interviewed her about her school and what went on there.

*Me:* Do you want to go back to school?

*Audrey:* Yeah. 'Cuz I want to put on my clothes and see my teacher Miss King.

*Me:* What else do you want to do?

*Audrey:* I want to see all those kids in the big room.

*Me:* What do you do in the big room?

*Audrey:* I will go sit down and eat our crackers and juice and peaches and apples...

*Me:* Then what?

*Audrey:* Then we have some oranges and french fries and hamburgers and milk and cake.

*Me:* After you eat, what will you do?

*Audrey:* I will have more crackers and...

*Me – trying to change the subject:* What other things do you do at school?

*Audrey:* I get some toys and my Easter clothes and my Easter shoes and go to the big room.

*Me:* What do you do then?

*Audrey:* I sit down and the kids sit down, then we go to the big room, then we go back and eat...

*Me – to avoid a long list of foods which I saw coming:* What do you do in the little room?

*Audrey:* In the little room we go sit down and then go back to the big room. In the big room I sit down with my Easter dress

and...

*Me – seeing an inventory of clothing was beginning:* Do you sing any songs?

*Audrey:* I want to sing the "Teapot Song."

*Singing:*

Mrs. Polly had a dolly who was sick, sick, sick.

So she called for the doctor to come quick, quick, quick.

The doctor looked at the dolly and he shook his head,

And he said, "Mrs. Polly, put her straight to bed."

He wrote on a paper for a pill, pill, pill,

"I'll be back in the morning with my bill, bill, bill."

---

might be someone you know, at least by sight. More intriguing, you never know what they'll say, because the paper poses thought-provoking questions a casual acquaintance wouldn't ask. It's a chance to spotlight all kinds of people.

Sometimes the question's as frivolous as, "What would you do if you were handed a million dollars?" More often it brings up a timely issue such as, "Are you satisfied with the education your kids are getting?" or "If you could tell the new mayor what to do first, what would you say?"

By asking serious questions, you kill several birds with the same stone. The paper reaches out to people who would never think to write a story, and it convinces them that your group values their opinions. The interviews are fun to read, while they also challenge readers to imagine their own replies.

One caution: While framing questions, think about the answers you're likely to get. If you ask the wrong questions, they could hurt you.

A variety of opinions is fine. But don't pose a question that'll tempt most readers to dump on a goal or activity of your group that isn't well understood. Once you've printed their opinions, people are less likely to change them. And you'll have a hopping mad reader on your hands if you do an interview and don't print a word of it.

### Was it worthwhile?

When your group sends someone off to a conference or meeting, you owe it to readers to tell them what that delegate got from it. Yet many reports from meetings read like "What I Did This Summer" – a laundry list of events.

To get a more interesting article, pose hard-hitting questions to conference delegates. Then selectively quote remarks that'll interest readers, as example C does.

### Four-year-old speaks out

That's right. Even a four-year-old can shine in print, if you ask her the right questions. Example D appeared in a newsletter encouraging mothers to send their children to Head Start programs.

The newsletter interviewed mothers whose kids participate in Head Start, and reaped their enthusiasm. Finally one enterprising writer went a step further. The article reveals the little girl's excitement about school – and it's cute as a button.

# 12. Get the most from photos

## Why every paper needs photographs

### They're grabbers

Big, striking photos attract readers. They help people picture what the organization's doing and why. And best of all, photos can show readers the paper involves them.

Print as many photos as possible of your members. And don't stop there. Include pictures of all different kinds of people, someone for every reader to identify with (Chapter 1).

### Say it with pictures

A good picture *is* worth a thousand words. And when a picture dramatizes an idea, the text doesn't need to repeat what the photo says. An article written partly with pictures is shorter, quicker to read, more powerful, and more fun to look at than a page full of words.

### The best proof

Don't expect people to believe whatever you say. Convince them with facts, interviews and logic – plus the right pictures. Photos may show just a part of the truth, but at least readers know what's before their eyes is real. Reading that a hall was filled to capacity isn't as impressive as seeing a photo with hundreds of animated people everywhere you look. TV news clips from the Vietnam War front did what no amount of writing could have done: they stripped war of romantic images and revealed the horror and brutality.

### Finding a photographer

Almost everyone takes vacation shots of the family. Hold a contest to discover the amateur talent among your readers; then train newcomers on how to use their skills for the paper. Expensive cameras are nice, but even the simplest can yield useful photos.

To make pictures tell a big part of each story, editors and writers should think of useful pictures *before* the story is written, and then work closely with the photographer to get the right shots.

Think ahead, and send a photographer to all your group's events.

• To find photos of other groups and ideas, try *Impact Visuals* (p. 159). A monthly packet showing current photos costs $15 a year; or for $25, they'll

Seeing is believing; proof that a worker was injured

UAW local 259

A good moment

Someone your group
doesn't like

Jerome Friar

CHRISTIAN
KNIGHTS

Room half empty

Room half full

Avoid a standard shot like this

promptly research a specific need and send a bundle of photos. Either way, they charge $35-$45 for each photo you use.

# The camera sees what it wants to

Before the photographer goes on a "shoot," the editor should explain the goals of the paper or newsletter, why the story is important, and what you're looking for. Otherwise, a photographer could miss all the excitement of the main event as he or she zeroes in on intriguing shots of people looking lonely in the hallways.

When a reporter and photographer cover the same event, coordinate things so you'll get photos of everyone interviewed, and ones that illustrate ideas those people express.

## The camera doesn't lie; it exaggerates

Photographers aren't neutral observers any more than the reporter is (p. 20); they pick and choose what to show. The same room is either half-full or half-empty, depending on how the photographer looks at it. If you're glad so many people showed up, pick the most crowded bunch, and take a close-up. If you're upset there weren't more people, capture rows of empty chairs in front. If you'll admit it's a boring affair, show people snoozing. If not, capture the audience at an exciting moment. If someone's a bad guy, catch him or her grimacing.

Seeing selectively is different from making things up, however. If a meeting called to protest poor snow removal attracted only three confused neighbors, don't try getting the three to look excited for the camera. Take photos of people and cars stuck on snowy streets instead, urging support for the next, hopefully better organized, protest.

# Make your group's events look interesting

If you don't think before you shoot, you'll find yourself printing nothing but boring clichés. Who wants to see a parade of speakers hugging the podium, the same old officials holding awards, and committees sitting behind a long dreary table, month after month? Here's how to avoid photos that make political action (and your group) look duller than a doornail:

## Look for action

When your team wins, don't line everyone up against a wall with the trophy. Show the team in action.

To take a picture of union president Tom Cruise, visit him on a busy day. Don't let him dress up in a suit and tie and plunk himself behind a desk, looking like the company personnel director. Capture him acting out the job, serving the people who elected him.

Hang around long enough to snap the "prez" visiting the workplace, speaking at a meeting, talking on the phone, discussing a problem, or just plain on the move. Staging a typical activity works better than police-style mug shots, but not everyone's a good actor.

## Make speeches come alive

You may not think there's much action in a speech. Granted, the action is subtle. It's in the gestures and the expressions on people's faces. When you shoot each speaker, include the hands and capture as many moods and gestures as possible.

● **Show the speaker with the audience.** If you forget the audience, you'll get photos that make it look like the speakers are up there all alone, as isolated as if they were in their offices.

When the audience does appear, too often it's just the backs of heads. It takes some doing, but look for an angle where you get at least part of the faces of both speaker and audience. It'll be near-impossible to get that shot if the front row or two of the audience is empty or the podium is too far from people. If you arrive early enough, see if you can move the podium before the program starts; or ask people to fill up the front rows.

Then wait patiently for your moment. If you just pop in, take a picture and take off, you'll likely get an audience that looks half-asleep. Sooner or later they'll clap, laugh at a good joke, or otherwise look alive. Don't be shy. Stand in front of the audience and take head-on shots of the whole group.

Sometimes the situation is hopeless, when look-alike speakers just stand there reading while everyone else examines their papers. Unless you're exposing the dullness of the event, look for photos that dramatize the *issues* the event deals with. After the speech, stick around. If people rush the podium to chat with the speaker, that could be the shot you need.

### Get close-ups

If you're too far away from the speakers, that big clunky podium could end up dominating each photo, making all the speakers look the same. To capture the gestures and faces that make each speech special, don't be shy. Move in close.

If you shoot a group that's too far away, everyone will look like little ants. Get close enough to a few people so that their faces stand out bigger than everyone else's. That will help draw the casual viewer into the scene.

### Try different angles

Move around so that each speaker and each event or person interviewed is seen in a different way, from a different spot. For variety, hold the camera different ways, to get both tall and wide shots of the same subject.

If tables and other lines in the photo go straight up, down and across, they just echo the lines of type and columns on the printed paper, and don't attract attention (example A). To get dramatic diagonal shapes instead, shoot from an angle – the side, above or below. For example, to shoot a bunch of people sitting at a table, stand to the side so that the table goes diagonally across the photo like example B. (That also gives you a nice, big face in the foreground.)

Make someone look sinister or bigger than life by crouching down and shooting up. Diminish that person or make someone look vulnerable by standing on a table and shooting down.

### Catch someone looking right at you

Whoever's looking at you will end up peering into the eyes of the reader browsing through your paper. This "eye contact" can startle readers, making them feel involved. Just make sure the expression on the person's face is meant for the reader.

Suppose you snap a furious tenant

UAW Solidarity

Show members doing something

UAW Solidarity

Show your officers doing something

Toledo Union Journal

Speaker & audience

Brent Nicastro

Speaker is all alone

Brent Nicastro

Show speaker chatting with audience

Brent Nicastro

Example A
Table straight across

Photographer was too far away

Example B
Table at an angle

UAW Solidarity

Catch crowd moving

Capture the excitement

Reader could feel threatened

Eye contact

Props help tell the story

ranting and shouting about how her rent is too high and her landlord is terrible. If the tenant's looking right at the camera, she'll be ranting at the reader. Instead of sympathizing with her, your reader will feel threatened and unjustly accused.

## Avoid "grip-&-grin" shots

If you keep taking the same tired shot, over and over again, of your leader presenting a check or plaque to someone as they shake hands, your group will start looking like a bunch of robots who spend all their time at ceremonies stiffly clasping hands. Instead, show the person holding up the check and looking excited. Or catch someone hanging the plaque on the wall, surrounded by merry well-wishers. Think up shots that dramatize how the money was raised, or why the check or plaque was awarded. Capture spontaneous good feelings, not frozen grins.

## Use symbols

Ask members to wear union or group T-shirts or buttons. (If they wear union caps, push the bills up so light hits their faces.) Show a person's job or family roles by including work tools, fellow workers, children or pets. When picturing a protest or picket line, ask people to hold original hand-made signs rather than pre-printed ones.

To get the right symbols, ask the person you're shooting for ideas.

## The right background

Shoot "on location" when possible, so the background tells part of the story. If people are protesting a dirty, polluting incinerator, look for a shot where you can see smokestacks spewing filth into the air behind them.

## Take lots of pictures

Experiment. Film is pretty cheap, even if prints aren't. Take dozens of pictures from every possible angle and camera setting. Even when you're new at the game, something's bound to come out right. P. 108 tells how to pick the shots you'll make prints of.

## Illustrate ideas that inspired the meeting

If you're upset about government priorities, show the governor in his limousine or plotting with business advisors. Next to the gov, print photos of people suffering from service cutbacks – waiting endlessly for the bus or trying to get health care. If the meeting is called to protest against lower electric rates for business, show downtown highrises all lit up at midnight.

# Dreaming up shots to illustrate an article

Suppose you live in a working-class community where a university just built a new campus, crowding the neighborhood and straining city services. Yet the community doesn't have access to libraries or the cultural advantages the university brings. What do you photograph to go with the story?

If you didn't think much about it, you'd just shoot the university buildings. But there's almost nothing duller than a building; you can do better.

## Picture something most people don't see

Although the neighborhood sees the outside of the buildings often enough, what about inside? As it turns out, local kids sneak inside out of curiosity; probably their parents would like a glimpse too. Shoot bustling offices and hallways, the theater, the library.

## Take pictures of people

Shoot teachers, students, administrators and opposition community leaders. Capture them involved in activities the article mentions, like teaching or protesting. (For a public place or non-profit paper, you usually don't need people's permission – p. 32.)

## Find symbolic shots

The article says the university causes overcrowding; so wait at the door for classes to change. As students swarm toward you, take a picture. Or find a nearby traffic jam at rush hour.

The article says neighbors won't have access to libraries and cultural events. Take a shot of the cop checking student IDs at the library; photograph students walking to the theater while neighborhood people walk in the opposite direction; or snap local kids ogling at the campus, in front of a STOP sign.

## Start a collection

Take advantage of other people's pictures by clipping photos from magazines and newspapers, and keep track of the issue and page (p. 32). P. 159 gives you ideas on how to use clippings.

## Special assignments

### Shooting a crowd

Once you've got the turnout you hoped for, how can you make it look special?

• **Get them moving.** Stand at the doorway when the crowd pours out of the room or catch demonstrators marching, before they stop to hear speeches.

• **Show the magnitude** of a huge crowd, even if most people are tiny specks. Take close-ups too, of different types of people.

The ideal photo looks slightly down from a knoll to catch some people close up while also revealing the hugeness of the crowd. Everyone's either moving toward you or looking your way.

### Staged photos

Make up illustrations for the camera to shoot. For example, when Barney O'Rourke retires, show what he'll do with his new freedom (example C).

*9to5 News'* big event one month was a fairly technical court case. No automatic picture ideas there. But the group worked hard to write an exciting headline for the story, starting with "Publishers Cited for Discrimination" and progressing to "9to5 Brings Publishers to Court."

Inspired by that vivid new headline, the group acted it out. 9to5 members borrowed toy handcuffs and a friend, went to the courthouse, had a few laughs, and got a great photo: example D. Such success comes when everyone – reporter, headline-writer and photographer – works together.

## Camera technique

### Is black-&-white best?

If you're not printing a full-color publication (p. 62), use black-and-white film. Although modern printers do a much better job with color photos than in the past, color photos can still look fuzzy or dark when printed in black-

Rick Reinhard

Show the services being cut back

Example C

Example D

Symbolic shot of plant closing

Get people into the photos

Industrias Thompson de M
SUBSIDIARIA DE
SWF Auto

Earl Dotter

Rick Reinhard

Vertical photo with close-up; looking up at subject, with background telling part of the story

Horizontal photo with no close-up

Background helps tell the story

Everything's in focus

Background has distracting details

You need a lens with a fast shutter to get action like this

This was a color photo

and-white. What's more, red comes out the same as black. So if the photo shows a dark face with redish highlights, that person could end up looking like "The Shadow," with no features.

Color film is tempting to use because you can get it developed within an hour almost everywhere. If you don't have your own darkroom it could take a long trip or a long time to get black-and-white shots printed. One solution is to use Ilford XPI black-and-white film. It's expensive, but can be processed at those quickie color labs.

Otherwise, the best black-and-white film for indoor/outdoor, daytime/nighttime shootings is Tri-X or T-Max 400. For color shots, try Kodak Gold ASA 400. In most cases, you won't need a flash.

## The camera

Many of today's automatic "point and shoot" cameras are idiot-proof (if you aim them the right way) and do a fine job. They automatically adjust the focus, lens opening and speed, and adapt to dim lighting with built-in flashes. If the camera has a *manual override*, you can fiddle around with all that whenever you don't feel like trusting the camera.

For the best success, invest in a name-brand 35 mm (millimeter) single-lens reflex camera. A good camera could cost you $200 to $300. Read the manual carefully, and keep it handy for reference. Then practice, practice, practice – shooting your family, pets and anything else in sight. Look into cheap adult education or camera-store photography courses to help you get started on the right track.

## The lens

Use a 50 mm *lens* for most shots, switching to a 24 or 35 mm *wide angle* lens to cover a big crowd or other broad shot. If you can't get close or don't want to make people nervous by shooting in their faces, use an 80 or 90 mm *telephoto* lens. With natural light, that'll focus sharply on the subject and soften the background. A *zoom* lens gives you all three lenses in one.

## The right lighting

When possible, shoot outside on a cloudy day or in a room with lots of natural light. When you're outside, gather people on the shady side of a building, so the light is even and won't get in their eyes. If people are in the sun, stand so the light comes at them from the side, just over your shoulder. Otherwise, the sun will make them squint, and will cast weird shadows on their faces.

Many cameras have built-in *light meters*. Otherwise, a hand-held one tells how to adjust the camera to the exact brightness of your subjects.

To take your light meter reading, aim the meter at the faces and look for a medium tone, more light than dark. If the people are too far away, use the zoom lens to get a reading. Or take it from your own hand, put in the same lighting as the subject's face(s).

If you're using an automatic camera, make sure the spot in the center of the viewfinder is smack in the middle of someone's face.

## The lens opening & shutter speed

The light meter tells how these should be set. Many cameras adjust both automatically, but give you the option to fiddle with them yourself if you want.

The *shutter speed* decides how long it takes the camera to freeze an image, while the *lens opening* opens enough to let in the right amount of light (*f-stop*). If you set either by hand, the other automatically adjusts.

For normal "still" shooting, keep the shutter speed at $\frac{1}{60}$ second. To capture a sports play or other action shot, set it to a faster speed.

If possible, buy a camera with a lens you can adjust down to f/2.8. A lens opening of f/5.6 or f/8 gives good overall detail. But if you choose *aperature priority* and set it as low as f/2, you can narrowly focus on one subject, blurring the background. Choose f/16, and distant objects become sharp and clear.

## The background

Watch out for distracting details. When possible, move people away from that pile of stacked-up chairs or boxes. Shoot from an angle that doesn't catch the junk, or keep it to the side so it can be *cropped* off (p. 160) later.

The ideal background is darker than the subject and has no details brighter than the main characters. If you're shooting black-and-white and there's a blue sky above, make it come out greyish instead of white by putting a yellow *filter* over your lens. Do *not* shoot a dark-skinned person in front of a white background – or you'll get a black shape where the face belongs.

To highlight a subject and blur a busy background, get as close as possible and try a lens opening between f/2 and f/5.6. Take several shots, each with a different lens setting.

### If you need more light

If the lighting is terrible, load up with 1000 ASA color film or T-Max 3200 (or 1600 ASA) black-and-white film – or use a *flash* or *strobe*.

A flash also helps you pick up the highlights in a dark face. But a flash or strobe that only points straight ahead can cast ugly shadows on people's faces. Ask people wearing glasses to turn their heads a little to the side so the flash won't reflect. In a meeting room, set a strobe manually. (With the automatic setting, the strobe hits the nearest thing, leaving the background dark.)

It's worth paying $75 to $85 extra for an adjustable flash you can point instead at a white ceiling. Pay another $100 for a *power pack*, and you can quickly shoot again and again, without waiting until the flash is ready.

### Keep the camera steady

Hold your breath a second or bend your knees while clicking the shutter. At shutter speeds of less than 1/60 second, rest the camera on a surface to keep it still. Never jab at the shutter, just calmly squeeze it.

### Put people at ease

Don't get so carried away with camera technique that you make people feel like guinea pigs, being tested with light meters and what-have-you. You'll get better results when people feel at ease

Flash was bounced off the ceiling

*Jackson Hill*

Focus is on background, front is blurred

*Russ Marshall*

Focus is on subject, background is blurred

*Rick Reinhard*

with you. If people look away and avoid the camera, explain who you are and why you're there.

### Get their names

Before you rush from the scene of the shot, take down the names of key people and make sure they're spelled right. Add a little note telling what photo(s) these people appeared in and who was where, so they can be identified later in a *caption* (p. 108).

You can get a good shot like this if people feel comfortable with you

*Earl Banks*

Watch out for reflections on glasses

Oh-oh! The eyes were closed

## When the photos are shot, what next?

### Develop the film

• The one-hour shops (which take color film and Ilford XPI) often make prints on the light side. If you ask, they'll darken them up. If the prints don't look right (and it's not because you sneezed as you pulled the shutter), most will develop them again for free.

• **Darkroom magic.** The quickest way to get high-quality photos is to find someone with a darkroom – or set up your own. Then you can fiddle with the

*contrast,* the range of white, greys and black, by using *filters* and special variable-contrast paper. To give so-so pictures a strong black-white contrast, develop them on #4 or #6 paper.

• If you're using black-and-white film and live near a decent-size city, you can probably find a professional lab to process film within about six hours. Kodak labs now handle black-and-white film. Or try a mail-order company listed in a photo magazine.

• If you've got color shots that must be printed black-and-white and you want top-notch quality, don't give color prints to the printer. Instead, take the negatives to a professional lab (or

Nice personal momento, but doesn't tell you about the conference

Jean-Claude LeJeune

This gives the right message

Photo is too dark & out of focus

your darkroom) and use Kodak Pana-lure paper to make black-and-white prints.

## See what you have

If possible, don't pay to get prints made of every shot, including that beauty of someone's bald spot. If you're using a full-service lab or darkroom, ask for a *contact sheet* (costing about $5 beyond the basic $5 charge for processing the film) of each roll. It'll show the whole roll in miniature, so you can pick which shots to make into prints. Use a magnifying glass to check the detail. Do key people have their eyes closed, or did someone move so the head is blurred?

• If you can't get contact prints from the local drug store and don't print your own, get the negatives developed before ordering prints. Hold a roll of film negatives in front of a light so the light bounces off the dull side of the negative, and the picture will look something like a print.

## Pick your favorites

• Choose photos that look exciting and do a good job of illustrating points the article makes. Sometimes a series of photos can tell a whole story on its own – with the help of a few captions.

• Look carefully at the faces. Are they grimacing or lost in darkness or brightness? If so, use another photo.

• Examine each shot for a full range of tones, from pure white all the way to pure black. If either the brightest white or the darkest black looks grey, the photo will be dull, and lose even more quality when printed.

• Check for crispness. If the original photo's out of focus and blurred, printing will make it worse.

• If a photo is the wrong shape for the page or is full of unneeded clutter or space, don't despair. You can trim the edges by *cropping* (p. 160) or make the background disappear (p. 160) during layout.

If you're using an offset printer (p. 60) or a copier that can reduce or enlarge photos, don't worry about getting prints the size they'll appear in the paper. Make them bigger, at least 5"x 7". P. 162 explains how to "size" photos to fit on the page.

• Choose more photos than you'll actually print. Pick ones that could be trimmed into a variety of shapes (tall or fat), so layout workers will have leeway in designing each page. Pick some with people looking to the left and some with people looking to the right or straight at the camera.

## For mimeod & copier-printed papers

Choose photos that're very simple, with sharp blacks and whites defining key figures, not much grey, and no clutter in the background. If your copier has a "photo" adjustment or your stencil-cutter (for mimeo) makes halftones, better yet. That can make simple photos look great. P. 161 gives more tips.

## Write a caption

The caption (or *cutline*) should be short and *add* to what the photo says (telling who's who, for example), not repeat it. Most readers aren't sight-impaired, so let the photo tell as much of the story as possible. If you bunch several photos on the same page, try writing one caption for them all (example F on p. 143). If the article explains the photos, you may not need a caption at all.

Jean-Claude LeJeune

Needs cropping

Cropped photo

Contact sheet

# 13. Writing for the people

Start writing only after you've thought through what you want to say.

You can't say everything in one article, and every issue has as many different slants as there are people thinking about it. The key is to find an angle you can get excited about. Once a topic interests you, you can make it sound interesting to someone else.

If nothing appeals to you about the topic, talk to people, find out more. If you've still got nothing, maybe the article isn't worth doing.

Either on paper or in your mind, *outline* between two and six main points you'll concentrate on. A typical article might be organized like example A.

## Are you ready?

In looking over your outline, you may realize you don't have the facts or quotes to make the main points hit home. Do more digging before you begin writing. Chapters 10 and 11 will help.

How can pictures help get your main points across? After all, let's face it: People are more attracted to pictures than a page full of words. Today's TV viewers are not only used to getting information from pictures; they *expect* pictures to help explain what's going on. The better each picture works, the fewer words need be said.

What facts can be told through charts and graphs? How about taking photos of a key event? Do you have pictures lying around that could hit the spot if you added the right caption? How about a clever cartoon? Chapters 12 and 18 show how to turn such ideas into reality.

## Begin to write

When you know what must be said in words, then write. Take one point at a time and prove it before you move on to the next. Be yourself. Let the words flow, and make your feelings and ideas as vivid as possible.

This first draft will never be perfect. You'll use it as a launching pad for several rewrites, and no one will ever see it. Right now the key is not to freeze as soon as you touch a keyboard or a pen's in your hand. And don't worry if the beginning sounds awkward. Most people start slowly and then rework the beginning later, when the article's done.

### Prove your points

Don't expect people to believe you just because you're sincere; people with a lot more influence might be saying something quite different. Prove each idea with facts, your own experience, and interviews. Think about your audience (Chapter 1) and whether you challenge deep-seated beliefs; tread very carefully when you attack those.

So you can concentrate on your main points, avoid getting into related problems and tidbits of knowledge. When you're in the thick of things, everything may seem crucial, and limiting yourself to a few points isn't easy. Just keep in mind that your audience isn't nearly as interested in the subject as you are.

### Rewrite everything

Brilliant writing doesn't spin miraculously out of anyone's head. Example B shows how slowly and painfully a paragraph from p. 91 of this book evolved.

• **Put a little distance between yourself and the article.** If the moments and hours agonizing over this word or that point are still fresh in your mind, you won't want to change a thing. And chances are, changes are necessary.

So when it's all said and done, put the

Example A

1. What the biggest problem is.
2. Where the problem came from and why.
3. What's being done about it.
4. What should be done about it.

## First draft

If there's any way to check your statistics and interpretations, do so. And don't forget where your source is coming from. If, for example, a newspaper that's usually very docile towards its advertisers carries an exposé of business and political wrongdoings, it's probably so true and blatant that they can't ignore it, even though it runs against the paper's general policy. In this case, I'd believe the paper. When they print stories that make the business scene look pretty rosy, you have every right to be suspicious. This is what they want to believe.

Example C

Mankind
Girls (for grown-ups)
Workmen's compensation
Bring the wife and family!
Chairman

## First draft

(And find another source) confirm controversial (or to explain
~~If there's any way~~ to ~~check~~ your statistics and ~~interpre-~~
what they mean. You can trust a for some facts more than for
~~tations, do so.~~ And don't forget where your source ~~is coming~~ others.
Do the facts jibe with its normal bias? cap commercial must cater
~~from. If, for example,~~ a ~~newspaper~~ that's ~~usually very docile~~
(and accept "business as usual.") But when that same paper
~~towards its~~ advertisers carries an exposé ~~of~~ business ~~and~~
or failure that more credible
~~political~~ wrongdoings, it's probably so true and blatant that
because contradicts
they can't ignore it, even though it runs against the paper's
normal bias.
~~general policy. In this case, I'd believe the paper.~~ When
it gives a
~~they~~ print stories that make the business scene ~~look~~ pretty
glow (Examine the facts and look for other opinions.)
rosy, you have every right to be suspicious. This is what
After all, they're printing what
they want to believe.

(move up)

Example D

*Instead of this:*

The situation of inflation in the basic necessities, including food costs, health care, energy and housing, is a primary problem area for most Americans, leading to a sense of powerlessness, and causing daily decision-making, and even subsistence, to be both difficult and anxiety producing.

*Try something like this:*

Does the clicking and beeping of the supermarket cash register leave you penniless? Does the price on the gas pump spin around at breakneck speed every time you fill up? Are you afraid to open the bills in your mailbox? With today's inflation, it's hard just to survive.

Example E

## Overworked? Underpaid?
## Or just a little irritated?

Are you tired of being your boss's "girl"? Have you fetched so much coffee that you feel like a personal maid? Are you doing more work than any man in your office but getting paid less? Were you just passed over for another deserved promotion? Stop screaming at the Ladies' Room walls, because help is on the way.

---

article aside. Play with your kids, watch TV, or spend a whole day thinking about something else. When you come back fresh to the article, pretend you're a typical reader seeing it for the first time.

• **The first person to edit your article is yours truly.** Use your outline as a checklist to make sure the main points come across clearly and convincingly. If you wrote passionately about a point that isn't in the outline, either change the outline, drop the point, or make it into another article. If you repeated things, misspelled words or gushed a bit, don't panic. The secret to good writing is to keep plugging, rewriting partly by trial and error and partly by learning the nuts and bolts in this book.

If parts of the article are in the the wrong order, cut them out and tape them where they belong.

• **Then turn your story over to someone else.** Show it to your editor or a friend who knows your readers. And whatever you do, *don't* be afraid of criticism. It can only strengthen your writing. Chapter 14 gives editing guidelines.

Before you hand over your article to be edited, make sure you've kept a copy for yourself. That's your only insurance against someone losing the whole thing – or butchering the original by over-editing.

### Everyone needs editing

Two heads are better than one. You can reread what you wrote 'til the cows come home and never realize that someone else could miss the point entirely, or find a different meaning for a word you thought was crystal-clear (p. 118). Better to be misunderstood now, when no harm's done and you can change it, than when it's printed and too late.

---

# Nuts & bolts of writing

## Tell it like it is

Most of us learned to write in school, where we tried to impress someone – the teacher – not communicate directly with our neighbors or fellow students. The more complicated the language we could muster, the better the grade we'd get. We'd learn to discuss other people's ideas, but rarely to enjoy and express our own ideas and experiences.

To communicate with a real audience about what's important to you takes a different kind of writing. Who cares if you impress your reader? If readers get bowled over by how brilliant you are, it just may make them feel dumb; they haven't learned anything useful and certainly didn't enjoy the experience.

Luckily you don't have to look far to find a better way. When you have a conversation with someone, you speak directly and with enthusiasm. That's the tone your writing needs. Writing may be harder, because you have to be careful about your facts and don't know who you're talking to. Readers can't ask questions, and you can't watch their faces. The better you picture your audience, though, the closer you'll get.

## Remember who you're writing for

Start writing the way you'd discuss the subject with a typical person in your audience. If you're having trouble, find someone to talk over your ideas with, and talk until you've gotten them translated into your own words. A good writer begins with what people care about and slowly moves them toward what the writer wants to say.

Imagine that the reader is looking over your shoulder. When the reader would interrupt with: "But so-and-so says the opposite," or "Why did you say that?" or even "Who cares?" answer the reader's concerns, point by point.

Don't assume people understand your organization, or even that they're sympathetic. It's not always easy to face the fact that what people *should* know or feel isn't always what they *do* know or feel.

Build on what you personally have in common with your readership, but recognize where you're different.

Use Chapter 1 as a checklist to make sure you include everyone. Do you use words that make some readers feel left in the cold? The words in example C suggest that women don't exist – even though women outnumber men these days. Can you find a substitute? Then check example F.

## Paint word-pictures

• To keep readers interested, give them images – familiar things they can imagine seeing, hearing, feeling, smelling or touching as they read along. That'll make your information hit home. Example D shows how to transform a boring description into one that strikes a responsive chord.

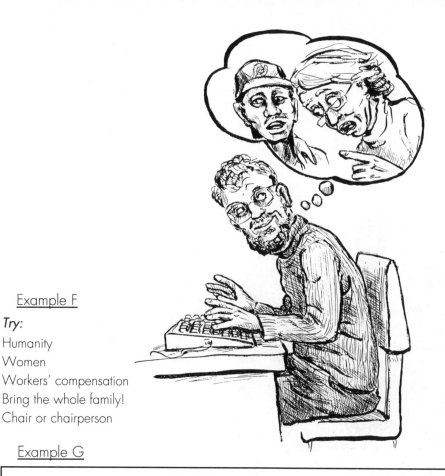

Example F

*Try:*

Humanity

Women

Workers' compensation

Bring the whole family!

Chair or chairperson

Example G

### The Emergency Call

It's past midnight. You've put in a long day at Chevrolet but now it's time to head home.

You know the traffic will be jammed on Norfolk as hundreds of other second-shifters go their separate ways. So you stop for one beer across the street. When you leave, traffic is relatively light and the lot is nearly empty.

After the usual drive home you enter the house quietly, because the wife and kids are usually asleep at this hour. Not tonight!

The kids are sitting in the kitchen and your wife is at the table, tear-swollen eyes glaring at you. For what? You ask, "What's wrong, what's everybody doing up?" Your only answer is icy stares.

After what seems like hours the story finally unravels. The hot water tank drain started to leak badly at 6 o'clock that evening. Your wife phoned the plant 15 minutes later when the leak got worse and she didn't know what else to do. She had called you at work once before, but that was almost 14 years ago. She wouldn't call unless it was an emergency.

It was an emergency now. The leak became a torrent as the drain faucet broke open further. The floor drain couldn't keep up with the flowing pipe; so water began to form a pool around the drain area.

The children became afraid as the pool got larger and larger. Mom reassured them Dad would be right home, because the person she talked to at the plant said they would contact Dad's foreman and get him home right away.

At 8 o'clock the water level had risen higher and the kids' bare feet splashed as they scurried around trying to get everything off the basement floor. They hardly noticed the tiny splashes from the tears that rolled down Mom's cheeks and mixed with the water, rising ever higher.

At 9:30 p.m., over three hours since the harried wife telephoned an emergency call to her husband, he still wasn't here.

Frantic, she appealed to helpful neighbors, embarrassed that her husband hadn't yet arrived.

Why wasn't he here? The message was passed on to the member's foreman. But the foreman "forgot" to tell the man he had an emergency call. It slipped his mind. Unbelievable, truly unbelievable that something so important about a man's wife, children and home should be so easily forgotten.

The present procedure for notifying an employee about an emergency call stinks. It cries for improvement and must be changed. This family's agony must not be repeated.

The strikers returned to their jobs with a lot of apprehension about the kinds of relationships that would develop between the formerly antagonistic groups.

Example I

UPI

Example J

*Can you find a substitute for these big words?*

| | |
|---|---|
| assistance | revenue |
| initiate | provide |
| anticipate | utilize |
| equitable | receive |
| request, inquire | beneficial |
| designate | compensation |
| purchase | implementation |
| annual expenditure | prior to |

Example K

*The government's version:*

Welfare recipients are entitled to a fair hearing if the recipient disagrees with any decision, action or inaction of the Department of Public Welfare. Notification in writing in advance of any action to reduce or withhold the recipient's check is required. If the recipient disagrees with the action but does not file an appeal before the effective date of the action, the change will be made. The welfare recipient has 30 days from the date of the notice to request a fair hearing but the welfare office must be contacted to request a fair hearing.

*The newsletter version:*

## Welfare: you can complain

When you're on welfare you have the right to protest whatever the Welfare Department does, or neglects to do, and to get a hearing.

If it plans to stop or cut your check, the Welfare Department has to notify you ahead of time. You have 30 days from the date on the notice to ask for a fair hearing. If you don't say anything before the 30 days are up, you lose your right to complain. And if you don't complain before the change is supposed to happen, that change goes through.

Example L

## Why do people emigrate from Latin America?

The March wind blows harshly up the treacherous Mona Passage toward Puerto Rico. Ten men and women huddle against the gunwales of their small inboard.

Isabela's teeth chatter. She has never been to sea before; her 22 years have passed in a tiny village near the giant sugar plantation owned by Gulf & Western.

Antonio, his back to the engine housing, is lonely and worried. The opportunity to leave his native Dominican Republic came quickly; he could not arrange to bring his family with him. He shakes his head thinking of the hard times they will suffer in the next few months. But the stories he has heard of life in North America – the luxuries that people take for granted, the wages that immigrant workers can send home – lighten his despair.

Antonio does not know yet that his American Dream is a dream. He has not felt the exhausting drudge-work, the rock-bottom wages and high prices, the job insecurity and constant fear of deportation which illegal immigrants face in the United States.

His eyes are on the choppy sea to his left. The wind is high. But it is at his back; it is pushing him toward United States soil.

Example E appeals to the common experiences of a particular audience.

• **Try seducing your audience** with a new experience, as examples G and L do. With example L, the reader goes on the ride, feels the gunwales, hears the wind and chattering teeth, sees the choppy sea, and shares the dreams.

• **Substitute things you can see** or feel for abstract ideas. A person "hits the ceiling" or her "blood boils" when she's mad. A "fly-by-night" company isn't legitimate, and a "debt ceiling" describes debt limits.

Instead of, "The Boston real estate market is based on speculation," try: "Big Boston landlords trade property back and forth as if people's homes were a pack of baseball cards."

But be consistent; don't double-expose your pictures. You can't put that "can of worms on a back burner" unless you're ready for a terrific stench.

## Little words are better

Never fear big long words.
Big long words mean little things.
All big things have little names,
Such as life and death, peace and war
Or dawn, day, night, hope, love, home.
Learn to use little words in a big way.
It is hard to do;
But they say what you mean.
When you don't know what you mean,
Use big words –
That often fools little people.

Example J shows words to watch out for. Try to translate these fancy words into simpler ones. Then look at example T on p. 115 to see how you did.

Big, vague words can be downright misleading. In example M, the writer used "security" to mean job security, keeping people from being laid off. But how do you know "security" doesn't mean "safety"? The word has both meanings. You could think the whole hubbub is about safety, and understand nothing.

## Avoid cover-ups

Cautious bureaucrats and managers often use big, vague words because they're insecure and want to sound more important than you and me; or they don't have all the information and are covering up; or maybe they don't want *you* to have all the information, couching it in vagueness so no one will bother them.

Don't imitate them. Vague bureaucratic language always comes from trying to humble a reader rather than communicate directly.

The Pentagon, for example, concocts vague words to make war an abstract "science." During the Vietnam War, Colonel David Opfer complained to reporters, "You always write it's bombing, bombing, bombing. It's not bombing. It's air support."

"We never say assassination," Watergate burglar and ex-CIA agent Bernard Barker told a CBS special. "We say 'termination by prejudice.'" Spying is "intelligence gathering."

And what does it really mean when the police "subdue a Pennsylvania picket?" That was the caption on the photo in example I.

When you turn to the government for information, you might get something written by one of those nervous bureaucrats. Look for cover-up phrases and instead of repeating them, find out what's really happening. Do your readers a favor, and edit out the gobbletygook, as example K does.

You might be guilty of your own cover-ups too. If you're upset or uncertain about your topic, you could sidestep it, as example H does.

Now what does "a lot of apprehension about the kinds of relationships that would develop between the formerly antagonistic groups" mean? It means "afraid there would be fights."

If you fear that people won't take you seriously, you can fall into the same trap, puffing up your words to sound official. Example M suffers from that problem. Remember: if readers get useful information and ideas from your paper, they'll respect your contribution. So relax. Show you aren't afraid of your audience by being straight with them.

## Use active sentences

Most fuzzy writing uses passive sentences instead of active ones. A *passive sentence* removes the actor from the action. "Somebody did this or that" is an *active sentence*. "This happened," "That was done," "There was this," and "That was done by somebody" are all passive structures that make an action vague and dull.

People often use passive sentences to sound more "objective" and official. It doesn't work; the article usually sounds pompous, and as exciting as stale toast. Try your hand at twisting the passive sentences in example P on p. 115 into

example P on p. 115

Example M

In the past several months there has been a considerable amount of discussion on all levels about the many problems that exist in the assembly division which have a great impact on the security of our union members.

Example N

### Cover-up wording

| The official language | The translation |
|---|---|
| "Data presently collected by the government is not sufficiently specific or timely to allow meaningful interpretation of price changes and profit margins throughout the system." <br> – U.S. House Agriculture Subcommittee | "We don't know if price hikes are caused by higher profits." |
| An "energetic disassembly" <br> "rapid oxidation" <br> – Three Mile Island officials describing the 1980 nuclear plant accident | an explosion <br> a fire |
| "I was provided with additional input that was radically different from the truth." <br> –Lt. Col. Ollie North testifying on Iran-Contra Scandal | "We lied." |
| "Involuntary conversion of a 727." <br> – American Airlines annual report <br> "Controlled flight into terrain." <br> –National Transportation Safety Board | plane crash <br><br> plane crash |
| "enhance the efficiency of operations;" <br> "eliminate the redundancies in the human resources area;" <br> "negative employee retention." | corporate terms for firing workers |
| "A pre-dawn vertical insertion." <br> – U.S. State Department | 1983 U.S. invasion of Grenada |
| "Major malfunction." <br> –NASA control center narrator | 1986 Challenger space shuttle crash |
| "Vertical pressure applicators." <br> – U.S. Pentagon supply order | screwdrivers |
| "A final balancing change order resulting from monetary adjustments in bid items as provided for in the Contract Documents under the sections dealing with 'measurement and payment' requires a simple majority vote by the Board if the contract amount is not being exceeded or if such adjustments are made pursuant to the supplemental work allowance item of the Contract Documents." <br> – Santa Clara County Transportation Agency memo | "The board is being asked to agree to the amount of work done on a project and the appropriate payment." <br> – Scotty Bruce, deputy director of the transportation agency |

active ones. In one example you must add people to make the sentence active; in others, making the sentence active makes it shorter. In all cases, the active sentence says more. Example R gives answers.

## Don't browbeat people

Don't hit people over the head with conclusions. Begin with what interests

### Editing clues

*These phrases contain extra padding. If you find them in your articles, be merciless.*

| Instead of this: | Replace with this: |
| --- | --- |
| They noticed *the fact that* she went. | They noticed that she went. |
| *The truth is that* she wasn't warned. | She wasn't warned. |
| That *caused a lot of* disappointment. | People were disappointed. |
| They discussed *the situation of* poverty. | They talked about poverty. |
| *This means that* elections will be held. | |
| *In any case,* elections will be held. | Elections will be held |
| *It is expected that* elections will be held. | |
| We *sent a* protest *to the effect that* it wasn't fair. | We protested that it wasn't fair. |
| He went *in order* to investigate. | He went to investigate. |
| *There was* alarm about this. | We were alarmed. |
| I'd like to *try to* go. | I'd like to go. |
| It's *very* unusual; | |
| It's *pretty* unusual; It's *a little* unusual | It's unusual. |
| It's *kind of* unusual; It's *really* unusual. | |
| *Make plans* for the march | Plan the march |
| A *more appropriate* response | A better answer |
| She *is saying that* he was fired. | She says he was fired. |
| *On a regular basis* | Regularly |
| *In a careless way* | Carelessly |
| *You should* file a grievance when... | File a grievance when... |
| They are | They're |
| You have | You've |
| Did not | Didn't |
| to know *about* the situation | to know the situation |
| to set *up* policy | to set policy |
| An *unexpected* surprise | A surprise |
| The *basic* fundamentals | The basics |
| I'm *presently* too busy | I'm too busy |
| The hiring *procedure* | Hiring |
| Remarks *of a hostile nature* | Hostile remarks |
| Some *of your* problems | Some problems |
| Questions *in regard* to the party | Questions about the party |
| Questions *concerning* the party | |
| *In the event that* she goes | If she goes |
| People *who are* unemployed | Unemployed people |
| Facts *that are* important | Important facts |
| The movie *which* I like best | The movie I liked best |
| Activities *of this sort* | Such activities; These activities |
| *It's a* machine *that* makes | The machine makes |

*them*, and then give readers the evidence to believe as you do; by the time you get to the punch line, they'll feel like it's their own idea.

Likewise, don't use the words, "obviously, clearly, surely" and "of course." If something's clear, you don't have to say it's clear. When you use those words you're trying to railroad people, to force them to believe something by implying, "Look, this is obvious, and if you don't see it, you must be dumb."

## Avoid technical words

Every professional and skilled worker uses words that have precise meanings in the trade, but lose all sense when they meet the public. Professionals get so used to talking shop that even when they try to speak clearly, they throw in terms we can't follow. Although we could all benefit from their knowledge, we shouldn't need to learn a whole new language.

• **Activist lingo.** The hardest in-group language to catch are the words you, as an activist, use every day. Do you talk about "Paragraph 76," "Title 10," "OSHA" or the "FCC," without explaining what they are? What's normal language for activists could sound like Greek to the reader.

• **Don't get overwhelmed by information** from lawyers and other specialists. You may not dare to change what a lawyer or doctor says for fear you'll get it wrong, even though you don't understand a word of it. But if anyone's going to learn from your paper, you have to. Otherwise you'll end up with a monstrosity like example Q.

• **Don't let such experts write articles** – unless the whole audience is fellow professionals or skilled workers in the same field. Instead, *interview* them, asking them to explain until you understand them. Then write an article in words the audience can relate to. Show the expert your article to make sure the translation is accurate.

• **Always think twice about using a technical word.** People may think they understand it without knowing the real meaning. Instead, substitute the definition for the word. Rather than "many mechanics are under-employed," say "many mechanics have to settle for part-time, low-paid or unskilled work."

If you think the word's important enough for people to learn, then define it, as example S does. But don't overdo the use of unfamiliar words, or you'll seem to be writing in a foreign language.

## Keep paragraphs short

You may have learned in school that each paragraph should contain a complete idea. But short paragraphs are easier to read. And if your paper has narrow columns, a long paragraph runs halfway down the page and looks really impossible.

End paragraphs every three to five sentences, at a good place to pause. When you finish writing, go back and break apart any long paragraphs that slipped through.

## Avoid run-on sentences

After you've finished writing the story, read it over to see if you find long, complicated sentences which you could rewrite into two or three simpler sentences that would be less confusing and easier to read and give readers a good chance to catch their breath between ideas, rather than stringing them on so that if the readers lose the train of thought they have to read the whole sentence over again. Gasp.

"Take two" of that run-on sentence would be: After you've finished writing the story, read it over. If you find long, complicated sentences, rewrite them into two or three simpler sentences that'll be easier to read. It'll avoid confusion and give readers a chance to catch their breath between ideas. When you string readers on, they have to read the whole sentence over again if they lose the train of thought.

Don't make every sentence the exact same length and structure, however. A little sentence variety makes reading less monotonous. A good technique is to occasionally underline a point with a tiny, blunt sentence. That's style.

## Don't repeat words

Reading the same word over and over gets boring. When you're done writing, go back and see how many words you've used more than three times, maybe circling them in pencil. Try to change some without hurting the meaning, especially if the same word appears twice in a sentence.

## Don't put yourself down

An article written by you is your opinion, so you don't have to keep reminding people with phrases like, "I think, I believe, in my opinion, it seems to me, as I see it, our organization feels

that . . ." These phrases water down an idea and make you sound uncertain. If the idea doesn't stand by itself with the evidence you show, drop it; don't fudge.

Don't start with phrases like: "My report for this month is about . . ." or "In this column I'd like to explain . . ." You're just talking to yourself. Cut the chatter and get to the nitty-gritty.

## Take out the fat

Listening is easier than reading. When you talk with people, they enjoy watching your face and following your laughs, frowns and gestures, even if you're longwinded. But no one looks forward to reading a long, overweight article.

When you finish writing, look for every word, sentence, phrase or idea that isn't necessary, and cross it out. And don't repeat yourself. If you're tempted to repeat an important idea so

*Cutting an article to the right length*

### Example P

*a.* A committee has been elected by the workers.
*b.* The meeting was arranged to see what could be done about teenage crime.
*c.* He was released from the hospital on Feb. 10.
*d.* There has been a meeting arranged which will be attended by Save Our Water leaders and city officials.

### Example Q

*What the lawyer says:*
With respect to the processing, disposition and/or settlement of any grievance initiated under the Grievance Procedure Section of this Agreement, and with respect to any court action claiming or alleging a violation of this Agreement or any local or other agreement amendatory or supplemental hereto, the Union shall be the sole and exclusive representative of the employee or employees covered by this agreement.

*The newsletter translation:*
The Union is your bargaining and grievance representative in all areas covered by the contract.

### Example R

*a.* The workers elected a committee.
*b.* Parents arranged a meeting to see what they could do about teenage crime.
*c.* The hospital released him on Feb. 10, or: He got out of the hospital on Feb. 10.
*d.* The Save Our Water group arranged a meeting with city officials.

### Example S

The Citizens' Action Program is asking for a "lifeline" electricity rate; by "lifeline" they mean a special low rate for the basic electricity everyone needs.

### Example T

| The big words: | Use this instead: |
| --- | --- |
| assistance | help |
| initiate | start |
| anticipate | expect |
| equitable | fair, just |
| request, inquire | ask |
| designate | choose |
| purchase | buy |
| annual | yearly |
| expenditure | spending, cost |
| revenue | money |
| provide | give |
| utilize | use |
| receive | get |
| beneficial | helpful, good |
| compensation | pay |
| implementation | action |
| prior to | before |

it won't get lost, you've probably smothered it under too much junk. Instead of repeating, throw out the garbage.

As you get used to writing, you'll know your bad habits and will find the overweight areas easier. A slim article not only saves the reader's time – it also leaves you room for pictures and looks easier to approach.

If you trim the article in example U to less than half its length, you'll catch the most common fillers. Example O on p. 114 gives clues on what to look for. Example V shows one way to cut it.

After you've written your first draft, skim example O on p. 114. If you find similar words in your draft, be brutal.

## What if the article's still too long?

No article should run more than two pages long or gobble up room needed for pictures. (P. 85 tells how to plan article lengths.) But suppose you spent hours editing every word or idea that wasn't needed, and can't cut more without amputating the heart of the article?

Break it into pieces. If you're saying we need a law to grant new parents time off the job, for example, take the facts on how other countries have such laws, and make that into one article. The story of how June Cleaver lost her job when her two sons were born could be the second article. A third article will explain your group's lobbying efforts and the law you want passed.

Print these as a series, either in one paper or over several issues.

## Write the first paragraph last

The first paragraph should grab readers and arouse their interest in the whole story. It's called a *lead* (pronounced *leed*).

Don't clog up your lead with the dates and names of everything and everyone. That's a real turn-off. Instead, put yourself in the shoes of people in your audience and ask yourself, "So what? Why should anyone care about this article?" A good lead makes the story seem exciting.

You probably won't write a good lead on the first try. Don't worry about it when you start writing. Often the story isn't firm enough in your mind yet.

When the article's done, look it over for a startling fact or quote, like example W. Or start with a familiar experience the reader can share, like ex-

### Example U
*Edit this article to half its length without losing the meaning:*

You may have noticed the fact that applying for unemployment compensation payments can become a long and pretty tedious process. In order to make things a little easier for yourself, be sure not to forget to bring along all the necessary information when you make your very first visit to the Division of Employment Security. In connection with this, you should try to obtain a notice of separation before you leave from work on the last day. This kind of notice will allow you to obtain your initial compensation a lot faster. If you are someone who was dismissed or had some kind of difficulty with your employer, it is important that you maintain as many records of an official nature and correspondence in writing as you possibly can; this is because your eligiblity itself may have to be verified.

### Example V
## How to apply for unemployment

Signing up for unemployment pay can take time and energy. To make it easier, bring the facts and papers you'll need when you first visit the unemployment office. For instance, you'll speed up your first check if you get a separation notice before you leave work. If you were fired or had trouble with your boss, keep official records and memos so you can prove you're eligible.

### Example W

"I guess we're supposed to lay down and die." In a note to Senator Smile, Ms. Lillian Balmer of Louisville, Ky. told the tragic story of the acute, unmet medical needs of citizens all over the nation.

### Example X

"Everything causes cancer." "You can't fight it, so you might as well relax and enjoy life." How many times have you heard comments like that?

### Example Y

If you've driven down Soldier's Field Road recently, you probably saw an around-the-clock picket line in front of WBZ studios. You've been witnessing a local dispute of national importance.

### Example Z
## The wrong questions

Congress is well into an election-year effort to "reform" the food stamp program. Unfortunately, they've so far proven only that if members of Congress ask the wrong questions, they'll come up with the wrong answers.

amples X and Y. Some leads ask a question. Others compare a new fact with something people already know. Some leads introduce a theme, like the "wrong question" idea in example Z. That theme continues to organize the writer's ideas throughout the article.

In example B, you'll get a snappy lead if you just cross out the first sentence. Your motor's just warming up when you starting writing, and often the first sentence or two can be scratched out later.

Example A, however, is duller than a doornail. The writer forgot the "so what" question and tried to bunch all the facts into the first sentence.

## End with a bang

Don't let your article dwindle off at the end. Leave people with a new idea, possible solutions, where to go from here, who to get in touch with, or a good quote. Summarize your main points at the end *only* if the article's highly technical or you can do it with a quick quote.

For more help with writing, look at *The Elements of Style* by William Strunk, Jr., and E. B. White.

# Try a new approach

Variety is the spice of newsletters and papers. Instead of just listing the important events coming up next month, arrange them into an attractive calendar. Example C shows an article written in diary form. Chapter 12 shows how to make others into a photo essay.

Ridicule absurd policies with a poem (example D) or cartoon strip (p. 158). Or dream up a funny fantasy.

Make a series of facts look lively by introducing each with a *bullet* (a big dot, like on p. 90). Or make instructions look easy to follow by dividing them into separate steps, like on the box on p. 118.

Present facts as charts, or questions and answers. Help readers learn useful terms, your group's history, or legal rights by making them into a game – a quiz, or a word search puzzle.

Make up a recipe for success, or print the letter you'd like to send to the boss or phone company. Or start an advice column, whether it's real or a spoof. Print a questionnaire for readers to fill out and send in.

Get ideas across through riddles and jokes. List your group's New Year's

Example A

On October 14, Katie Elsila, a Boston City Hospital employee and a member of City Women for Action, spoke before the President's Commission for Women. The Commission held hearings in Boston at the New England Life Hall on issues that are of special concern to women, such as economic justice, crime and violence, consumer problems, child care, and child abuse.

Example B

At Boston City Hospital, employees have expressed growing concern about security. During the month of August, two nurses were robbed on the way to their cars, and one of these women was raped.

Example C

## "Next window, please"

Dear diary,

*2/6/91, 8:45 p.m.:* After $40 worth of food shopping, my arms wrapped around my grocery bag, I was pushed aside by a tall stranger.

After he quickly disappeared into the crowd, I discovered $50 worth of food stamps had been stolen. What am I going to say to my wife?

Well, dear diary, I explained the whole story to my family. My wife (dear woman) asked me to notify the Welfare Department for help.

*2/7/91, 12:45 p.m.:* Dear diary, I gathered my cards and I.D. together and called the Welfare Department on Hancock St. and explained the terrible situation.

"C'mon down," the familiar voice said, "and I'll try to get some help for you."

*1 p.m.:* Arrived at the welfare office, filled out a report and was told I could not get any kind of aid unless I reported to local police.

*1:45 p.m.:* After jogging up Dorchester Ave. to police station in 18-degree wea-

ther, I filed a report. I quickly jogged back to Hancock St. with the police report.

*2:10 p.m.:* Dear diary, I finally made it to Welfare Dept. "Ah, they'll help me now," I thought. I wasn't asking for money, just one week's supplement in food.

*2:20 p.m.:* I saw the same person and he said, "fine." He picked up the phone and asked me to wait in the lobby.

I was pretty well exhausted and I guess he must've seen me panting and sweating.

*2:30 p.m.:* The man came out of his office, called me in. Said he had a hard time reaching the Salvation Army. "Wow," I said to myself, "got to take a street car to South End. Can't jog that far – I'm a sick man."

*2:40 p.m.:* Dear diary, get this! After the guy got through talking with Salvation Army person on the phone, he tells me that I must produce all past paid bills to Salvation Army for them to give me any assistance.

"Well," I said, "ask Salvation Army if they will feed four members in my family so's I can accumulate some past bills?"

*6:00 p.m.:* Dear diary, this evening I will find a way to feed my family – somehow!

Example D

## I'm a machine

I think a green button I'll wear on my nose
Push it and away to work 0000-00-00 goes.
Yes, I feel like a machine on the shop floor.
They want me to leave my mind out the door.
I wish they could work on this line one day,

They'd know then they owe us more than just pay.
After all, we workers helped put them up there,
Can't they at least look down and care?
Sometimes I feel like yelling, "But look, I'm me!"
If they look a machine is all they can see!

Finding time to write

Resolutions, write a Valentine to your favorite hero, or make a "Wanted" poster about your group's next target.

# Write an exciting headline

People glance at the headlines to see what the paper's about. If headlines or pictures don't grab them, many will turn away, without reading another word.

Coming up with good, simple headlines is one of your biggest challenges. Don't just top each article with a label. Take the time to write headlines that lure people into eagerly reading one article after another.

## The creative process

Don't get your heart set on a particular headline right away. Let your imagination go, writing down all the possibilities you can think of, even if many turn out awful. Then pick the best, and see if you can improve them further; or combine the best of two so-so headlines to get one great headline.

### Example E

Tests show Somerville kids' lead poisoning

### Example F

Are you a victim of sex and wage discrimination?

### Example G

1. Rent control at City Council

2. City Council could bring disaster!

3. City Council could bring disaster to tenants!

4. City Council attacks rent control

5. Can rent control be saved?

### Example H

6. Can we save rent control?

7. Can you afford rent de-control?

8. Can you afford huge rent hikes?

## What makes a good headline?

**1.** It tells what the article's about. Being clever is nice, but not as important.

**2.** Don't try to cram everything the article covers into the headline or it'll be so vague it's boring. Instead, pick a highlight from the article that's sure to attract attention, and focus on that.

**3.** Trim it down to three to eight words long; if you need to add more, put the overflow into a smaller *subhead* (p. 74).

**4.** Make it active, not passive. Tell what's *happening*, not just what *is*. Instead of "Recycling plan," say something like: "Earthfirst wins recycling plan" or "City must recycle waste." Use the *present tense* ("wins" instead of "won") even when it's a done deal.

**5.** Stick to short, simple words. Use abbreviations only if everyone knows what they mean. Choose specific words that hit home over vague ones.

**6.** Avoid using words that have double meanings, unless both meanings apply. Scrutinize every word carefully, to make sure it couldn't be taken to mean something else.

Example E topped an article about kids poisoned by lead-based paint in older homes. But since the word "lead" has another meaning (sounding like *leed*), the reader might think kids are going around poisoning everyone. Example F could also be misunderstood.

**7.** Set headlines in big, bold type, so they jump out at readers (p. 142).

**8.** After the headline's written, cut out every unnecessary word.

**9.** Pinpoint what's interesting to readers. If the article answers an important question, why not make the question into a headline?

Suppose you need to mobilize tenants after your city council threatened to kill rent control. Start by writing several headlines, like those in example G. Look them over one by one.

Headline 1 is short, but not exciting.

It's so vague it doesn't suggest what happened or its urgency. Headline 2 gives the flavor of the news. It contains an active verb (p. 113), so it sounds more exciting. But it gives you no idea what the meeting was about. Headline

3 says more, but it's too long. How about headline 4? That's short, active and informative. It's fine, but you can do even better.

Put yourself in the reader's place. Why would anyone read an article about rent control? What questions are on people's minds? Headline 5 raises one they might be thinking about.

The next three headlines (example H) grew out of trying to improve headline 5. Headline 6 makes the question more personal. Headline 7 appeals directly to the reader's stake in keeping rent control. And headline 8 says it better, like regular speech.

# Looking at examples

## What about example I?

When you finish reading article I about the police-community meeting, don't you wonder if anything actually happened? Most of the article could have been written beforehand.

Who spoke up? What did people say? What are the "increasing problems"? Why did the meeting leave the writer with frustration? Why did it leave the writer with hopes? If you were telling a friend about the meeting, you'd answer those questions.

Maybe the article was written this way because nothing did happen. In that case, rewrite it to say that directly, covering points like:

1. People expected to work on such-and-such problems at the meeting;
2. The meeting didn't accomplish much on those problems;
3. Why it was a bust;
4. How future meetings could be better.

Explore these points by interviewing people after the meeting. You'll get a lively discussion of problems and possibilities, not a cover-up.

If you don't want to discourage people, tell them how important it is that they help make the next meeting better. Make people feel they were missed, but don't guilt-trip them. After all, if you make readers feel too uncomfortable, they can just stop reading.

## How about example J?

Article J is more informative, but it needs to be reorganized.

Most newsletters carry reports from leaders sent to various conferences. The

Example I

## Police - Community Committee meets

On Tuesday, October 30th, about 40 Charlestown residents attended the Police-Community Steering Committee meeting at Station 15. The purpose of the Steering Committee is to bring about a dialogue and better understanding between the police and the community.

As acknowledged by Dept. Supt. Peter Donovan, the committee will afford an opportunity for citizens to become actively involved with police to provide better service. Another purpose of the meeting was to form three separate but interwoven committees:

• Communications
• Program Development
• Program Implementation

Each committee will define and set up its priorities and goals. It's important to note that everyone is equal and all will have a chance to participate in generating ideas.

The members of the Steering Committtee are adults concerned about increasing problems in our community. We must not forget that the youth must also become responsible for helping improve communications.

The meeting left one with frustrations, but also with hopes of effectively working with the police to bring about solutions to the increasing problems.

Example J

## Workers' Compensation and you

The week of April 27 through May 2, Deb Olson and I attended the annual Community Action Council seminar on workers' compensation in Columbus, Ohio. The guest speakers included administrators from the Bureau of Workers' Compensation and the Industrial Commission of Ohio. The Director of the Bureau informed us that the Surplus Fund is in very good shape, no matter what anyone may say to the contrary. In explanation, the Surplus Fund is the monies available to pay medical bills and temporary total to claimants unable to work. This fund is financed through premiums collected from employers and interest on investments. The Director of Operations further stated that Ohio's Workers' Compensation or The Ohio Plan, as it is popularly known, would be able to pay its bills well into the next decade if not another penny is collected from Ohio's employers. We also learned that the Bureau processes 1,000 new claims every day.

The Industrial Commission of Ohio interprets workers' compensation law and instructs hearing officers on the correct enforcement of these laws. As you may already know, Ohio's legislature passed a new law last year, and the Industrial Commission must write permanent rules for everyone to follow. Through conversation with the two labor representatives on the Industrial Commission, I learned that permanent rules have not been written on that section of the new law regarding temporary total. I feel that this part of the new law, if enforced as written by the legislature, would have the most adverse effect on claimants injured and unable to work. Nobody knows for sure when these rules will be written by the commission. One thing I am sure of though, is that employers in Ohio can't wait. I will keep you updated on this.

As always, this seminar is very informative and helpful to the 158 workers' compensation representatives from plants and offices throughout the state of Ohio.

Finding out your article needs editing

Example K

number-one goal may be simply to let people know you didn't play 18 holes of golf during meeting hours. But if all you can say is that you showed up, you still haven't justified the trip. The report should explain why it was – or was not – worth sending you there.

What skills, contacts, and information have you gained to help you better serve the members? Article J tackles that goal, and passes along key facts the writer learned at the meeting. But most people won't read them, because the beginning will turn them off.

Can you honestly get through the first few sentences of article J without thinking of all the other exciting things you have to do, like emptying the dishwasher? That's because the writer starts with a list of dates, names and titles that don't mean diddly-squat until you know

why the meeting's important. The article needs a *lead* (p. 116), a beginning that highlights something of interest.

How's this: "More than 1,000 Ohio workers file new claims for workers' compensation every day. Can Ohio Workers' Compensation (popularly known as the Ohio Plan) afford to pay those claims? Yes, the director of operations told the annual Community Action Council seminar on workers' compensation last month."

But after readers get into the article, some will get lost. What does "temporary total" mean? Although the author is familiar with the term, most readers aren't. The author tries to explain how the system works, but this confusion can spoil the whole article. The author should define that term, and also give a little background on how a law that could hurt workers got passed.

It's mostly a matter of changing the order of facts and sprucing them up so they're easy to approach Also, chop apart the long paragraphs.

### Does article K work?

Article K about the VET program is on the right track, but it's frustrating. You'd like to believe conclusions that are so heart-felt, but why should you? The writer insists the VET program helps veterans, but he doesn't show how.

The writer is so anxious to make you see things his way that he won't give you a chance to look over the program yourself, to like it, and then to get angry on your own that such a good program is being scrapped. He doesn't mean to, but he's browbeating you.

The writer of the VET story also goes out of his way to hide his sources: "Under most circumstances this has proven to be . . ." "There is concern that . . ." and "These demands are not felt to be unrealistic." Then out of the blue he refers to "our" usefulness. In fact, he's a vet who's been through the program. Why didn't he say so?

The writer refuses to be up-front because he thinks he should be "objective" and impersonal. If he'd instead write a personal story telling why he went into the program, how it helped him, and how he saw it help other vets, the article would be 100% more convincing. Example L shows how another writer began an article on adult education by showing her own excitement at going back to school.

---

## U. Mass VET program in danger

The VET (Veterans Education Training) program at the University of Massachusetts is the only one of its kind in the state. It helps inner-city vets of the Vietnam era – and it's being thrown to the wolves by the government. It is now in the hands of the University to decide if it will survive past June.

This program is a must for the vet to further his higher education. The purpose of the program is to help the veteran both academically and emotionally through the transition period of going back to school after a long absence. Under most circumstances this has proven to be a big step.

It seems that the federal government feels that our usefulness has been used up in their war.

The VET program is not the only thing at stake here. There is concern that the cutting of this program can only lead to the downfall of other programs set up to help people of the lower-class urban districts so that they can reach out through education to help themselves and their communities.

The Veterans Union at the University of Massachusetts has sent certain demands to Chancellor Golino, and they have a firm hope that these demands will be met. These demands are not felt to be unrealistic, because it is the responsibility of the University, as a public university, to serve the people.

We have asked that the program will remain at the University, and if necessary funded in its entirety. Also, a guarantee that the other programs which serve urban students will not be closed.

Programs of this nature are a necessity in a community like Dorchester, not only for the veteran but for everyone who has been neglected due to lack of money or academic skills. If we allow the doors to close on the veteran it will only be a matter of time before it's impossible to receive an education. Needless to say, this means that the people of Dorchester and similar communities will be denied a right they have paid for with their tax dollars – and in the case of the veteran, sometimes with social and emotional stability.

Example L

---

## My dream came true

On February 9, I re-entered the world of education. As I walked into Room #105 at the union hall, feelings of self-consciousness and apprehension flooded over me. For 30 years I had dreamed of completing my high school education and receiving my diploma. Through these years I had attempted three times to attend school;

but education couldn't be my number-one priority because of other obligations.

My big chance came in the autumn of 1989 when I received a questionnaire from the union. It asked if I would be interested in furthering my education and what goals I wanted to achieve. My dream was going to become true!

– From UAW Local 662, Sandra Lovett

# 14. The how & why of editing

## Why should you edit?

Editing pulls the paper into shape. The editor catches mistakes, clears up confusion, and makes sure the paper's interesting, beginning to end.

- **If you don't edit articles** because you're afraid to hurt people's feelings, your paper will be a hodge-podge. Some articles will insult readers by being, for example, sexist (p. 4). Some articles will be so long no one will read them, while others won't make sense. Some will push ideas your group doesn't endorse, some will have the facts wrong, and others will be boring. To produce a top-notch paper you must edit. But that doesn't mean barking orders or chopping people's articles into smithereens.

- **Editing helps make the paper a group effort.** If people are concerned only with their own articles, they work alone and don't get to know the group or its priorities. Editing raises issues that should be discussed and keeps members of the group in touch.

- **The editor does writers a favor.** As you help members write well for your publication, they gain an invaluable skill and become more self-confident. That strengthens your group.

- **Set the political direction** of your publication through editing. See that articles mesh with the point of view your group's organized around, and don't slip in views your group opposes. (See p. 22 for more.) A writer may assume, for example, that companies always make a profit from electricity and get all wound up figuring what's a fair profit, without knowing public power is possible and what's more, your group endorses it.

## Who should edit?

Once you've agreed that articles should get edited, who's the editor? Here are methods you could try:

- **One editor.** One person has the job of editing everything for a particular issue. The job can rotate from month to month, or it can remain with the same person. If your group has paid staff, one staffer might become editor. The editor would still show articles to other people to get their advice. Clear controversial articles with other leaders or an expert.

- **An editor for each story.** At the first planning meeting (p. 80), assign each story an editor as well as a writer. This process might make articles less consistent, but it encourages a closer relationship between writer and editor. It gives everyone valuable experience without overloading one person.

• **An editing meeting.** Some publications hold a staff meeting the date articles are due (p. 81). Everyone shows up early to read the stories and write comments. Edit for overall content, approach, and what to cut or expand at such a meeting; but avoid getting into details, or your meetings will turn into marathons. And people might get so carried away with their own ideas, they forget the writer has rights and feelings.

Editing at meetings makes sense only when your group is very close, personally and politically. Even then, assign individual editors to finish going over each article and to work personally with the writer.

# How to edit successfully

## Editing without tears

If you follow these guidelines, you can edit the most sensitive writer's article without overdoing it.

• **Prevent problems from cropping up.** That's easier than trying to cure them when they're full-blown. Make your editorial process clear to everyone *before* they start writing. Tell new writers they'll get edited and how it'll help, so that when it happens they won't think they failed.

So people won't start out confused, discuss their article ideas and goals *before* they put pen to paper. Encourage new writers to read Chapter 13 on writing. And type a brief summary of your paper's goals and *editorial policy* (p. 22) to distribute to all new writers.

Encourage everyone to type article drafts double-spaced, like example E on p. 134. That way you'll know if the article fits where it belongs (*copyfitting*, p. 86). And it allows room for minor rewriting.

• **Whatever you do, don't edit by whim.** Don't change a word or sentence to something else just because you like it better. You're tampering with people's personal style, and they have every right to be annoyed. When you want to change something, make sure you've got a good reason; then explain it so the writer understands and learns from it.

• **Don't criticize every little thing** down to the last unnecessary word. People learn from getting edited, but not if the experience discourages them. A new writer has a delicate ego and probably fears he or she can't write at all. Don't confirm that fear.

Pick out the most important problems to get changed, and let the rest go. To sweeten the medicine, look for the writer's strong points, and praise them.

• **Criticize in a constructive spirit.** Don't just say, "that's boring." Figure out why it's boring and what could liven it up; then say: "That point would interest people more if you . . ."

• **Avoid rewriting the article yourself.** Only the writers know what all the facts are and what they're trying to say. The editor's job is to draw out of a writer the missing facts, to get the writer to explain confusions, and to suggest revisions and see if they're correct. Often when you ask a writer to explain something, the writer will say out loud exactly what should have been written.

When the writer's at a loss, then suggest your own revisions. If you say a sentence should be clarified but the writer can't think of anything better, the writer might insist the sentence is great as is. Dream up an improved version of that sentence, and it'll break the impasse, opening the writer's mind.

• **Never – ever – make major changes** behind the writer's back. If you're really too busy to go over changes with the writer, don't change anything. Picture what it's like to spend valuable free time writing a story. You look eagerly to the day when you'll see it in print and can show it to friends. When the paper comes out a story appears with your name on it, but it isn't your words.

How would you feel? Embarrassed? Taken advantage of? Worse yet, suppose the editor misunderstood one of your points and rewrote it with clear wording – so that the point's *clearly* wrong. It makes you come across as a fool. Would you want to write for that publication again?

When an editor single-handedly changes something, you're presuming to know everything the writer knows. It's an insult to the writer. If you don't have time to sit down with the writer, at least make a phone call to get changes approved, or to clarify a point.

## What the editor does

Editing is a matter of reading and watching your own reactions. It's a test

## Example A

While doctors' salaries average over $80,000 a year, for most working people, minor surgery will wipe out all savings.

## Example B

While minor surgery could wipe out the savings of most working people, doctors' salaries average over $80,000 a year.

run, to see if the story reads well.

Mark with pencil in the margin or on a separate piece of paper points that need rewriting or can be crossed out. But don't get your heart set on changes. They're tentative, until the writer either approves each change or solves the problem in another way.

When you meet with the writer, explain your reasoning behind each change. Usually you can solve the difficulties together, then and there. Send the writer home to revise the article only if it needs more research, it's too long to work on together, or the writer insists. Leave the meeting with solutions, not just mistakes.

## Modern marvels

If you have a computer and get articles from people who also have computers, you can edit them right on the machine. (However, if the machines aren't *compatible*, you may have trouble – p. 46.) The writer copies the article onto a floppy *disk* (p. 47), and you slip that into your machine.

Don't start massacring the article right away, or you might delete half of it by mistake. Make a copy on the screen to work with, so you can check your changes against the original.

● **If you and the writer both have** *modems* (p. 55), the writer can send you an article over phone lines – from the computer next door or one at the opposite end of the earth. Although you could figure out all the codes to send such "mail" yourself, it's easier to subscribe to a *network* (p. 89) that offers *electronic mail*. Just make sure your writers belong to the same network.

When you've typed your editing suggestions into an article on the computer, send it back. The writer then sends you a rewritten version; it could all be done within an afternoon.

## What an editor looks for

Pretend you're a typical reader looking at the article for the first time and ask yourself these questions:

● **Did you understand it all the way through?** If you're confused for a while and only start to get the idea at the end, some facts or ideas are probably in the wrong order. A less sympathetic reader won't take the trouble to figure out what the story means.

Did you get confused because the writer seemed to be concerned about one thing, and ended up talking about

another? Did the writer leave out steps in the reasoning so you don't see where a conclusion came from?

● **Can you tell what the main point of the story is?** Or does the writer beat around the bush? Do some sentences seem beside the point? Get the writer to tell you why those sentences are needed. If the writer can't defend them, the sentences are probably side-tracks.

If the writer tells you what the sentences were supposed to do, that should help the two of you figure out what's not getting across. Ask the writer to say it to you in a different way.

● **Do you find yourself reading a sentence twice?** Look at example A. It sounds funny. If you missed that tiny little comma, you'll read ". . . salaries average $80,000 a year for most working people . . ." and it'll throw you off. The sentence needs to be rearranged into something simpler, like example B.

● **Does the story put you in the mood the writer intends?** And does that mood suit the goals of the paper? Suppose I read an article exposing all the gory details of city corruption. If it sounds so overwhelming I want to hide in a closet or pour myself another drink, it's not doing me – or the people fighting city corruption – any good. The article should make me feel angry and capable of changing things, not defeated and scared.

Likewise, an article attacking government corruption shouldn't leave your readers hating government. Give readers the sense governments can be changed, with specific ideas, and that the government is *worth* changing.

- **Does the language sound as natural** as someone talking to you? Or are there words readers wouldn't understand? Look over the writing guidelines on p. 111, and use them for editing, too.

Example D sounds like it was lifted straight from a police department news release, not a conversation. Example E is more direct and tells how the change will affect people.

- **Does the article raise questions that are left hanging?** If the questions are important, the writer should answer them, or suggest where the answer lies. A helpful editor will give the writer tips for further research. If the questions are beside the point, get rid of them.

### If editing doesn't work

Once in a blue moon you could feel the wording the writer insists on is intolerable – when it's racist or otherwise insulting to your audience (Chapter 1). Or the writer might insist on contradicting your group's beliefs, flat out.

In that case, you have three choices:

**1.** Suggest to the newspaper committee that the article be dropped;

**2.** Print the article as a letter to the paper instead, possibly followed by a polite Editor's Reply; or

**3.** Print it under the writer's name, and add an Editor's Note explaining this is an individual's view and that you welcome other views. Then don't ask that person to write for you again.

Example C

---

## Pandel workers win union

1. It's not every day that a company in Lowell unionizes, but that day has finally come for Pandel-Bradford. Approval of the union by the government and management has just been given to the United Rubber Workers. As Pandel union leader Walter Dufresne puts it, "It's the best thing that's ever happened at Pandel."

2. Now that the union has been officially recognized, a Contract Committee has been selected by the workers to draw up a contract. Union representative Dufresne explained, "First we draw up a contract, then present it to the workers for approval. If they don't like it they can change it. The people are going to have their say. Then we give it to the company and allow them time to study it. They tell us what they don't like about it, and we start what's called negotiating."

3. The union expects the negotiating to begin around February, and the actual contract probably will be signed in March or April, if there aren't major hang-ups.

4. Some of the key issues will be "equal time for equal work," and pay. A union spokesman says, "in the last two years I got a .35 wage increase. That doesn't carry you too far. We won't be going for peanuts, that's for sure."

5. At the same time that the Contract Committee is preparing a contract to be negotiated, Union members will be signing up other workers to join the union. The union emphasizes the fact that "almost everybody should sign up. The stronger the body, the better the negotiating power."

6. Since the union election last April, workers have waited nine months for approval of the union. Dufresne summed it up when he says, "It's hard to believe it's finally in, we've worked so hard. But now the real work's going to start."

---

# Can you edit this article?

When you read example C, you'll find it has basic flaws. For starters, it doesn't tell how the union was won. Instead of asking Walter Dufresne questions that evoke the thrills and chills of organizing, the writer let Dufresne's current thoughts about negotiating a first contract dominate the whole article.

If you had time, you'd ask the writer to call up another worker – one who's not tied up with negotiations – and ask how they won the union. Quoting more than one person also dramatizes the point that a union is a group.

But let's get real. When it's deadline time, you often must make the best of what you've got. Assuming that, how would you edit this article? Try your hand at it, and then look over example G on p. 126, the edited version.

### Step-by-step editing

Although the point of the article is summed up by the headline, "Pandel workers win union," the first paragraph acts as if the union just happened. First it says the "company. . . unionizes." Then it says that government and management have given their approval. Even union leader Dufresne says the union "happened."

What did the writer really want to say? Probably something like this: "It's not every day that Lowell workers can unionize a company, but that day has finally come at Pandel-Bradford. A United Rubber Workers local has just won recognition from the government and management. Pandel union leader Walter Dufresne called the victory 'the best thing that's ever happened at Pandel.' "

But the new first paragraph still doesn't answer a key question: When did the workers vote in the union? We don't find that out until the last paragraph, after all the talk of the future.

Wouldn't it be better to put that last paragraph second? When you try it, you find it works. Yet the reader still doesn't know enough to share in the excitement this victory should inspire. Why was the union needed? And how did Pandel workers succeed? Ask the writer to add campaign highlights before the Dufresne quote. "But now the real work's going to start" forms a perfect introduction to the rest of the story.

● **Paragraph 2.** Unnecessary words plague the first sentence of paragraph 2. The union being recognized has been mentioned twice already, so the beginning of this sentence isn't needed. Saying the Contract Committee will draw up a contract repeats itself, especially when the sentence after this begins, "First we draw up a contract." You could just say, "A contract committee has been selected by the workers." But it's shorter and more powerful to say, "The workers selected a contract committee." (See *active* sentences, p. 113.)

"Already" makes the sentence flow better and makes it seem like things are moving. There's no need to say who Walter Dufresne is again. He's appeared in every paragraph, so the reader should remember. The rest of the paragraph is fine. So is the next one, except for the *run-on* sentence (p. 115), which is easy to fix.

● **Paragraph 4.** Unless you work at Pandel, you don't know what "equal time for equal work" means. Putting quote marks around it doesn't help. If this issue is important enough to include, explain it. In the next sentence, ".35" looks funny, because people don't talk in decimal points.

If that mysterious spokesman just happens to be Dufresne again, don't try to hide it; say so.

● **Paragraph 5.** "While" is shorter than "At the same time that." To say that while the committee is doing such-and-such, "union members" will do so-and-so makes it sound like committee members aren't part of the union. "Other members" gets rid of that problem, and eliminates repetition of the word "union" as well.

In the last sentence, "the fact that" isn't needed. "The union" is probably still another alias for Walter Dufresne.

## Thirty words shorter

With these revisions we've made the story stronger and cut out 30 unnecessary words. That may not sound like much, but it helps make room for more meat: facts, pictures and quotes.

# Style, grammar & punctuation

Don't get tied up with these details until articles are done. This last step is window-dressing, and doesn't need the writer's okay unless the grammar or spelling is so confusing you have no idea what the sentence says.

## Nit-picking

Many little decisions, like when to spell out numbers, just aren't important to a small newsletter. But others, like correct spelling and punctuation, clear up areas that could confuse or distract the reader. And to convince your audience you're competent, use acceptable English so nothing looks "funny."

Be wary of rewriting everything into perfect grammar, however. If you're determined to be correct, you could end up with "To whom would we give the job?" and ruin the style of the writer. "Who would we give the job to?" may not be the Queen's English, but it sounds more natural.

How much you nit-pick about grammar and other details depends on what your audience and writers are comfortable with. Each paper sets up editorial guidelines, usually through an informal understanding of what's important. A large group may need to write down what is and isn't accepted. Some make up a style sheet to give all writers. Go over the stylistic rules that follow, and see which ones you could use.

Example D
The MBTA announced it will begin a new evening security program.

Example E
More police will patrol subway stations after 5:00 p.m.

## Example F

*Don't say:*

Sharon Ruiz, financial analyst and mother of two lovely children, won the quality award.

*Unless you'd also say:*

Mark Baldwin, programmer and father of two lovely children, was the first runner-up.

## Example G

Edited article from p. 124

# Guidelines for writing in style

## Keep the style consistent

Keep names of your group and others consistent. Don't refer to the Nine-to-Five Women Workers in one place and the 9to5 group of women office workers in another. It's confusing. Instead, use the same form every time.

## When to abbreviate

Don't clog up your article with the constant repetition of long, official names like the National Organization for Women. You can abbreviate: NOW.

• **Use initials to abbreviate**, not bits and pieces of things that are normally spelled out. Don't make Charles into Chas. or Organization into Org., unless it's very common slang.

• **The first time you mention an official name**, write it out. To clue people in that you'll be abbreviating from now on, follow the name with the abbreviation in parentheses. For example, when it's first mentioned, write National Organization for Women (NOW), the Cost-of-Living-Adjustment (COLA) or the Department of Public Works (DPW). The next time it comes up it'll be NOW, COLA and the DPW.

• **Exception:** You needn't spell out initials that everyone in your audience knows, like U.S.A. or AFL-CIO.

• **Slang.** If most people refer to a place or group with a short slang term, like Mass. General for Massachusetts General Hospital or the unemployment office for the Department of Employment Security, don't bother with initials. Use the common term, defining it when it first comes up (if necessary): "They went to Mass. General [Massachusetts General Hospital] to visit him."

• **Don't overdo it.** If you mention EPA (the Environmental Protection Agency) in the first paragraph but don't refer to it again for several paragraphs, define it again the next time it comes up. Only a dedicated reader will hunt through paragraph after paragraph to find out what on earth EPA is – and that dedicated reader will be annoyed.

Don't abbreviate everything in sight, especially if the abbreviations aren't commonly used. Articles should be written in English, not a made-up language of abbreviations.

• **Periods.** When do you put a period between initials of an abbreviation? Leave those periods in for *dates, geographical places* and *people*: Oct., U.S.A., N.Y.C., Mr. But you don't need periods to abbreviate *organizations* and *things*: AFL-CIO, DPW, GNP, COLA, FBI, ABC News.

## Always abbreviate these

The following abbreviations are so widely used they wouldn't confuse anyone. So use them every time:

• **Exact dates:** Feb. 15 is better than February 15.

• **Use Corp., Co., Ltd., and Inc.** when they follow a specific company or group name: The Itek Corp., Jordan Marsh Co., Citizens Forum, Inc.

• **When you name a city or town,** abbreviate the state: Montgomery, Ala.;

### Pandel workers win union

*[This article is shown with handwritten editing marks. The printed text reads:]*

1.  It's not every day that a company in Lowell unionizes, but that day has finally come for Pandel-Bradford. Approval of the union by the government and management has just been given to the United Rubber Workers. As Pandel union leader Walter Dufresne puts it, "It's the best thing that's ever happened at Pandel."

2.  Now that the union has been officially recognized, a Contract Committee has been selected by the workers to draw up a contract. Union representative Dufresne explained, "First we draw up a contract, then present it to the workers for approval. If they don't like it they can change it. The people are going to have their say. Then we give it to the company and allow them time to study it. They tell us what they don't like about it, and we start what's called negotiating."

3.  The union expects the negotiating to begin around February, and the actual contract probably will be signed in March or April, if there aren't major hang-ups.

4.  Some of the key issues will be "equal time for equal work," and pay. A union spokesman says, "in the last two years I got a 35¢ wage increase. That doesn't carry you too far. We won't be going for peanuts, that's for sure."

5.  At the same time that the Contract Committee is preparing a contract to be negotiated, Union members will be signing up other workers to join the union. The union emphasizes the fact that "almost everybody should sign up. The stronger the body, the better the negotiating power."

6.  Since the union election last April, workers have waited nine months for approval of the union. Dufresne summed it up when he says, "It's hard to believe it's finally in, we've worked so hard. But now the real work's going to start."

*[Handwritten editing marks include: "Lowell workers can unionize", "local has just won recognition from", "called the victory", "The workers have already selected", "move up", "what's that?", "who?", "while", "other", "who?", "What happened during the campaign?"]*

Somerville, Mass. *Don't* use the postal codes (AL, MA) instead.

- **In full addresses,** abbreviate St., Blvd., Ave., etc.: 14 Connecticut Ave., 5 Putnam St. But you'd walk down Putnam Street, not Putnam St.

- **Abbreviate titles** like Mr., Dr., and Rev. when they go before a name. When you first mention a person, use the full name, such as Dr. Gladys Corona. After that, you can call her by her title: Ms. Corona or Dr. Corona.

## Numbers

Write out numbers one through nine. But don't bother writing out 10, 65, 153 and everything else higher than nine.

- **Exceptions:** Don't write out numbers for addresses (6 Cooper Way), the time of day and date (5 p.m., Sept. 14, 1944), page and chapter numbers (page 3), percentages (6 percent), highways (Route 9), the temperature (2 degrees), money ($4), ages (4 years old), channels (Channel 2), unions (SEIU Local 9), sports scores and voting results (10 – 3), and names like DC-9.

Don't put a "th" or "rd" after dates (May 3); but add those letters to all other numbers where you hear the sound, like the ninth inning or 11th floor.

- **When you start a sentence** with a number spell it out, even if it's a biggie (except for dates). Forty-three starts a sentence, and 43 comes in the middle of one. 1985 is a date.

## Titles

You add stature or respect to someone when you use his or her title, especially if it's a big one. So talk about Mr. Bush or George Bush more often than President Bush if you want to trim him down to our size.

Would you be tempted to say something like: "Mr. Delaney told Ellen something or other?" In that example you showed Peter Delaney more respect than Ellen McGrath, feeding right into stereotypes of power and prestige. Replace it with "Delaney told McGrath . . ." or "Mr. Delaney told Ms. McGrath" or "Peter told Ellen."

Avoid titles that highlight sexist stereotypes: spokesman, stewardess, Mrs., Miss, etc. Likewise, forget the old rule that said anonymous people are always men: "Everyone should take *his* seat." Replace these sexist traditions with terms like spokesperson, flight attendant, Ms. and "everyone should take *a* seat" or: "People should take *their* seats."

Granted, the substitutes for sexist grammar aren't always as natural-sounding as the original version. But when inequality is built into our language, using everyday language takes a back seat. It's more important to use words that won't offend or push aside large groups in your audience (p. 4).

## Spelling

Keep a dictionary handy and look up words you're unsure of. But how, you might ask, can I look up words if I don't know how to spell them? There's finally an answer to that age-old question. Buy a small *spell-check* hand-held computer for around $50, and when you don't know how to spell a word, type your best guess on the computer. If you're wrong, the machine will suggest the word you're groping for by listing similar – but correctly spelled – words.

If you have a *word processor* (p. 37) or a personal computer with a *word processing program* (p. 50), a spell-check system may be built right in.

## Capitalization

Capitalize every proper name or official title of a specific person, place or thing. For example, Steel Workers belong to the United Steel Workers of America – a particular union with a proper name – but steel workers are all people employed by steel companies.

General Electric Corporation isn't just any electric corporation. The meeting hall isn't an official name; but the John P. Dowdy Memorial Hall is a capitalized name. A safety-and-health committee becomes the Local 89 Safety and Health Committee if that's its official name.

Even in official names and titles, don't capitalize the tiny common words like *and, or, of, in, to, with, for, the, an, a* – as in example H – unless one of those tiny words begins the sentence, or a line of a headline (example I).

The Education Department, Bill of Rights, Easter, Fifth Annual Report on Housing Needs, Eastern Standard Time, Dorchester District Court, Montreal City, State Senator Eloise Backman, Red Cross, Baptist Convention, and Chairperson Spinoza are all official names of specific things or people. But when you refer only to the department Kathie O'Kray chairs, or to the director,

Mr. Delaney told Ellen

Peter told Ellen

<u>Example H</u>
Bank of the Commonwealth
The Bill of Rights

<u>Example I</u>
Bank of
The Commonwealth

the capital letters disappear.

The South is a specific area of the United States, not just any place to the south of where you are now. In fact, if you're in Florida most of the South is north of you! The Thirties names a specific depression-era decade, but when you mention someone in his or her thirties, it's not a specific name.

A Democrat belongs to a particular political party, whereas a democrat is anyone who believes in democracy. Brazilians, Africans and Eskimos are people from specific countries, continents or nationalities; but blacks and whites are less precise. When you mention defense attorney Joyce Chaffee, she could be defending anyone and it's not her official title; U.S. District Attorney Albert Kowalski is a title.

These rules can be confusing and have changed over the years. Modern society capitalizes less often then what you may have learned in school.

## For more information

If you'd like a manual on style to keep around the office, try the Associated Press Stylebook and Libel Manual published by Associated Press, 50 Rockefeller Plaza, New York, N.Y. 10020; or the Canadian Press Stylebook put out by Canadian Press, 36 King St., E. Toronto, Ont., M5C 2L9.

---

### Example J

*Incomplete sentence:*
Thanks given to the Paskal family for their enthusiastic collection of donations.

*Complete sentence:*
(somebody)    (does something)
The speaker thanked the Paskal family for their enthusiastic collection of donations.

### Example K

| Present | Past |
|---------|------|
| I look | I looked |
| You want | You wanted |
| They agree | They agreed |
| She wastes | She wasted |

### Example L
Some exceptions:

| Present | Past |
|---------|------|
| I say | I said |
| He thinks | He thought |
| She writes | She wrote |
| We go | We went |
| She makes | She made |
| You speak | You spoke |

### Example M

*A picture is* worth a thousand words.
*Pictures are* worth a thousand words.
*She goes* to meetings regularly.
Her *friends* rarely *go* to meetings.
*He realizes* the importance of this.
The *delegates realize* the importance of this.

### Example N

*Joan has* made a promise.
The *leaders have* made a promise.
*A window was* broken.
*Windows were* broken.

# Brushing up on grammar

## People talk that way

In some parts of the country and among some groups, people just don't talk according to the rules. If your whole audience does very well without following grammar, you may decide not to worry about it. But if you want to reach beyond that audience, then it's time to brush up.

Here are common mistakes, and rules to help you correct them:

## Complete sentences

Edit partial sentences into complete ones, with a subject and an action (*verb*). That makes them livelier and less confusing as well as proper. The basic form is: somebody (or thing) does (or is, did, will do, will be, was) something. Example J shows the difference between a complete and incomplete sentence.

*Exception*: Don't change tiny incomplete sentences if they emphasize a point and sound clear and natural. "Good work, Ann!" is fine. So is: "He says we should solve our problems individually. Fat chance."

## The past

When something happened in the past, you normally add an "ed" to the *verb* (action). If there's an extra "s" at the end of the verb, drop it before you add "ed." If there's already an "e" at the end, just add a "d" to get your "ed" ending, as example K shows.

As example L illustrates, this rule has an annoying number of exceptions. A decent dictionary puts all exceptions to the "ed" rule next to the normal (*present*) version of the verb. To find out the spelling for the past of "buy," look it up and you'll see "bought" next to it. If there's nothing next to the verb, just add the standard "d" or "ed."

## The "s" rule

Normally you'll add an "s" to a word when you mean there's more than one (*plural*): friend becomes friend*s*. But if the word ends in "s," "sh," "ss," "ch," "x" or "z," add an "es" for the plural: lenses, ashes, stresses, churches, boxes. An "o" ending usually gets an "es" too: heroes. An "f" ending gets changed to "ves" for the plural: self, selves. Then there are the hundreds of exceptions (like person, people, or child, children) that make writing in English so much fun – your dictionary can help.

When you have more than one subject doing something, that changes the *verb* (action) too. One person *does* something. Two persons *do* something. The trick is to keep your eye on the "s" ending. A tenant protest*s*. But two tenants protest. The rule of thumb is, you get only one added "s" ending for each action. So if the subject (actor) is just one thing or person, it usually doesn't end with an "s" (tenant). The verb, or action, gets an "s" instead (protest*s*). More than one subject usually ends with an extra "s" (tenant*s*), so the verb doesn't (protest). Example M shows more.

There are exceptions, but that's the general idea. Sometimes the word for more than one subject doesn't end in an "s," like "people." But so long as there's more than one subject, the action (verb) has no extra "s." A person run*s*, but people run.

The "s" rule applies to something happening in the present to someone or thing not involved in the conversation. When "I," "we" or "you" does something, (I *like* it, you *like* it, we *like* it) or when you discuss the past or future, the verb (action) never gets an extra "s"; it stays the same: The group *will show* a film, several groups *will show* films, the group *showed* a film, several groups *showed* films.

But "has – have", and "were – was" follow the "s" rule even when you're talking about the past (example N).

---

# Those little punctuation marks

## Apostrophes (')

● Whenever you leave out one or more letters or numbers (a *contraction*), an *apostrophe* (') fills in. "It is" becomes "It's." (But when "the group does *its* share of organizing," "its" is just an adjective. It doesn't stand for "it is," and gets no apostrophe.) 1975 is '75. "Come on" can become "c'mon."

● **Common contractions make your writing flow better.** "It is a necessary step" sounds stilted compared to: "It's a necessary step." But don't get carried away and write in dialect: "The winnin' numba' is a hu'dred an' twen'y." That makes it look like some accents aren't really English. A British person might be tempted to write *all* American and Canadian speech in dialect form, but we'd find it insulting.

● **Things become adjectives** with the help of apostrophes. The women's union gets an apostrophe because it's a short, turned-around version of the union *of* women. Again, something has been left out. The same holds true for example O in the margin. A word describing something ends with an 's if it could be turned around into an *of, for, by, from* or *in* phrase instead.

When the expression is very common and you no longer hear an "s" sound, drop both the apostrophe and the s: the company car, the building superintendent. If the word already ends with an s, just add the apostrophe all by itself, as example P shows.

● **To make a single letter plural,** throw in an apostrophe: p's and q's. But 727s, 1950s, and VIPs don't get apostrophes.

---

### Example O

The building**'s** superintendent.
(superintendent **of** the building)
The men**'s** room (room **for** men)
The radiator**'s** heat
(heat **from** the radiator)
The park**'s** trees (trees **in** the park)
The city**'s** downtown area
(downtown area **of** the city)
Dooley**'s** painting (painting **by** Dooley)

### Example P

The prisoner**s'** rights (rights of prisoners)
Ms. Jones**'** eviction
(eviction of Ms. Jone**s**)

### Example Q

They grieved for three reasons: pay, discrimination and harassment.

Their case was as follows: etc.

### Example R

Negotiators set this schedule: First they picked a date; next they . . .

### Example S

Tenant union demands were listed by the committee: stairway repairs, a safer heating system and storm windows.

---

## Colons (:)

A *colon* introduces a longish list, explanation or illustration, as in example Q. Follow a colon with a lower-case letter *unless* it's a whole new sentence, like example R.

## Semicolons (;)

If the list following the colon is short, use commas between items, as in example S. If it's long and/or complicated, use *semicolons* (;) between separate things, as example T does.

## Dashes (–) & semicolons

Either one can replace "and" when you add a phrase or sentence to explain the main sentence: "I went down there; we found quite a mess." But the dash gives stronger emphasis to the addition: "We went down there – what a mess!" A dash can also introduce a sudden correction of what you start to say: "He's shy – or is it snobbery?"

To reprint a quote that stands on its

---

### Example T

Tenant union priorities were: repair of all stairways that could be dangerous; replacement of the rundown heating units with a safe, central system; and storm windows for every apartment.

Groups sponsoring this benefit are: District 925, SEIU; Seattle Chapter, Earth Now; the Women's Committee of the Legal Aid Society; etc.

### Example U

"You may be disappointed if you fail, but you are doomed if you don't try."
– Opera singer Beverly Sills

### Example V

The women (including many who admitted they'd voted for him) were shocked at Councillor Washout's ignorance.

The women – including many who admitted they'd voted for him – were shocked at Councillor Washout's ignorance.

The women, including many who admitted they'd voted for him, were shocked at Councillor Washout's ignorance.

### Example W

*Right:*

Secretaries who won't bring Mr. Allan coffee in the morning don't get raises.

### Example X

*Wrong:*

Secretaries, who won't bring Mr. Allan coffee in the morning, don't get raises.

### Example Y

You can get treated by that clinic if you live in the neighborhood, and it's open until midnight.

### Example Z

You can get treated by that clinic if you live in the neighborhood and can prove it.

### Example A

He said he didn't know.

### Example B

He said, "I don't know."

### Example C

She asked if you made out your taxes yet.

### Example D

She asked, "Did you make out your taxes yet?"

### Example E

They say we're "unqualified," but they won't say how they decide who's "qualified."

### Example F

"We were stunned" is good grammar, but "she were stunned". isn't.

own, use a dash to show who said it – like example U on p. 129.

## Commas, parentheses & dashes

All three of these can set off a phrase that's *not essential* to the main sentence. Where you use which stems partly from your personal style and partly from subtle differences between them.

The parenthesis ( ) is the most extreme and can even interrupt one sentence with a completely different one: "Councillor Washout objected (he objects to everything the women's group proposes) and raised a petty point." But be careful; if you overuse the parenthesis, your writing will be choppy.

Suppose you start with the sentence: "The women were shocked at Councillor Washout's ignorance" and want to insert in the middle that many of them had voted for Washout. Example V shows your alternatives.

As you can see, each parenthesis, dash or comma comes in twos: One opens the phrase and one ends it.

Which of these alternatives would you choose? The parentheses (the first) make the added phrase look less important because it's removed farthest from the main sentence. But you may find commas, the third example, too shy to handle a phrase this long. The dashes – the second example – are bold and demand attention.

So in this example, your best choice is probably dashes – the second alternative. But they're all correct.

Remember, if a sentence is *too* complicated, all the commas and dashes in the world won't make it work. Break it into two sentences instead (p. 115).

Surround a phrase in the middle of a sentence with commas, dashes or parentheses *only* when it isn't essential to the sentence's meaning. Example W doesn't talk about all secretaries, only the ones who refuse to bring Mr. Allan's coffee to him. The phrase is necessary, so it gets no commas.

Example X shows what happens when you make the mistake of surrounding that phrase with commas. Since the commas mean the phrase isn't necessary, try the sentence without it: "Secretaries don't get raises." The commas make the sentence imply that *all* secretaries won't bring Mr. Allan coffee, and none of them gets a raise.

That's just not true. So don't throw around those little commas carelessly.

## Other commas (,)

A comma tells a reader when to pause. Use a comma when you combine two complete sentences with "and" or "but," like example Y. But don't bother with a comma when the "and" phrase is *not* a complete sentence (example Z).

## Quote marks (") & questions marks (?)

Use quote marks only when you repeat an exact quote, like examples B and D. In example D the whole question is repeated, so it ends with a question mark. Example C isn't an exact quote and doesn't get quote marks or the question mark. When you quote a whole sentence, as examples B and D do, capitalize the first word of the quoted sentence. The comma or period at the end goes *inside* the quote marks (example B).

Use quotes to repeat precise words or phrases you'll use for an example or take from an article, etc. (examples E and F), especially if you want to emphasize that these aren't your own words. If the quote is more than one paragraph long, put quote marks before each paragraph; but don't put them at the ends of paragraphs until the last one, when it's finished.

## Hyphen (-)

● Feel free to make up new words by combining old words with each other or with *prefixes* like anti-, re-, pro-, co- and super-. If the new word doesn't show up in your dictionary, seal the two parts together with a hyphen: anti-inflationary, pro-military, ex-tenant, super-serious. But don't make up a new language. Create words only when there's no clear alternative and when the meaning of the new word is obvious.

● If you use two words together as one adjective (to explain the thing or person that follows), link them with a hyphen. Otherwise people might get confused for a moment. Although "high rent apartments" could be a single story tall, you might think they're "high apartments." But when you hitch the words that act together with a hyphen, the reader knows immediately what you mean: "high-rent apartments." The same goes for cost-of-living increase, roll-call vote, and full-time president.

**130**

# 15. Tips for typing or typesetting

You've picked the kind of typing and typesetting you'll use (Chapter 5) and have written the articles (or leaflet). If you haven't designed the paper yet, turn to Chapter 8 for help. Most articles will be set in the same type style (p. 69). Chapter 2 explains how to design an effective leaflet or brochure. What next? How do you transform the raw *copy* (what you've written) into neat, finished columns?

## Figuring column widths

P. 68 explains why you should divide pages into columns instead of typing straight across. To figure the width of each column, take the width of the whole page (usually 8½" wide), subtract the side *margins* (p. 68 – usually ½" on each side for a total of 1"), and subtract the *gutter(s)* between columns (p. 68) – usually ¼" each. Chart A shows the column widths for typical page designs. (As p. 68 explains, each pica equals ⅙".)

## Make galleys first

Whether you're doing all the typing yourself or using a typesetter, the first step is to set the copy into *galleys* – long one-column wide strips of type (p. 40). Don't try to put columns next to each other yet. You'll arrange them onto pages later, with the help of Chapter 16.

## Do you have to copyfit?

Wait a minute. Before you type the whole thing (or get it typeset) ask yourself: Do you first need to *copyfit* to make sure it all fits in the available space on each page? Not if you were very good and planned the length of your articles (or leaflet or brochure) as p. 85 suggests, before they were written.

If you didn't, you run the risk of producing a publication that's horribly crowded or too long. Or you'll have to chop everything down to the right length after it's typed or typeset. Once you've figured out how to chop out half the words, you could end up either retyping big sections and piecing little bitty pieces of galleys together or paying the typesetter a fortune to make changes and print out new galleys.

### When can you avoid copyfitting?

● If you've written all the copy yourself and are typing it on a word processor or computer, you can chop everything down to size after it's typed.

Once you type it all into long galleys, measure the total length of each galley and add them together. That tells you how many *column-inches* you've got. (Some computer programs have a little ruler that helps you measure galleys on the screen. Otherwise, print them out to measure them.)

Find out how many column-inches you can easily fit onto a page by following steps 3 through 5 of the box on p. 86 (substituting the word "brochure" or

## Chart A

| Size of page | Columns per page | Width of each column |
|---|---|---|
| 8½" wide (standard or legal-size paper) | 2 | 3⅝" (22 picas) |
| | 3 | 2⅓" (14 picas) |
| 7" x 8½" (legal-size paper folded in half) | 2 | 2⅞" (17 picas) |
| 11" wide (tabloid) newspaper | 3 | 3⅙" (19 picas) |
| | 4 | 2⅓" (14 picas) |

**These typewriter keys haven't been cleaned**

Typed with old nylon ribbon

This typewriter has a ribbon that's too old.

Typed with clean keys & carbon ribbon

This is typed with a carbon ribbon you type through once.

Draw margin widths on a separate sheet

. . . and use that as a guide

Example B
All-cap type is harder to read

COMPANY FREEZES WAGES

Company Freezes Wages

What can happen when you don't hyphenate

What does the CAP Committee do? We work for you. How? One way is to investigate anything that could prove harmful to our community. Recently we conducted an investigation concerning the Louisiana Army Ammunition Plant (LAAP). There was a

"leaflet" for "newsletter" if necessary). Multiply that times the total number of pages you want. Does that number match the number of column-inches you've written? If you've written too much, chop the galleys down to the right length on the machine and print out a new copy.

● If you're doing a brochure or leaflet on a computer or word processor and have space to spare, you can change the column widths (within reason – p. 68) or size of all the type at whim, after it's typed, to make it fit on the page(s). But don't shrink type smaller than 9 or 10 points. And don't mess with the style of a newsletter or paper, or you'll ruin it.

● If there's no limit to the length your paper or brochure can be and you don't care if one article spans several pages, you don't need to copyfit. Just get everything typeset into galleys, and arrange them onto pages following the steps on p. 138.

# If you're using a typewriter

Clean the typewriter keys so the letters won't fill in, using typewriter cleaning fluid or a *kneaded rubber eraser* (p. 150). And use the same model typewriter for the whole job. You're ready to go once you've installed a carbon ribbon or brand-new nylon one.

## We all make mistakes

If your typewriter has a self-correcting ribbon, just backspace over goofed-up letters and type again. If not, keep handy a roll of *correcting tape* and *tabs*. If you prefer *typing correction fluid*, be patient and let it dry before retyping.

Typing something to be printed gives the lousy typist other second chances. If you discover you've massacred more than one line of a paragraph, keep typing. Once you're done, retype the paragraph separately and mark clearly where it goes, crossing out the botched-up paragraph. They'll be pieced together during paste-up (p. 154).

## Stick to a column width!

Set your margins to the exact width one column should be (p. 131), and put the machine on single spacing. Roll in plain, white paper. Onionskin or erasable isn't sturdy enough. Type a single-column *galley* (p. 40), on only one side

## Time to copyfit

● If you're fitting other people's articles into limited space, it's not fair to chop them into smithereens at the last minute. And it's dangerous – you could unwittingly leave out the best part. As p. 122 explains, all changes should be cleared with the writer.

If you're making a leaflet, all the copy should fit on one side of paper, with plenty of room left over for pictures, space, and headlines (p. 142).

● Anytime you're not using a computer or word processor and have limited space, you must copyfit.

● The first step is to get one page of copy set in the type and column-width your style calls for. Then turn to p. 86 and do what it says (substituting "brochure" or "leaflet" for "newsletter" if necessary). If you have too much copy, edit it and clear your changes with the writer before you get the whole thing typed or typeset.

of each sheet of paper.

Once the margins are set, don't *ever* hit the margin release key to sneak in an extra little letter or comma; that'll throw the whole column out of whack. If you can't help cheating, set the margins narrower.

To help you stay within the margins, take a separate piece of paper and a ruler, and draw two straight lines all the way down the page, exactly one column-width apart. Roll this paper into the typewriter behind each sheet you type on; the dark lines will show through as a guide. Set the margin width where the lines are, and you can see exactly how much room you have.

When you approach the end of a line with a word too long to fit, *hyphenate* it (p. 133) in the middle. That'll make the column look even, and it'll help you fit more words on each page.

● Avoid all-caps like the plague. Don't be tempted to abuse the shift key and type a string of capital letters to make something stand out better. As example B shows, that instead makes it hard to read if it's more than a couple of words long or in a *serif* type style (p. 69). Instead, underline the words. If your typewriter can only make jaggedy underlines, use a drawing pen (p. 152) and ruler to underline key phrases.

● To get bigger type for headlines,

see p. 38. For display quotes (p. 72), type at half the column width you really want, and add rule lines (p. 75) above and below the quote. Then find a copier that can enlarge things (p. 59), and copy the quote at 200%. (You may have to take two shots to get it that big.)

# Using a computer, word processor or typesetter

• If your machine (or program) can automatically *hyphenate*, make sure that option is turned on. And check the hyphenated words – every so often the machine makes a mistake. If the machine won't hyphenate, break words into pieces following the rules above.

*Warning:* Some typesetters don't hyphenate *ragged right* type (p. 67), leaving you with horribly jagged columns that waste valuable space (example C). Either pay extra to have the typesetter hyphenate by hand or change your style so columns are *justified*.

• Don't get carried away with using boldface, underlines and italics. Use them only for occasional emphasis – just a word or two at a time. Otherwise, they'll disrupt the page layout, attracting attention away from the beginning of the article.

If you're tempted to set a paragraph in boldface to stress its importance, maybe it belongs at the beginning of the article instead. Or maybe you've overloaded the article with junk that isn't important, and should cut out the fat.

As explained on p. 132, using all-capital letters is an even more serious sin.

• Don't switch type styles or sizes or column widths around when you're cramped for space or get tired of the monotony. That'll just make your publication look jumpy and haphazard (p. 66). Either edit articles to fit the pages

---

## Tips for typing & typesetting

• Retype reprints. If you "borrow" an article, retype it so it doesn't disrupt your paper's style.

• Type that goes into a box (p. 76) should be 1½ picas (¼") narrower than

Tips for typing or typesetting

---

### Where to hyphenate

**1.** Break words into logical pieces or sounds you hear when pronouncing them slowly. For example: "de-prived" (not dep-rived), "head-line" (not hea-dline), "rea-son" (not reas-on). If you don't hear "ed" as a separate sound, avoid breaking it off. For example, "fi-gured" is better than "figur-ed."

**2.** Don't break up one-syllable words like school or phrase.

**3.** Don't break words into one-letter pieces even when it's logical. It looks weird. That rules out "a-mend," "i-dea," or "ide-a."

**4.** Don't hyphenate more than two lines in a row.

---

or add pages to fit the articles.

### Line space & leading

*Leading* (pronounced "ledding") is the amount of space added in between each line of type to keep the bottoms of one line from touching the tops of the next. Add the leading to the *point size* (p. 67) of the type to get *line spacing* – the jump the machine makes when going from one line to the next. With a typewriter, you get proper leading automatically; but when you go up-scale you must set your machine or tell the typesetter exactly how much leading you need. Chart D shows suggested leading for basic type sizes.

*Don't* squeeze lines of type close together so you can fit more; it'll make reading annoying and uncomfortable. Some styles call for extra leading in special areas, like display quotes.

### How big should the headline be?

When possible, lay out the whole page before "sizing" headlines. P. 142 tells how to get headlines the right size for each page.

---

Example C

Not enough hyphenation

That shows what kinds of
priorities the
administration has, and how
it devalues our
contribution to prosperity.

Much better

That shows what kinds of
priorities the administration has, and how it devalues our contribution to
prosperity.

Too much hyphenation

That shows what kinds of
priorities the administration has, and how it devalues our valuable contri-
bution to prosperity.

Type without
leading is hard
to read and annoying.
It makes you feel
uncomfortable.

Type with leading
is easier to read
and more relaxing
to look at.

This type has too

much leading for normal reading.

It looks spacy,

which could be fine for display quotes.

Typed display quote

was down, they went back to
the old way, not for quality,
but quantity.
                --Ron Clark

"I didn't believe
a word... "

    I didn't believe a word they
said, as far as this place is
concerned, they don't do any-

---

Chart D

| How many lines will fit? | | | |
|---|---|---|---|
| If your type will be: | Suggested leading | Line spacing | You'll get this many lines of type per column-inch |
| 9 point | 1 point | 10 point | 7.2 |
| 10 point | 1½ or 2 point | 11½ or 12 point | 6¼ or 6 |
| 11 point | 2 point | 13 point | 5½ |

the normal column width, so the sides of the box line up evenly along the column edges.

- Once you've found the right graphic (Chapter 18), try *wrapping* the type around a picture (example E). That (also called a *run-around*) means setting part of a column or two narrower than usual. The hard part is figuring where to put a narrow section of a second column so it ends up next to the first one. Typeset full columns first, put them next to each other on the page, and then sketch where you want the graphic to go. Reset both columns narrower at that spot. (If you have a computer and *scanner* – p. 55 – insert the graphic on the computer screen.)

- Don't indent anything more than one or two lines. Otherwise it'll look like the column suddenly switched to a narrower width, and throw off the style of the page.

- When you list several things, use little *bullets* rather than numbers to introduce each one ( p. 73). This paragraph, for example, starts with a bullet. With a typewriter, try asterisks (*).

### Headline tips

- When a quote appears in a headline, use just one quote mark on each side, like example I on p. 136.

- Kern headlines, which means tightening the space between letters as much as possible. Some letter combinations, like "Wo" or "Ka," need extra tightening (example G). And if there are no y's, g's or other letters that descend below the type line, don't put *leading* between lines of the headline.

- Don't justify (p. 67) lines of a headline, display quote or other big type, and don't hyphenate headlines.

- Avoid serif all-cap headlines (p. 69).

# How to communicate with a typist or typesetter

Sending your job to a professional typesetter probably won't liberate you from typing. All copy should be neat and easy to read – and that usually means typed – so the typesetter can whip through without making mistakes. If the typesetter has to wade into a handwritten mess, it'll take forever and

## Marking up copy to be typeset

Teens speak out

It seems every time you pick up a newspaper or magazine or turn on the news any evening, you hear of a teen either being murderd or committing suicide. why? Why are so many teens losing their lives? "PEER PRES-SURE", the pressure put on them by their cohorts/friends or people who they feel they have to fit in with to be cool and accepted. Some people even go so far as to do drugs or skip school. That's not cool, that's dumb. When you're a teen, you feel that if you aren't cer-tain group, your life is over. But that just isn't true.

--By Stacey Hammond, 9th grade, Southwestern H.S.

Center this word or phrase within the column

Indent a space equal to the room a capital M takes up (called one *em*)

These two letters are switched; *transpose* (meaning switch) them back

Take out this word or words

Take this out and close up the space

Add this letter or letters

Capitalize this letter or word

Add space here

Make the capital letters under this mark lower case

Add a dash here

Substitute this word or phrase for what's below it.

Whoops – I crossed this out by mistake; please leave the original as it was.

Don't start a new paragraph here. Just *run on* from one sentence to the next.

Make this capital letter lower case

Set this in bold type

Start a new paragraph here

I left out these words. Please put them here.

Make this word or phrase italics

Add 3 points space between these two lines (or you could make it 6 pts. etc. by changing the number).

Make this Flush Left, ragged right

cost you a fortune and a headache, fixing all the mistakes.

Even when you don't use a typesetter, it may be worth learning a few simple typesetting rules and terms (example F), so you can clearly indicate how the type should look and how mistakes should be corrected.

### Preparing copy for typesetting

Type copy on one side only, double- or triple-spaced so there's room to write instructions or make small changes. If handwritten copy is all you can offer, write neatly on lined paper, leaving every other line blank. And capitalize only the letters that should be typeset as capitals.

Clean up messy copy by whiting out blobs and cross-outs with *typing correction fluid*. Write corrections clearly with a dark marker, using the marks in example F. Retype the worst sections, and tape corrections over the mess. If paragraphs are in the wrong place, cut and paste them in order, rather than drawing little arrows all over the page.

Label each page at the top with a word to identify the story and the page number. Put "-30-" or "#" at the bottom of the last page. Above all, keep a carbon or xeroxed copy. With all the chaos that goes into making a publication, valuable copy does get lost.

If your style calls for subheadings (p. 72), insert them in the copy now. And send all the photo captions (p. 74) to be typeset along with the articles.

### To get the type you want

All typesetters use a few simple symbols to indicate the style and size of type, column widths, etc. Since that prevents confusion, the symbols are worth learning.

To order a column of type for the book you're reading, example H shows what to write above the first page of copy. And here's what it means:

- **T.R.** – That's *Times Roman,* the *typeface* you picked. You can get away with abbreviating most typefaces, within reason. If you're ordering a variation of Times Roman, say so right after the T.R. *Ital.* means *italics, b.f.* means *boldface, Lt.* means *light,* and *X-b.f.* means *extra-bold.*
- **10/11.5 pts.** – That's 10 point type with 11.5 point line-spacing.
- **x 14 pi.** – This translates as "times 14 picas," and it means the column will be 14 picas wide.
- **FL & FR** – *FL* stands for *Flush Left,* which means the left-hand side of the column will be even all the way down the page. *FR* means *Flush Right,* so the right-hand side will be even too; in other words, the column is *justified,* straight as an arrow on both sides.

If you had wanted the right-hand side of the column to be uneven, or *ragged* like typewriter type, you'd write *FL, rr (Flush Left, ragged right).* For special effects you could even order type that's *FR, rl (Flush Right, ragged left)* – but that's harder to read.

### Marking copy

That's not all you need to tell typesetters. How should they handle subheadings, mistakes, spacing and special type? Example F shows the marks for that, too. Consider copying this for all your writers, editors and/or typists.

Discovering the importance of proofing

Flush left, ragged right          Flush right, ragged left

Example G

Spacing that looks fine with small letters
We ko

Looks funny with big letters

# We ko

The same letters kerned:

# We ko

Example H

10/11.5 T.R. x 14 pi.
FL + FR

Messy copy

Cleaned-up copy

---

# Proofreading

Picture this: You rush to the printer to pick up 5,000 brochures you need right away. But when you get them, you discover that the brochures don't make any sense – because a crucial paragraph is missing. It can happen.

Don't wait for a disastrous experience to teach you the importance of proofreading. Always proofread carefully, even if you finish pasting up in the middle of the night and have to get to the printer at nine the next morning.

If you work on a computer, print out a copy to proof, so you can see what you're doing. Proof each article at least three times.

## 1. Proof when copy is typeset or typed

No one types perfectly. So read every word, looking for errors.

- **Make sure the type style** is right. First, measure the column width with a ruler. Then, check the typeset column against a sample of the type you want, to see if it's the right style, size and line spacing. If you used a typewriter and any of this is wrong, get the whole thing retyped before you proofread further.

- **Then look for big mistakes.** The hardest errors to catch can be screwed-up headlines, or sentences left out altogether. Unless you know the article in-

Audi-Figuerola to Congress:

# 'Stop aid to brutal nations'

Example I

Example J

---

## Proofreading marks on typeset galleys

*Marked type:*

Teens speak out

It seems every time you pick up a newspaper or magazine, or turn on the news) you hear of a teen either being murdered or committing suicide. Why? Why are so many teens losing their lives? "Peer pressure", the pressure put on them by their friends or people who they (they) feel have to fit in with to be cool and accepted, some people even go so far as to do drugs. That's not (cool) that's dumb. Hang in there

When you're a teen, you feel that if you aren't a member of a certain group, your life is (over.) You can't see things getting better. But as a teen myself I know they do and will, if you just hang in" and be patient. LIFE WORKER gives you the CONFIDENCE and reassurance in yourself STET that you need. They make you feel good about yourself. I know that's what it did for me. See, I don't feel I have to change myself to fit other people's needs. If they don't like me the way I am, that's too bad for them.

By Stacey Hammond

*What the marks mean:*

|  |  |
|---|---|
| b.f. | Set this in bold type |
| | Break the headline into two lines here |
| | Indent a space equal to the room one capital M takes up (called one *em*) |
| | Add a hyphen here |
| | Add parenthesis here |
| | Get rid of extra space, leaving just a little between words |
| | Take out this letter and replace it with this one |
| | Add a dash here |
| ( ) | Close up the extra space between lines |
| tr | *Transpose* ( switch) these two letters or words |
| tr | |
| | Add a period here |
| cap | Capitalize this letter or word |
| med | Change from boldface to medium |
| <# | Add this much space between these two lines |
| ][ | Center this word or phrase |
| | Close up *all* the extra space |
| | Put an apostrophe here |
| rom | Change from italics to the *roman*, or regular version of the type. |
| e | Add this letter, word or letters |
| FL | Move line over to make it *flush left* with the others |
| cc | Put a quote mark here |
| | Start a new paragraph here |
| l.c. | Make the capital letters under this mark lower case |
| STET | I crossed this out by mistake; please leave the original as it was |
| run on | Don't start a new paragraph here |
| ital | Make this word or phrase italics |
| l.c. | Make this capital letter lower case |
| # | Add space between these two words |
| | Put a comma here |
| | Take out this letter, word or words |
| FR r.l. | Flush right, ragged left |

---

side out, check the galleys against the original copy, word for word. This is slow reading and takes two hands, as you keep your place on the original copy and on the typeset column with both forefingers. Or, ask someone to to read the original copy out loud while you examine the galley.

The mistake in the above paragraph is particularly tough to catch. Can you find it?

● **After you've read the article,** examine each letter and word, looking for "typos" like switched letters. Don't read what the article says this time through; it'll distract you. Just look at each word by itself. If you need a trick to keep you from reading normally, examine each line of type backwards, right to left. If you're unsure how a word is spelled, check it against a dictionary. Are words hyphenated correctly? (p. 132)

● **When you find a mistake,** you'll use many of the same marks to indicate corrections as you did to prepare copy for a typesetter. Example J shows a marked-up galley of type.

### How to mark corrections

When you return the corrected galley to be fixed, typists or typesetters won't read the whole thing; they'll look only for your corrections. So *don't* retype the copy. Make sure corrections pop out by marking each one in the margin as well as within the column, just like example J.

If it's set with a typewriter, be careful not to write over and mess up words and lines that are fine as is.

### 2. Proof the corrections

After you've corrected all the mistakes, get a new set of galleys full of corrections. (If there are only a few corrections it may not be worth paying a typesetter to print out a whole new set of galleys. Instead, get little bits of type you paste into the galleys by hand. P. 154 tells how. That's also how you paste corrections into typed galleys.) Now you must trouble-shoot these.

Examine the galleys you corrected, hunt for every mark you made, and make sure each mistake got fixed. If the corrected galleys are wrong too, mark them, send them back, and try again.

### 3. The last proofing

Proofread once again after the entire page is laid out and pasted up. See p. 155 for details on the final proofreading.

**136**

# 16. Laying it out

When the paper has been designed (Chapter 8), and all the articles are typed into columns or typeset, and you've collected the *graphics* (illustrations, photos and cartoons), it's time to lay out each page.

## What is layout?

Good layout rarely calls attention to itself. Instead, it makes reading your paper an irresistible and pleasant experience. Pictures and headlines jump out at readers, beckoning them to each page; stories are easy to read, and key information can be found quickly.

The page that looks impossibly complex is the easiest to lay out – you just throw everything wherever it can be sandwiched in, and force readers to fend for themselves. Many won't bother. But the page that looks simple – like everything just fell into place with ease – may have taken hours to lay out.

Good layout involves trial and error, and it always takes twice as long as you'd expect. Often you try one arrangement after another to see which works best. The time is well spent, because you're saving all your readers the aggravation of searching through a hodge-podge of bits and pieces, trying to figure out what's what.

## The #1 danger: too much type

To keep the paper from looking like a crushing bore, don't let article type gobble up much more than half the page area (*page guidelines*, p. 70). If your budget limits you to a set number of pages each issue, your best bet is to make a *dummy* (p. 78) early on. That gives you a rough plan of each page, so you can assign exact article lengths *before* people start writing.

Too much type

1. Measure total length of articles

2. Measure height of the page area

3. 20 column-inches × ½
   = 10 column-inches

4. $\dfrac{130 \text{ column-inches total}}{10 \text{ column-inches per page}} = 13 \text{ pages}$

5. 12-page paper

Layout sheet

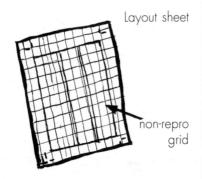

non-repro grid

If you didn't make a dummy, follow the steps below. If the number of pages is limited, be prepared to leave articles out, or cut viciously to make everything fit. Remember, though, if you're using a typesetter, cutting articles after they're typeset will cost you.

And how will you explain to hard-working writers that their articles had to be chopped to bits because you didn't plan ahead and assign them an exact length? The next best thing to planning ahead is to be flexible about how many pages long the paper is.

## When the number of pages is flexible

If you have no dummy, start with *galleys* (p. 131) of articles set into single long, strung-out columns. If you're setting up pages on a computer, that means converting all articles to the style you want – the right type, column width and line spacing (p. 67). Here's how to figure out how long the paper should be:

**1.** Gather the articles that must go into this issue of the paper, and measure the total length, stringing them all together. That's the total *column-inches* (the number of inches long they are, one column wide). If you're using a computer, either print out the galleys to measure them, or use a "ruler" displayed on the screen.

Measure each article separately, then add them together. Suppose the total is 130 column-inches.

**2.** To find out how many column-inches fit on a page, measure the height of the page's type area (the height of the paper minus top and bottom margins), and multiply that times the number of columns per page. For a 2-column 8½"x11" paper, the type area would be around 10" tall. Multiply 10" times the 2 columns to get 20 column-inches

**3.** How much type do you actu-ally want on a page? If you filled every column-inch with type you wouldn't even have room for head-lines, never mind pictures and space. If you want the average page to be just half-full of article type, multiply the number of column-inches per page (step 2) by ½ – your guideline for article type per page. In the example, that gives you 20 x ½, or 10 column-inches of type per page.

**4.** Divide the answer from step 3 into the number from step 1. That tells you the minimum number of pages needed for the paper you want. In the example, divide 10 column-inches into 130 column-inches to get 13 pages.

**5.** Round that figure up to the next multiple of four. With a folded newsletter, each page is attached to three others – two pages on either side of the sheet of paper. You have to work with multiples of four – 4 pages, 8 pages, 12, 16, etc.

In the example, your 13 pages could be expanded to a 16-page paper full of space, big headlines and graph-ics – with a few added *fillers* (p. 140), if you want. Or if you squeezed it all into 12 pages, the paper wouldn't be too crowded. Pages would be 54% full of article type – just over half.

# Get ready for layout

## When you do your own paste-up

Look over Chapter 17 to see what paste-up tools you need. Set up the equipment before you start layout, so that as soon as pages are in final form, you can paste them down.

## When the printer puts pages together

Never, ever, ever, ever just dump your articles off at a printshop and ask the nearest warm body to decide where everything goes. Layout is your job, not theirs; it's a key to getting across infor-mation. Deciding which article gets the big headline and the best placement, what comes next, how to place graphics, what to do if an article is too long – all that depends on *your* knowledge of your topic and readers. And in this TV age, *visual* communication is as important as words themselves.

Once articles have been typeset into *galleys,* ask for *layout sheets* the size of your printed pages, with column widths blocked out. (If the printer doesn't have any, draw up a sample layout sheet and xerox a copy for each page. See p. 150)

You'll need scissors, scotch tape, and a ruler to cut xeroxed "proofs" of the galleys and tape them down on layout sheets, showing the printer exactly what goes where. The printer uses your *rough* layout as a guide to make neat finished pages, and then gives back *page proofs*, for you to okay or correct.

### When you lay out pages on a computer

This is possible only if you've got a desktop publishing set-up (Chapter 6). With the help of Chapter 8, you've designed a *master* page – a blank page showing the standard format for column widths, margins, rule lines, page numbering, etc. that your style calls for. That pre-designed format should be sitting on your computer screen as a little page, waiting for you to "copy" it (Just push the right key and click the *mouse*, p. 48) to make each page.

If you don't want to keep re-inventing the wheel, create a set of blank page layouts covering the possibilities you're likely to try. You'll set up one layout for a full-page article with display quotes, for example, and several other set-ups

for cases when two or more articles are on the same page.

*Caution*: Just because the program lets you tilt type, stick lines everywhere and switch type styles at whim doesn't mean you should. Showcase the *information*, not your whiz-kid technology.

If you use a top-of-the-line word processor, you'll probably do some layout on the machine, and the rest by hand.

Distribute type
onto each page. . .

Then lay out a page or two

Computer master page

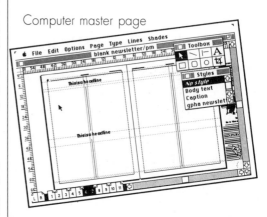

# What goes on which page?

### It's easy with a dummy

• Spread out a bunch of blank pages (or more precisely, layout sheets for pages – p. 152). Put facing pages (like pages 2 and 3) next to each other, so you can see how they work together. (Later they'll be put in a different order for printing – p. 155). Number each page.

If possible, make xeroxed "proofs" of all type and graphics, and use those to safely play around with layout ideas. Take your graphics and type (or proofs) and distribute each piece onto the correct page.

• For computer layout, make enough copies of the blank *master page* (above) for this issue of the paper, and number each one. The hard part is that you probably can't open up and see more than one of those pages at a time on the computer screen. Each time you open up a page, check the dummy to find out which articles and pictures belong there.

### When there's no dummy

Set up the right number of pages. Then take each typeset or typed article, starting with the most important stories, and place it on a page. (If you're working on a computer, it may be easier to make a list of articles and their lengths and figure out what pages they'll fit on with a pen and paper first, before pouring them into pages on the machine.)

When half to two-thirds of a page is full of article type, move on to the next page. Whenever possible, keep articles complete on a page or double-page. (If readers have to flip to a back page to find the last two paragraphs of an article, you'll lose them. And a paper that has bits and pieces all over the place will look awful.)

The exception is the front page – by continuing a front-page article inside the paper, you encourage people to open up and read the whole paper.

### Plan the whole paper

Don't worry about exactly how the type is laid out on any page until you know there's a place for every article, and you've distributed all pictures and

Front page

Back page

Centerfold

A "rough" sketch

Too many attention-getters

graphics onto the proper pages. Have plenty of *fillers* handy: funny quotes, home-made puzzles, or members' recipes that could be used in any issue. And be prepared to "kill" minor articles – or save them for the next issue.

Graphics don't have to be the exact right size to fit on the page. Just leave space for them, and you'll *size* them later; p. 163 explains how. If you don't have a graphic for each page, p. 160 tells how to get something from nothing.

# What goes on special pages

Put your best articles and pictures on right-hand pages (p. 78). And plan to make the front, back and center pages different from the rest.

## The front page

The front page attracts people to the whole newsletter or paper – or it turns them off. Since its purpose is to encourage people to pick up and open the paper, the best front pages usually have little or no article type – headlines and pictures are the attention-getters.

The front page needs a *banner* (p. 70) to remind people who you are, something big and flashy (graphic and/or headline) to strike their attention from afar, and "teasers" about the rest of the paper – at least two headlines and/or a "what's inside" listing.

## The centerfold

The *centerfold* (p. 76) is the largest continuous sheet of paper. This is the only place where a big headline and/or graphic can stretch right across both pages. Reserve it for a long feature article or several related articles, so the whole area works together. If you plan to print color on the front page, you usually get color on the centerfold and back page too, at no extra charge (more on p. 146).

## The back page (p. 76)

If your paper's a self-mailer, leave room on the back for the mailing label. If you insist on putting the mailing space on the front page, *screen* it so it isn't too disruptive. (P. 145 explains screens.) For more on the mailing area, consult p. 172.

Don't underestimate the importance of the back page. It may be the first thing readers see, and if it gives people a bad impression, they might toss the paper aside as "junk mail." Don't squander it on advertising or article continuations.

# Once you know what's where

To save time and minimize mistakes, put page numbers and other set-up information (p. 74) on each page right away. For group layout sessions, think of other tasks, like setting transfer lettering (p. 151), to separate out and teach to newcomers.

## Layout can be fun

Gather as many helpers as possible, and give yourselves time to play around with each page. Group layout sessions are fun, since it's easy to talk and work at the same time.

Each experienced person takes a page or double-page to work on. Some people like to do a few sketches (*roughs*) of how a page should look. Others start right away, playing with type and graphics on the layout sheet.

## For computer layout

If you're laying out the paper on a computer, you may find yourself working alone. If you want company, gather a group to roughly lay out galleys of type and pages just as they would for a printer, and then use those roughs as a guide for finishing the layout on the machine.

To lay out each page, "call up" the page (open it up, so you can see the full page), then call up the galleys of articles you typed, and zap the right article(s) into the page.

Once an article is on the page, you can move it from column to column in a jiffy; see how it looks running up and down two columns, three columns – whatever you want. Try a headline in one size and then give it a whirl in a bigger size. (But don't switch type *styles* – that'll destroy the paper's style.) If an article's too long, do last-minute editing on the page. (But don't butcher someone else's writing; see p. 122.) Leave space for pictures.

To see a "thumbnail" view of the whole paper, use the "print" command in PageMaker (p. 51) and it'll show you up to 36 pages in miniature.

When the layout is just right, print out a *hard copy*. The computer printer spits the page onto a sheet of paper, and you paste graphics (pictures) onto the hard copy. It'll take a few tries to get the page just the way you want it. When you're ready to print out the finished page, try a sturdy, heavier paper with a slightly glossy finish. Office and computer supply stores sell good *laser paper* for use with laser printers (p. 53).

# Attract people's attention

When someone glances at the top of a page, something of interest should jump out and demand attention. This could be a headline, picture or other graphic. To do the job it must be big, dramatic and simple enough to make sense at a casual glance; it should inform people about the article, as well as interest them.

## Don't let them compete

Just one headline or graphic should stand out on each page or double-page as the first thing the casual reader notices. Then it leads right into the most important story on the page. Decide now what it'll be.

If you try to make everything stand out, nothing will. The page will look too complicated, and may come across as shouting at, rather than calling to, the reader. Instead of helping each other, graphics and headlines will compete with – and detract from – each other.

## Layout isn't democratic

Some people balk at these rules, because they seem undemocratic. Why should one picture or headline be more important than any other? The fact is, it's physically impossible to be democratic about looking at a paper – You can't see everything at once. Something has to catch your eye, or nothing will. If nothing does, readers will just keep flipping through the pages with a glazed look on their faces, wondering when they'll find time to read all this.

Graphic leads into beginning of article

Graphic points the wrong way

## A picture with punch

If you decide to feature a graphic, make it big and put it toward the top outside of the page (the right-hand side of odd-numbered pages, the left of even-numbered pages). After calling for attention, it should lead the reader right into the headline that follows.

But first, take a good look at the graphic. Are people looking down, or to the right? Then place it so they're looking *in*, at the headline and article. If that's impossible, rearrange the page or *flop* the graphic – p. 164.

The headline adds to what's already said in the graphic; if it's completely unrelated to the idea in the graphic, it's confusing. The headline can be short and sweet, because it needn't repeat what the graphic says.

## One big headline

One headline should stand, big and bold, toward the top of each page or double-page. It should be set in a strong, simple typestyle – see p. 69 for more.

When the headline is also the big grabber for the page (more than any graphic), it – or the space leading into it – goes toward the top outside of the page. The graphic follows, often snuggled within one or more columns of the article (example A).

Example A

Headline attracts attention

Graphic attracts attention

Headline & graphic combined

Headlines compete with each other

Bad use of space

Better

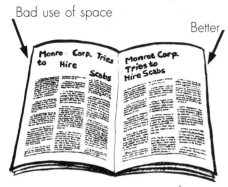

Example C

Headline split across two lines
stands out better

Diagonal in right place

Diagonal in wrong place

## What size headline?

If possible, don't typeset headlines until after each page is laid out. Or use a reducing/enlarging xerox machine to adjust headline sizes to the page layout. The size of the headline will depend on how many columns wide the article is, whether this is the main attention-getter on the page, and how crowded the page is.

The main headline should *not* fit comfortably into the page layout. If it's going to attract readers, there must be *tension* between the headline and the page. It has to be so bold it makes you a little uncomfortable. You'll keep that discomfort from annoying readers by leaving space around the headline.

Beyond that, the longer and more important the article, the bigger and bolder the headline. And a headline only a couple of words long needs a larger size type to make it as striking as a long headline.

• If you're doing layout on a computer, experiment with different size headlines right on the machine. If none is big enough, use a xerox machine to blow headlines up to the right size.

• If you're doing layout by hand, keep handy long samples of headlines in the typeface your style calls for (p. 69), in a variety of sizes.

Take each headline you wrote, and count the number of *characters* (p. 36) it has. Then pick a sample headline in the type size you want. Count its characters, until you reach the same number as the new headline has. Hold that over the page to see if it fits. If not, try another size – or rewrite the headline. If it's too long, try dividing part of it into a *subhead* – a smaller, possibly less bold, version of the same type style.

## Two-in-one

If your main picture has a simple area of white, grey or color, you can slip the headline into the picture by using *burns* and *drop-outs*. See p. 164 for how.

Or, if a graphic shows a simple idea, it could function like a word of the headline (example C).

## Space is powerful

One way to make your main headline stand out, besides keeping it big and simple, is to surround it with empty space. Don't make it small just to get space; but if your page isn't crowded, you'll have room to play with.

Never leave space at the bottom of the page because articles are "short." Move the articles down so the space is at the top, where it can work for you.

• Space can form a powerful (in terms of getting attention) white shape. Stand back and squint at any printed page. Since most of the page is smallish type, the overall look is dull grey. Anything black (dark headlines and bold graphics) or white (space and open graphics) stands out from the norm. Use strong black and white areas to direct readers' attention toward the beginnings of articles.

• Notice the shape of each area. Sometimes you can arrange space, for example, to form a white arrow pointing toward the top of the article. But if the space forms an arrow pointing out of the page, rearrange it.

• *Don't* dilute the space by separating everything equally; you'll just get a boring, monotonous look (example B). Group together words and graphics that belong together, with space surrounding them. Don't let space separate things that read together, like lines or words of a headline, or the headline and type underneath it. Leave extra space *above* the headline instead.

## Split that headline

Even when a major headline could fit in one line across the page, consider breaking it into two or three short lines, with empty space to the side(s). A headline designed within a square-shaped area is quicker to read than one that's strung out. And a headline spanning several columns dumps the reader at the top of the last column, far from the opening of the article.

Break the headline at logical points, as example D shows; try to keep the bottom line shorter than the top line.

## Diagonals

Anything slanted on the page attracts the eye. Check that areas of space and the diagonal shapes within photographs and other graphics are strongest at the top of the page, where they're needed. A strong diagonal can literally point toward the headline. Or the headline itself could be tilted.

Some computer page-layout programs can tilt headlines or anything else at an angle – or you may need a special graphics program (p. 54).

# Organize their attention

If there's more than one article to a page, decide which one people look at first, which second, and so on. Arrange them clearly in that order. Attention moves from the top to bottom of a page, and from large headlines to small ones, all in a consistent *typeface* (p. 65).

## Make it flow smoothly

After you've grabbed the reader's attention, lure people into articles with an easy visual flow – from big graphic to headline to subhead to the beginning of the article, for example. Don't suddenly plunk a picture in the middle of that flow just because you like the way it looks. Don't separate the headline from the article, for example, by sticking a picture at the top of the first column. Put the picture in a right-hand column or two instead, up top where it helps draw attention to the start of the article (example A on p. 141).

## Leave headlines alone

Never put two *separate* headlines or *unrelated* pictures right next to each other, or on top of each other. Use space, pictures and a clear layout to keep them apart. Otherwise they'll compete with – and detract from – each other. And the reader could get real confused about what goes with what.

Example E shows ways to avoid headline competition.

If you've got lots of short articles on the same topic, try putting a huge, striking headline across the whole page or double-page spread, and then top each article with a subhead that's half the size of the headline. Or use a "topic head" as the main headline – p. 74.

## Telling a graphic story

Choose one big, dramatic picture over several medium-sized ones. Even a lousy photo looks better if it's big.

- **The newsreel effect.** If several pictures will go with one article, then by all means group them so they'll work together like frames of a movie.

- But don't print those photos the exact same size and shape, lined up in neat rows. If you do, the little bands of space in between pictures will stand out more than the pictures themselves. Vary the size and shape of each picture; then arrange them in a clear, dramatic shape, maybe across the top or down a column along the side of the article.

- For every group of graphics, choose one appealing picture as the main attention-getter. Pick your simplest and best shot, and print it bigger than the rest, *cropping* it (p. 160) so the main face (or whatever) leaps out, nice and big. For your annual picnic, find a lovable kid's face to highlight.

- If the whole page is full of pictures, bunch them all toward the center, with areas of space around the fringes. And bunch the captions together, as in example F, so they don't interrupt the drama of the photos. But don't blow your whole wad on one page. Save a great photo for the front page, and maybe another for the back page, to lure people into the paper.

# Get pages into shape

## Lazy layout

The laziest layout approach is to just run articles up and down each column, as example G on p. 144 does – with disastrous results. That forces most headlines into tiny one-column widths. Some end up next to each other, while others fall at the bottom of the page.

A page is easier to approach when articles and graphics are designed into

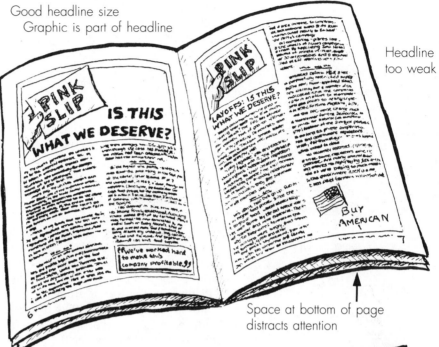

Good headline size
Graphic is part of headline

Headline too weak

Space at bottom of page distracts attention

Headline & graphic don't belong together

Example E
Ways to avoid headline competition

Example F
Page full of pictures

The wrong way     The right way

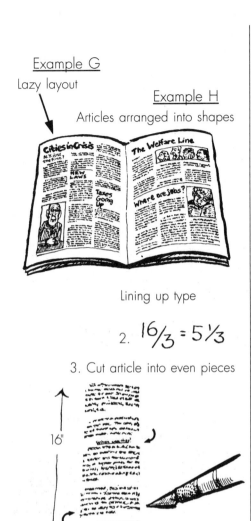

Example G
Lazy layout

Example H
Articles arranged into shapes

Lining up type

2. $16/3 = 5\frac{1}{3}$

3. Cut article into even pieces

16"

5. Orphan

6. Subheading at bottom

Orphan moved back

Subheading moved

Columns evened up

clear shapes. The reader can tell at a glance which headline, type and graphics go with which article.

• Shape all but the shortest articles into clear rectangles, spread evenly across two or more columns like example H. This also minimizes the distance the eye must jump when reading from one column to the next. The tops and bottoms of each article line up along invisible lines across the page. An even band of space separates each article from what comes next.

## Invisible lines

To make the main headline and graphic stand out, everything else falls in line – literally. The edges of everything (including boxes) – *line up* neatly with the edges of one or more columns.

Pictures at the top of an article can "float" in space. But all other pictures should be neatly boxed, with edges of each box running right along the column edges. (If a boxed cartoon is the wrong width, make a new box for it.)

If your headlines are *flush left*, they, too, start at an invisible line – the lefthand edge of the first column.

• At the bottom of the page you'll normally line up each column of type along the bottom *margin* (p. 68). Some styles instead call for a slightly uneven bottom margin, to create a pattern – letting the center or right-hand column run a bit shorter, for example. You have to know what you're doing to keep that from disrupting the layout. If you don't, don't risk it.

## Real lines (*rules*)

Use lines (p. 75) to *emphasize* the order of the page. But don't delude yourself into thinking you can get away with throwing lines all over the place to *substitute* for an orderly page – to separate headlines that don't belong next to each other, for example.

Lines come in widths from *hairline* to ⅛" or more. You can get smooth lines, wiggly lines, dotted lines, etc. But don't be tempted by those fancy sorts. Bold lines in the middle of the page or fancy ones (anywhere) call attention to themselves, disrupt the page, and distract readers from digging into articles. Stick with the simple ones.

---

### How to divide an article across columns

**1a.** If you're doing layout on a computer, even up the tops of the columns and just move type from column to column until it comes out even at the bottoms. Then move it down to the right place and skip to step 4.

**1b.** If you're laying out by hand, measure the length of the whole article, including subheadings and anything else below the headline – boxes, graphics that fit within a column, display quotes, etc. (If any are two columns wide, measure the height and multiply it by 2 before adding it in.)

**2.** Divide that total by the number of columns the article will stretch across. If an article 16" long is supposed to span three columns, divide 16 by 3 to get 5⅓."

**3.** Divide the article into pieces the length you figured in step 3, including graphics, etc. at the right spot. Then cut them apart. In this case, each portion should be 5⅓" long.

**4.** If type doesn't divide into precisely even pieces, you'll either:

• *Leave a one-line space* at the bottom of the first or last column(s), depending on your style. The style for this book, for example, calls for leaving a line of space under the first column, if the two don't evenly line up.

• *Add space above subheadings* or paragraphs, or within boxes and graphics in each short column until it gets as long as the other(s). Or junk a subheading or add a new one to make the columns line up.

**5.** If just a word or two at the end of a paragraph ends up at the top of a column, it's called an *orphan*. It looks funny and can be confusing. The easiest solution is to rewrite the paragraph, adding a few words to fill out the line.

If you'd rather not rewrite, move the orphan back to the bottom of the paragraph it came from or give it company by moving the next-to-last line of that paragraph up above it. Then line up the columns by adding space or a new subheading to the short column(s).

**6.** If a subheading falls at the bottom of a column, throw it out and re-adjust the columns to make up for the loss.

## Boxes

To keep a long article from looking impossible, pull out a tidbit of information and put it in a box. Charts and tables are made for boxes, but any little piece that stands on its own could be boxed. Consider adding a subheading to introduce it.

Keep the box within a column or two of the article, with the edge of the box lining up evenly along the edge of the column. To pull that off, set the boxed type a bit narrower – p. 133.

### Liven up long articles, don't destroy them

P. 72 shows other tricks to make long articles readable. Just don't get carried away, putting boxes next to each other or a display quote (p. 72) or two, plus subheadings and an enlarged letter. . . you get the picture. Don't let these gadgets fall right next to each other.

The best way to keep graphics, boxes and display quotes from getting disruptive is to place them at the top or bottom of columns instead of smack in the middle.

### Wrap-arounds

Here's one way to get away with mid-column graphics: *wrap* the text *around* a picture or even a display quote – like example I – so the reading keeps flowing alongside the picture or quote, without interruption. That can look great, but it means setting some type narrower to make room for the picture or quote. That's a snap if you're using a computer. If not, some type will have to go back to the typesetter or typewriter to be reset (p. 134).

### Screens and tints

As p. 60 explains, a *screen* of tiny dots can make you see grey. That can neatly set off a box, quote, or poem from the rest of the type, or highlight part of a

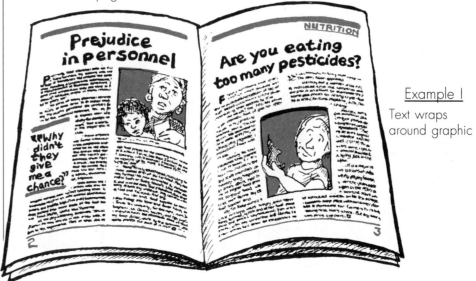

Bold line works because it's not in the middle of the page

Example I
Text wraps around graphic

Example J

| 10% screened box | 20% screened box |
|---|---|
| "If you know everything, you can't learn anything." | "If you know everything, you can't learn anything." |
| **30% screened box** | **40% screened box** |
| "If you know everything, you can't learn anything." | "If you know everything, you can't learn anything." |

Graphics in a clear shape

Scattered graphics

Collage

Group of graphics

graphic. Usually screens look best snuggled within lines, not on their own. As example J shows, you can order a 10% grey or a darker shade – but a screen darker than 30% will make type hard to read. Computer layout programs can also put screens over type, but the dots may be so big they'll make anything smaller than a headline irritating to read. Check it out.

# Keep their attention

If the reading is smooth and clear, it's easier to *keep* a reader's attention than to trap it in the first place. But some mistakes *will* lose a reader in the middle of an article. Here's a checklist:

## Confusion

The reader doesn't know what follows what, or can't tell what type goes with which graphic or headline. Headlines look like subheads, or captions look like they're part of the article. The style isn't consistent (p. 65).

## Aggravation

The page is too crowded; type is too close together, ugly or difficult to read. Information isn't well organized; there aren't occasional pauses in the reading, like paragraph subheadings (p.72).

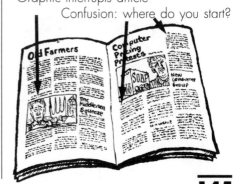

Graphic interrupts article
Confusion: where do you start?

Too big a jump to finish article
Messiness

Nothing lines up

Everything lines up

Confusion: what article does this type belong to?

Printing without black ink is rarely a good idea

## Interruptions

Anything that abruptly stops the flow of information can remind readers they have other things to do. Too much space in the wrong places can do it; so can big jumps from one word to the next – like from the bottom of one column to the top of the next.

Sticking a picture in the middle of an article, right across two columns, is a sure stopper. Is the reader supposed to leap across the picture to finish the article or jump to the top of the next column? Grrr!

When the reader loses his or her place, it's usually caused by something that could be avoided, like columns that are too wide (p. 73).

## Messiness

Type and lines are crooked; type or spaces are smudged; there aren't clear margins; something isn't lined up along columns; columns change widths for no particular reason.

## Boredom

Nothing's interesting to look at. Headline type is weak, and articles are too long. Everything's spaced out. Try the "squint test" described on p. 142. If the whole page looks like a mass of grey, it's boring.

# Check it all out

Once you think you've got a layout that works, take a minute to look at it fresh, as if you were a reader seeing it for the first time.

If you're laying out by hand, things that won't show when printed – like lines on the layout sheet or the edges of pieces of paper – could distract you from seeing how the page really looks. Stand back and squint, so those details fade out of view.

If you're using a computer, print out a *hard copy* (p. 56) of each page. Place facing pages next to each other and put graphics where they belong (or nearby), to help you picture everything together.

Once you've transformed yourself into the typical reader, how do the pages grab you? Ask someone else where they look first, what they think goes together, etc. to see if each page works. Are there distractions or confusions that throw you off? If it doesn't look right, go back to the drawing board – or the computer screen.

Remember, the purpose of words and design is to get across information as well as possible. Anything that interferes with this purpose, no matter how attractive, shouldn't be there.

# Using colored ink

As p. 62 explains, you can have the paper printed with a colored ink instead of black at little extra cost. However, the strongest contrast is still black ink on white paper; so to make the paper dynamic and easily remembered, stick with basic black as your *first* or only color. (The furthest you can safely stray is printing on an ivory or other bright, light-colored paper with dark brown or navy blue ink. That's a good choice for a brochure or leaflet.)

## The second color

Once you've decided that your first color is (usually) black, look into using a *second* color ink for highlights. The younger your readers, the more they're drawn to colorful publications.

Each color you buy costs extra, but you can save money by using a second color only on key pages, like the front and back. Since several pages are printed together (p. 155), that usually means you also get color for the centerfold, and maybe other pages. It depends on the size of the press.

Just as you can make many shades of grey by *screening* black ink (p. 145), you get other colors by screening colored ink, and/or mixing screens of black and colored ink. Put yellow and various screens of black together, and you get several shades of green. (However, screened colors never look as strong as pure colored ink.)

## What color ink is it?

That depends on the use. Don't just order "red" or "blue." Ask the printer to show you a *PMS (Pantone Matching System) color guide*, telling how to order hundreds of interesting shades. If it's a small printer, look at samples of basic colors they have on hand. If they can't mix colors in-house, the standard shade can save you $10 to $25 a job.

## More color

If you can afford to get fancy – and you know how to work with color – add a *third* color to the front and related pages. You get dozens more colors nearly for free by mixing all three and their screens. One step further – to a fourth color ink – and you've got a *full-color* publication. Mixing four basic colors gives you nearly every color under the sun, including full-color photos (p. 62).

## Now for the hard part

Working with color may be exciting, but it isn't easy. Your layout sheet just has black (type, etc.) on white. The colors you'll actually get are added later, when the printer puts colored ink on the plates (p. 62). You must picture the color(s) you want, and then show where they go; Chapter 18 tells how.

How do you know what happens when you mix a 20% blue screen with 100% red? If you're using lots of color, invest in a book that shows different color mixes. Or ask your printer for samples. If you're printing on cheap paper like newsprint, colors won't be as strong and rich as the color guide.

But control yourself. Don't get so carried away with splashing color all over the place that your paper looks more like an abstract painting than something to read.

## Tips for using color

• Use color sparingly, to emphasize a display quote or two, or a graphic. The big no-no is to put spotty little bits of color all over the page. Use color to highlight your paper's layout, not disrupt it. Use quiet colors for big areas, like the background of boxed type, and lively colors for simple highlights, like borders for photos. Just a colored banner (p. 70) and a delicate color line all around the page can be plenty.

• Use color consistently. If you put one display quote in color, make that your style for the whole page – or maybe the entire article or paper. Put all other display quotes in the same color.

• Since black on white gives you the strongest contrast possible, stick to black for most of the type. That means resisting the impulse to put key headlines in color. (Putting headlines in a strong color *could* work, but only if there's just one headline on a page, and

Too much color

Good use of color

CITIZEN TIMES

Focus on You

Covention calls for new organizing

INSIDE:
Seniors well represented –6   Woman make waves?
New delegates in awe –3   Youth speak out –5

Layout sheet

Printed page

Black headline stands out well

Colored headline isn't as strong

Some of the colors you get from mixing black & blue ink

| 100% blue | 10% black & 100% blue | 30% black & 100% blue |
|---|---|---|

| 20% black & 70% blue | 20% black & 50% blue | 20% black & 20% blue | 30% blue |
|---|---|---|---|

Photo printed over color

Photo knocked out of background

Duotone

plenty of space around the headline to make it pop out.)

• Full color (made from four basic shades) is the most dangerous of all. Calm down, and use it mostly for photos and other graphics. For the rest of the page, stick to black for type and again, just one or two colors for highlights and backgrounds.

That said, cheer up. Those few colors can be any shade your heart desires – any color in the PMS color guide.

• Avoid loud backgrounds that make type hard to read. You'll be driven to distraction, for example, trying to read small type printed over red. If red is all you've got, *screen* (p. 145) it for backgrounds. Printing red at a 10% to 30% screen turns it into pink.

• When you print one color on top of another, they'll mix. If you print blue ink on gold paper, for example, it'll come out green. The same thing happens when you use blue ink on an area covered with yellow ink. That's great if you want to get an extra color – green – at no extra cost. But if you really want a blue headline on the yellow back-

ground, tell the printer to *knock* the type *out* of the yellow area before printing it in blue. P. 164 explains knockouts.

• If you've got less than full color, be careful using color for photos. *Don't* print photos with colored ink, such as red. Once you lose the black-white contrast, you've diluted the photo's impact. For the same reason, avoid sticking a colored background behind a photo. A photo printed on a blue background, for example, will look washed out; what's worse, all the little people will be blue.

When you cover a page with a colored background, spare the photos. Have the photo area *knocked out* of the color, so the photo background is white.

• Duotones. Luckily for color lovers, there's one terrific loophole to the above rule: *duotones*. That means you print a photo with *both* black and a colored ink, so they blend to give you a *very* dark version of the colored ink – dark enough to stand out on white paper. If you do that with one photo, do it with others used in a similar way, so it becomes part of your design. Expect duotones to cost $30-$40 a shot.

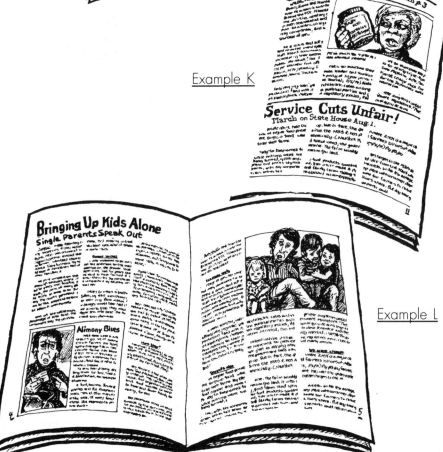

Example K

Example L

# Layout examples

Take a moment to look at these examples of newsletter design. Do the pages catch your attention? Is the reading smooth?

• Example K. This page is well organized, but there's a mistake in attracting attention. The top story is just a continuation, and it's misleading to attract readers to the middle of an article. Since the top is the first place a reader looks, don't waste it. There's a double-reason for switching the two stories here: Major headlines shouldn't fall below the center of the page. If you have two stories to a page, keep both headlines high by putting the longer article on the bottom.

• Example L. Here you can tell clearly that the second page flows from the first – it doesn't even need a continuation headline. The layout does the job with a band of space. If you glance at the upper right-hand page, the space directs your eye back to the left-hand page and the headline. Article type is lined up evenly across both pages.

# 17. Cut & paste-up

If you send pages to the printer for final paste-up, don't worry about getting things straight and neat – that's their job. Just put together rough layouts to show where everything goes, as explained in Chapter 16.

## Who needs paste-up?

If you use a computer with a desktop publishing system, the machine puts together near-finished pages and you won't mess with much paste-up. But you'll probably still re-order pages for printing (p. 155), or paste down *graphics* or special headlines, or make *silhouettes* and *overlays* to get special effects (Chapter 18). Skim through this chapter to see what equipment and tips you might need.

Where this chapter is a real "must" is for folks who take typed or typeset *galleys* (p. 40) and graphics and arrange them onto pages by hand. This chapter explains how to put it all together and make everything look right.

## Yes, it matters

If you just slap down type and graphics without making sure they're neat and straight, they won't be. Crooked type, uneven margins, and messiness attract attention to themselves, away from your message. Even if readers don't consciously notice that a line tilts upward, they'll get the feeling that things aren't quite right. And that you're a slipshod operation.

Paste-up begins when layout is done (Chapter 16). The pages you'll paste together are called *mechanicals*.

This chapter lists the equipment you need, and shows how to use it. Before you get into paste-up, review the method you'll use to print the paper (Chapter 7).

## The printing method

Photo offset printing gives the paste-up artist the most leeway. Material on off-white paper, such as news clippings, can come out fine when printed. Since the pale, *non-repro* shade of blue is invisible to the offset camera, use non-repro blue guidelines (p. 60) to your heart's content. Photos will be of excellent quality, so long as you *halftone* them (p. 160). And you can get all the special effects on pp. 160 to 166.

Messy page

Fixed up

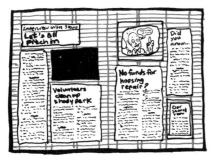

Mechanical

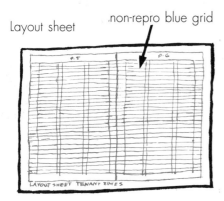

Layout sheet      non-repro blue grid

Layout sheet made from lined paper

Tape white paper on top

black lines

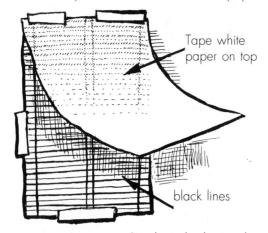

See-through plastic ruler

Picas

Inches

Metal ruler

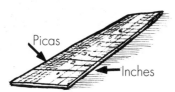

When pasting up for other printing processes, you may have to make a xerox or photocopy of the mechanical (plus anything else that isn't pure black on white), and touch up that copy before printing it (p. 58).

Find out what to expect from your printing machine – whether it's a paper plate offset, copier or mimeo – before you begin layout. Ask the printer. Or run off a sample that includes non-repro blue lines and things pasted on top of each other. If the machine picks up the lines or paper edges, try adjusting the controls to get rid of them.

# Kitchen table paste-up

When you're getting started and your budget is tight, or if you use desktop publishing, the simplest paste-up can do the trick. Buy what you need at a stationery or art supply store.

## Bare-bones shopping list

Here's the basic equipment you can't do without:

• **Layout sheets.** Onto these sheets of paper or cardboard you'll paste type, graphics, etc. They must be at least as big as final printed pages.

The ideal paper for paste-up is heavy and white, with non-repro blue grids on it to help you measure margins and straighten type. See if your printer provides layout sheets; or contact a Gestetner mimeo dealer and stock up on their pads of layout sheets. An art supply store usually sells pads of graph paper with a non-repro grid. (12 sheets of sturdy 9"x12" cardboard you can re-use cost $9.95.) The sturdier the paper, the better.

• **If you can't find printed layout sheets** or if your copy machine picks up non-repro blue lines, take a sheet of lined notepaper at least as big as printed pages will be, and with a black felt-tip marker and a ruler, go over the lines, making them dark and straight. Measure the *margins* for each page (p. 68), and draw them in.

Take this sheet to a copier and have 10 to 20 good, black copies run off.

To use it as a guide for paste-up, securely tape white paper over each xeroxed, lined sheet. So long as the lines show through, you're all set.

Paste up each page on the top sheet and when you're done, remove it. Keep the lined sheet for future use.

• **Rulers.** Although any ruler will do, the following types are especially helpful:

• *A metal ruler* ($5.50 for a 12" ruler) can be used with an X-acto knife (p. 152) to cut straight edges. (But don't get one with little ridges on the side.) Find one that measures in *picas* (p. 68) as well as inches. Once you get used to them, picas are easier to count.

• *A see-through plastic ruler* ($2.25) with grid lines printed across the surface can also help you straighten type.

• **Glue sticks** ($1 each) or one-coat rubber cement ($6.45 a quart). Rub a glue stick across the back of type and it'll stay tacky while you fiddle around straightening the type. However, there's a time limit. Once it sticks it's stuck, and hard to lift up.

If you use one-coat rubber cement, you won't have to rush to get each page straight before it dries. You've got all day or all week to straighten type and try this and that. Lift up the type anytime, and the cement always stays sticky.

Keep a bottle of *thinner* ($3.15 a pint) handy, and add it every so often to keep the cement from getting too thick. If type gets so stuck it won't budge, squirt thinner under the corners, and that'll loosen them.

Don't try any other kind of paste or glue. Most will stick through hell or high water, while you want something that lets you peel up the type after you've made a mistake. Some glue also ripples paper and ruins type. The fumes from spray glues can be downright dangerous.

• **Burnisher.** You'll use little plastic *burnishers* ($1.30 each) or rollers to rub the page to make everything stick. Or use the blunt end of a felt-tip marker.

• **Rubber cement pick-up** (75¢ each). Buy this to clean up excess rubber cement so it won't attract dirt. Or make your own pick-up by wadding together a ball of dried rubber cement.

• **Scissors.** The sharper the better.

• **Erasers.** A soft *kneaded rubber eraser* doesn't disintegrate all over the paper (40¢ each).

• **Pencils.** The ones that draw the lightest lines are best.

• **Frosted cellophane tape** ($2 a

## How to rub off transfer lettering

**1.** Set headlines on a separate sheet of paper, so you can play around with their placement on the layout sheet.

**2.** Draw a light blue or pencil guideline. Position the little guideline marks under each letter on the sheet of rub-off letters right over your blue or pencil guideline, so type won't be crooked.

**3.** Use a dull point (like the wrong end of a felt-tip marker) to rub the type from the sheet until the whole letter turns grey. Get all the corners and edges, but *don't* keep rubbing grey areas. When the rubbing is done, remove the plastic sheet of letters and tap the letter down with your finger.

**4.** This type is very delicate, so treat it gingerly – don't scratch or rub finished letters.

If a large chunk of the letter is missing, rub another identical one on top of it. If it's hopelessly crooked or botched, press some scotch tape on top and lift off the whole letter.

**5.** Position the next letter as close to the first as you can stand, with just a hair of space in between. (P. 134 explains headline spacing.)

When the headline's done, wax or cement the back of the paper, cut it out and put it on the page.

roll). Scotch makes a "Green Plaid" tape you can write on. Use tape with clean fingers and avoid getting the edge of the tape on type or a graphic etc. Steer clear of shiny tape; it picks up reflections.

• **Typing correction fluid** ($1.69 a bottle). Some are water soluable and easy to thin when they clog. For other brands, buy a bottle of *thinner*.

• **Black or red thin-tipped markers** ($1.19 each). Use these for drawing lines, cartoons, etc. When printed, red shows up as black. Ball-point pens draw lines that're smudgy and uneven. And blue pens *don't* show up well.

• **Rub-off transfer lettering** ($2.50 – $11.00 a sheet). If you don't have another way to typeset big headlines, stock up on these sheets of letters. P. 69 gives tips on choosing styles and sizes.

Unopened felt-tip pen rubs off letters

Rubber cement pick-up

Eraser

Pencil

Letters spaced too far apart

**far**

Scissors

Much better

**close**

Frosted cellophane tape

Fixing up broken letters

**on**

Glue stick

Rubber cement & thinner

Sheet of transfer lettering

Felt-tip marker

Typing correction fluid

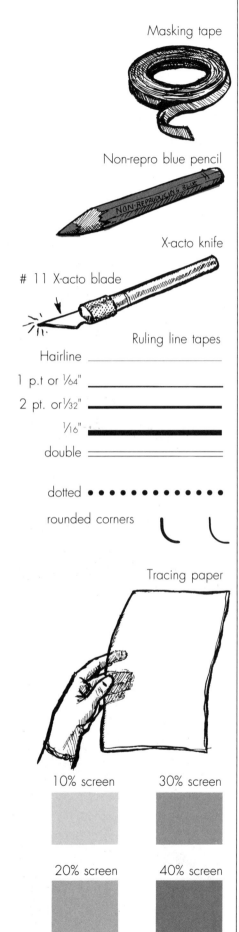

Masking tape

Non-repro blue pencil

X-acto knife

# 11 X-acto blade

Ruling line tapes

Hairline

1 p.t or 1/64"

2 pt. or 1/32"

1/16"

double

dotted

rounded corners

Tracing paper

10% screen

30% screen

20% screen

40% screen

## For a few pennies more

Add these inexpensive items to your shopping list, and paste-up will be easier and more accurate.

● **Masking or drafting tape** ($2-$3 a roll). Use this to fasten down the layout sheet; it won't rip the paper when you lift it off.

● **Non-repro blue pencils** (57¢ each) or pens (89¢ each). Both draw lines that don't show when printed.

● **#11 X-acto knives** ($1.35 each). This sharp little knife helps you cut smoothly, especially between lines of type or around graphics. So the blade won't break or scratch your table, cut over a cardboard surface. Keep extra blades handy ($2.95 for a package of 10), and replace them at the first sign of dullness.

● **Ruling (or border) tapes** ($1.89 a roll). If you don't have a computer that makes top-quality lines, these tapes will. Tapes come in widths from *hairline* to 1/8" or more. P. 75 explains why the fancy or superbold varieties will do you more harm than good.

The 1/64" (or 1-point) tape can drive you batty trying to get it straight, however. If it comes with a *carrier* (a band of clear tape on each side of the black line), it's easier to lay down straight; but the layout sheet must be 100% clean – no dirt, no hand-drawn blue lines, no nothing. A simple 1/32" (or 2-point) tape is your best bet.

● **Drawing pens** like Penstik or Nestler Tech-Liner ($1.50-$9 each). These give you sharp lines, and you can buy them in different widths.

● **Black or red paper.** If you're using a photo offset printer and want to make your own *silhouettes* (p. 154) where photos and other graphics go, use thin, sturdy paper, not the crummy "construction" variety. The protective black paper that comes in pads of acetate (p. 165) is perfect.

● **Sturdy tracing paper** (called *vellum* ($4.61 for 50 9"x12" sheets) will help you trace graphics or *size* photos (p. 162). It's also the cheapest way to make overlays (p. 166).

● **Sheets of screens, symbols** and other goodies ($3.89 a sheet) to spiff up cartoons, charts and other graphics. Companies that sell rub-off lettering (p. 151) also make sheets of just about every pattern you can imagine, plus all kinds of symbols, from dollar signs to little trees. Rummage through a catalogue for each brand. Computer programs also make screens and symbols (p. 51).

*Screens* look like grey, but they're actually black dots or lines. They come in shades from 10% (light grey) to 90% (a dark grey that looks black). Lighter shades (20% to 40%) are the most useful. They also come with dots of different sizes: An 85-line-per-inch screen has littler dots than a 46-line-per-inch screen. None, however, are as fine or useful as the printer's screen (p. 60). Never put store-bought screens on top of small type – the dots are so big they interfere with reading.

The screen is a thin layer of sticky plastic, attached to a backing sheet. Use it over an absolutely clean, smooth surface. If you put it over non-repro blue lines or paper edges, both could show up when printed.

To cut a screen the shape you want, cut a larger area with a sharp X-acto knife (but don't cut through the backing). Slip the knife blade under the plastic layer, lift it up, and place it on the graphic. Then cut the screen to a more precise shape with the knife, and throw away the excess (example A).

## Basic paste-up technique

### Get ready for layout

Find a work table that holds several pages at once, and clear the decks. Tape the layout sheets onto the table, and number each page. Place pages together that'll face each other when printed, such as pages 2 and 3. Even though pages will later be printed back-to-back, each page gets pasted on one side only of each layout sheet.

If the layout sheet is bigger than pages will be, measure the page size and draw its edges with a ruler and light pencil or *non-repro blue* (p. 60). Then measure *margins* (p. 68) from the top, bottom and sides of each page, and column widths (p. 131), and draw those guidelines with a ruler. Remember to put the *gutter* (p. 68) in between columns.

• Prepare the type for easy handling. With scissors, cut excess paper from article type and headlines. Cut ½ pica (⅛") away from the type itself, so it'll be easy for you or the printer to fix shadows cast by paper edges (pp. 58, 60). Since paper edges won't show up on printed copies (you hope), don't worry about cutting straight edges.

Then lay out the whole page (Chapter 16) before pasting anything down. Don't let page numbers or anything else wander into the outside ¼" edge of the page, unless you're *bleeding* graphics and backgrounds (p. 163).

## When layout is done

• Start paste-up from the bottom, so the bottom lines of type run evenly across the lower margin (or are consistently *un*even – p. 144).

Take each piece of type, turn it face down on a clean sheet of scrap paper, and coat the entire back with the glue stick or rubber cement – don't miss the corners. With a glue stick you'll need to work quickly. One-coat rubber cement lets you position and re-position the type as often as you like.

Put the type where it belongs, using the layout you did with xeroxed "proofs" (p. 139) as a guide. But don't rely on your naked eye to tell you if it's straight or crooked. Place a ruler vertically along the left-hand edge of type, to see if it lines up evenly with the rest of the column and with the guidelines on the layout sheet. *Caution*: Line up the edge of the *type itself* into a straight column, not the edge of the paper it's on.

Now place the ruler horizontally across the type, laying it straight along one of the layout sheet guidelines visible on either side of the type column.

With the ruler held straight on the page, see whether the lines of type follow the line of the ruler. If the type tilts a little, tug at its corners with one hand, while holding the ruler steady with the other.

• If the type you just put down is crooked, carefully peel it off the layout sheet and try again. If you're using a glue stick, you may need to re-apply a fresh coat of glue.

• Paste up the rest of the page the same way, piece by piece.

• Pasting two portions of type together into the same column of an article is tricky, because the distance be-

tween lines of type must be exactly the same (*line spacing*, p. 133). Hold a spare bit of type over the column, overlapping where the two pieces meet. Use the spare as a guide, so it shows how far apart type lines should be.

When you place two columns of an article next to each other, line up the top two lines of type with each other – see p. 144.

65 line-per-inch screen

85 line-per-inch screen

Printer's screen (120 lines per inch)

Patterned screen

Example A
Cutting a screen

Cut out each column of type

Straightening the type

Start pasting up from the bottom

BLACKS DENIED HOUSING

Getting the line spacing right

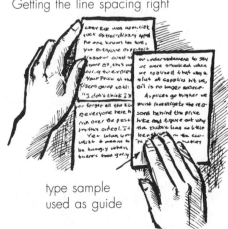
type sample used as guide

## The fine points

• **Correcting a typing mistake.** If just a word or so is wrong, retype the word (or so). If the correction is a different length, retype the whole line or end of paragraph. Cement (or wax – p. 156) the back of the correction and cut it out with an X-acto knife, cutting as close to the letters as you can get without touching. Place it over the mistake, hold a ruler across the corrected type as a guide, and use the blade of the X-acto knife to wiggle the correction around until it's straight.

To make sure a little correction stays in place try this instead: Hold the correction in place, and with the X-acto knife cut into both the correction and bottom sheet of type. While you cut the correction, you also make a hole in the type column where the correction goes. Then slip the correction into the little hole. This is called *stripping in*.

If you must replace a whole paragraph (or so), try this trick: If the first word of the correction is the same as the original, cut it from the correction with an X-acto knife; then use the original first word as a guide to get the spacing between the lines right.

• **If a headline is supposed to be centered** (p. 69), measure the center of the layout sheet or column, just above where the headline belongs, and make a mark.

Measure the width of the headline type, and then mark half that width out from your center mark, on either side. For example, if the headline is 3" wide, measure 1½" out from the center and make a mark. Use those marks to position the headline squarely in the middle.

• **Put boxes and other lines in place.** But first, draw straight lines lightly with pencil (or *non-repro blue* – p. 152) where lines should go.

When the type's pasted in place, clean the area that needs a line, and cut away any overlapping paper. If you don't have ruling tapes (p. 152), draw each line carefully with a fine marker or drawing pen and a ruler. If you mess up, paste a strip of clean paper over the botched-up line and try again.

If you're using a ruling tape, unroll a length of it longer than the finished line will be. Place it straight over the pencil line, with the ends of the tape extending beyond the line's ends. Then pull the tape taut, and with your thumb, press the ends down. If the line's crooked,

pick it up and try again.

Don't rub the line, or it'll wiggle. Instead, tap the tape every inch or so with your fingertip. Slice off the excess at either end with an X-acto knife.

## What about photos?

As Chapter 7 explains, a printing press doesn't pick up greys, and neither do most mimeo machines or copiers. If you lay a photo directly on the layout sheet, it'll come out *high contrast* – dark greys will turn black, and light greys will be bleached white. To see grey, have the photo *halftoned*, so it's full of tiny black and white dots that appear grey to the naked eye.

While you're at it, get the photo reduced or enlarged, so its sides (or a *cropped* area, p. 160) line up exactly with one or more type columns. P. 144 explains why and p. 162 tells how.

• **If you're using metal plate offset printing,** the printer will halftone photos. Draw a black or red *keyline* – a rectangle of thin, straight lines showing where the photo edges go, lined up neatly with column widths. Some printers prefer that you cut a black or red paper rectangle (a *knockout* or *silhouette*) and put it where the photo goes; its edges actually become those of the printed photo. (P. 60 explains why.) If an edge is crooked or ragged, repair it with ruling tape. P. 162 tells how to figure the exact size the keyline or rectangle should be.

• **Do you want a border line around the photo?** If the line's at least ½2" (or 2 points) wide, make a box with ruling tape (p. 152) or your computer right on the page mechanical. The printer will *double-burn* the photo into that border (*burns* explained on p. 166). If the border's narrower than ½2" or 2 points, the printer must scratch it into the negative. In either case, explain what you want clearly on the mechanical in non-repro blue – and again in a note.

• **For mimeoing, copying and paper plate offset,** you'll paste a copy or *velox* print of the photo on the mechanical. P. 58 gives the details.

## Final details

• **Burnish the whole page.** When pages are all laid out and straight as a pin, cover each page mechanical with a sheet of *tracing vellum* (p. 152) or other sturdy paper, and vigorously rub it with the *burnisher* (p. 150). Just to be safe,

Stripping in corrections

Centered headline
guideline marks

center

Putting down
ruling tape

## Re-ordering the pages for printing

Pages aren't printed in the same order as you read them.

**1.** To see for yourself, fold blank sheets of paper to get a little book the length of your newsletter or paper. Each folded sheet makes four pages – two on each side. Number each page and pull apart the "newsletter" to see which pages are printed next to each other. Use this as a guide.

Printers will often put pages in the right order for you. But if you're printing the paper via a cheaper method, you'll do it yourself. Here's how:

**2. Separate the pages** you put together for layout (except the centerfold – that never changes) and reposition them the way they'll be printed.

Match up page 1 with page 8 for an eight-pager, page 2 with page 7, etc. Odd-numbered pages (1, 3, 5, etc.) are always on the right-hand side; even-numbered pages (2, 4, 6, etc.) are always on the left.

**3. To put pages together** place a ruler across each double-page. Jiggle them around until the bottom margins of both pages line up. Then tape them together up the middle.

burnish every page again before taking it to the printer.

• **Clean each finished page** with typing correction fluid, the eraser, and the rubber cement pick-up. Don't rub over typewriter type or rub-off headlines, however – you'll just destroy them. Dab extra rubber cement or glue under any corners that aren't firmly stuck down.

Protect each page by taping a clean sheet of paper or tracing paper over it.

• **The last proofing.** You've laid out and pasted up the mechanicals, so they're ready to be printed. Well, not so fast. While arranging and rearranging type on each page, you could easily have switched paragraphs, left something out, or lost a correction. At the last minute, all your hard work can be bamboozled.

Proofread every finished page before rushing to print it. (Guidelines on p. 135.) Keep pages flat, and on the way to the printer, sandwich them between sheets of cardboard.

p. 2     p. 3

Cutting pages apart with knife & ruler

Facing pages 10 & 11

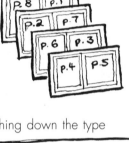

8-page newsletter

12-page newsletter

Burnishing down the type

Keyline for photo

Knockout for photo

Border line around photo

Hand waxer

Kneaded rubber eraser

Drawing board

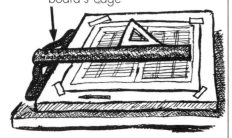
T-square & triangle

T-stem flat along
board's edge

Light table

# Tools to make life easier

The following tools are more expensive than the basic ones. But once you learn to handle them, you can do paste-up twice as fast, with half the frustration. If you plan to publish regularly, consider a one-shot investment in these time-savers:

## A waxer is wiser

Once you have a waxer, you'll swear off glue sticks or rubber cement. Wax is cleaner and easier to apply. And it'll *never* get type so stuck down you can't lift it up again – even years later.

A simple hand waxer costs around $40. To keep it constantly half-filled, buy extra wax ($3.50 a box). To use it, lay type or graphics face down on clean scrap paper – and we mean *clean*. If you get wax on type, it can destroy it.

Roll the hand waxer quickly across the back of the type or graphic in one direction, covering the whole area. (If you're too slow, you might burn thin paper, making it transparent.)

Cut out the waxed type, following the suggestions on p. 153. The type will be lightly sticky, so it won't fly all over the place every time you breathe. Now lay out the page. Since type is already waxed, you needn't lift it up again when you're ready to paste up.

When you're done, burnish (p. 154) each piece, so it'll really stay put. The motion heats up the wax and seals it.

The only way to clean sticky excess wax off the layout sheet is with a kneaded rubber eraser (p. 150).

## Drawing board, T-square & triangle

This trio straightens pages so nicely, you no longer need a grid on (or under) your layout sheet (p. 150). Anyone in your group who studied drafting knows how to use these tools.

• **The drawing board.** Buy one larger than your layout sheets, with at least one metal edge ($37.50). Put something under the far end, so the board tilts slightly toward you. Some boards come equipped with a horizontal guide that moves up and down the surface. Use that guide as you would a T-square.

Place the layout sheet on the board, with the metal edge to your left. (If you're left-handed, keep the metal edge to your right.)

• **The T-square.** Buy one with a stem at least as long as your drawing board is wide. The plastic ones ($6 for a 24" one) work okay, but the expensive metal ones are more accurate and can be used with an X-acto knife for cutting ($19.75 for a 24" one).

Put the stem across the layout sheet, and fit the "T" top snugly along the board's metal edge. The trick to using a T-square is to always hold the T-top so firmly against the metal edge of the board that the stem always gives you a perfectly straight horizontal guide across the layout sheet.

Sliding the T down, put the stem along the bottom edge of the layout sheet. Use the T-square to get the paper straight, then tape the sheet onto the board with masking tape.

Measure and mark the top and bottom margins. Hold the T-stem across each spot as you draw a guideline with pencil or non-repro blue. As you position type on the layout sheet, move the T-stem over it to see if it's straight.

• **The triangle.** Don't put the T-square along the top of the board to straighten columns of type vertically; most boards aren't perfectly square.

Buy a plastic *triangle* with a perfect 90-degree right angle, and you're in business. A big 8" or 10" triangle is far more useful than its little cousins, and costs around $2.65.

Hold the T-square tight along the metal edge of the board, and rest the triangle snugly on the T's stem. The vertical edge gives you a perfect line up and down the page.

Use the triangle as a guide, first to mark where side margins and columns go, and then to keep columns straight. As you slide the triangle back and forth along the T-stem, make sure the T doesn't slip.

## A light table

A light table shines upward through the paper, so you can clearly see what's underneath. It'll help you correct typesetting mistakes (p. 154), or paste up without using blue guidelines. It comes in various sizes: A 16"x18" one runs at about $140. Or make your own light table out of a horizontal pane of frosted glass with lighting underneath.

Draw or buy a grid with dark lines (p. 150), and tape it onto the glass. Tape the layout sheet for each page over the grid, and the lines show through as a guide.

# 18. Graphics & special techniques

## Why bother with graphics?

**A** *graphic* is a picture – a photo, cartoon or arrangement of type and symbols – that helps tell your story. The better the graphic works, the fewer words the story needs. After all, people are more apt to look at (and enjoy) pictures than a long, dry-looking article.

Graphics also dramatize key points in the story, and show the real people involved. These visual images stick in people's minds, helping them "picture" – and remember – what you're talking about.

Every page or double-page needs a graphic or two. If you're empty-handed, don't despair. The raw materials for the perfect graphic could be hidden in your files – or even the wastebasket.

## Where do graphics come from?

### Photos

Chapter 12 explains how to take exciting, informative photos – or steer a photographer down the right path. Whether you shoot original photos or clip them (p. 159), this chapter tells how to turn a good – or mediocre – photo into a terrific graphic.

### Charts & graphs

These help readers make sense of facts and figures. Rather than dig through complex numbers, where you could easily misread one billion to say a million, charts and graphs show you at a glance that the spending line goes up or that defense gets a third of the pie chart. Example C on p. 159 shows three main kinds of graphs.

Magazines often take it from there – transforming charts into fanciful illustrations where jagged lines on a heart monitor show our health ups and downs, bars become highways, and pie charts become round spaceships. Some get so carried away you can hardly tell what they're talking about.

Examples A and B show simple ways to spiff up charts and graphs. To fit a photo into the bottom of a line chart like example B, *silhouette* it (p. 165).

• **If you've got a computer**, it's worth buying a program like Cricket Graph (p. 54) to whip any set of numbers into a nifty graph. Just choose the graph you want, feed your numbers into a table for that graph, push the right

WHO VOTES IN AMERICA

Example A

Teenagers  Young adults  Middle-aged men  women  Senior citizens

Example B

HOME OWNERSHIP

1940 1950 1960 1970 1980 1990

$ex

These cartoons were all drawn by factory workers

Rick Flores, UAW Local 977

THIS REMINDS ME OF THE FACTORY WHERE I WORK!

Ken Owen, UAW Local 1999

UH,OH! WE'VE GOT A PROBLEM. THE EMPLOYEES ARE REALLY GETTIN' INVOLVED IN THIS JOINTNESS THING!

Jim Ehlinger, UAW Local 94

"Hey, mom! Break out the tranquilizers, Pop's line is on speed-up again!"

---

1. 1 pica = $500

2. $\frac{\$4,600}{\$500} = 9\frac{1}{5}$

3.

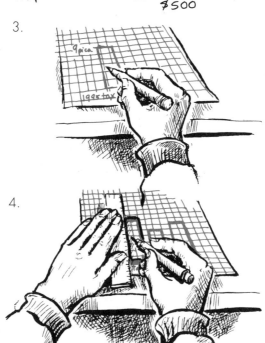

9 pica

1995 tax

4.

---

buttons, and presto! Your numbers become pictures. Then mess around with shading and other details on the computer screen until you like the way it looks (example D).

• **If you have to make graphs by hand,** keep a hand calculator and ruler handy for figuring. Use graph or layout paper with non-repro blue lines (p. 150) for plotting out the exact placement of lines and/or bars.

### Symbols

Take a big, bold dollar sign and use it to replace the "s" in "Sex," and you've made a statement. Look through magazines and sheets of symbols (p. 152) for other images to play with.

### Cartoons

Keep people laughing while they're learning or sharing, and they'll feel great about your group and its goals. Who's the cartoonist? In every group there's

---

## How to make a simple bar chart

**1.** Pick a number that will equal 1 *pica* (p. 68) on your chart – $500 for example.

**2.** Divide that number into each figure you want the chart to show. That tells you how many picas tall each bar should be. If you want the first bar to stand for $4,600, for example, divide $500 into $4,600 to get 9⅕. That means Bar 1 is just over 9 picas tall.

**3.** With a light or non-repro blue pencil, draw a bar slightly more than 9 picas tall on graph or layout paper. Label it ("1995 tax," for example) and move to the next bar.

**4.** Once all the bars are plotted out, use a felt-tip or technical pen and ruler – or border tapes (p. 152) – to make each bar straight and even. Typeset or type the labels, paste them and any pictures on, and you're done.

---

someone who doodles – or scribbles graffiti on walls. That could be just the person. Ask around; or hold a contest.

Even a primitive stick drawing can drive a point home in an amusing way. Encourage everyone to help think up cartoon ideas. Meanwhile, the budding cartoonist suddenly becomes an activist, develops a latent talent, and improves by leaps and bounds.

### Tips for cartoon drawing

• **Always use a pen** (preferably a drawing pen) or brush with black ink. Blue pens won't work.

• **Pencil won't show up either,** unless it's dark and drawn on grainy paper from an art supply store. Have pencil drawings *halftoned* (p. 154) to capture the greys, and add black highlights with a pen on the drawing itself or *overlay*.

• **For shading,** buy sheets of *screens* (p. 152) or put shapes to be screened on an *overlay* (p. 166).

---

# Clip & collect

### Cartoons & illustrations

• Collect a file of cartoons, clipped from everywhere. When in need, pull

one out and change the caption to whatever's perfect for the article. Rarely does a big time cartoonist worry about reprints for a small non-profit paper – p. 33. Or take a sheet of tracing paper and draw a similar cartoon yourself.

If the drawing has colors, it's a differ-

---

ent bird altogether. Run it through a quality office copy machine, fiddling with the "lighter – darker" controls to make the colors come out white, black or grey. If you get a good copy reprint that, *not* the colored version. If the copy looks awful you're sunk – unless re-touching with a black pen and typing-correction fluid will revive it.

● Subscribe to a graphics service. Some of the best are:

● *Carol Simpson cartoons*; 323 South East Ave., Oak Park, IL 60302.

● *Huck-Konopacki* labor cartoons; P.O. 3511, Madison, WI 53704-0511.

● *Bülbül*; P.O. Box 4100, Mountain View, CA 94040.

● *Ricardo Flores Graphics Packet*; P.O. Box 1044, Marion Indiana 46953.

● *Impact Visuals*; P.O. Box 404830, Brooklyn, NY 11240-4830 (p. 101).

● Or keep handy some "clip art." This can give you turkeys for Thanks-giving or a funny man holding an empty sign, which you fill in. While many look silly and bland, a little imagination can make most work – like example E.

Art supply stores usually stock clip art books, and computer stores sell clip art for use with desktop publishing (p. 54). Or write for a catalogue. Try:

● *Dover Publications*, 31 E. 2nd St., Mineola, N.Y. 11501. Clip art books start at $4.50.

● *CMS*, P.O. Box 5955, Berkeley, CA 94705. Each $28 "theme book" offers about 50 illustrations. Clip art on com-puter disks costs $79.

● *Dynamic Graphics*, 6000 N. Forest Park Drive, P.O. Box 1901, Peoria, IL 61656-1901. Art in book or computer disk form. Prices start at $49.50.

## Clipped photos

Don't bother clipping printed color photos from other papers. Reprinting them will give you a dark, weird mass.

Since every printed black-and-white photo is already *halftoned* (p. 60), in theory it can be clipped and reprinted, as is. In reality the quality will slip, espe-cially if it's on junky paper.

Rather than take a chance, keep track of the publication you clipped each photo from (with page number), so you can ask for an original print along with reprinting permission (p. 32). Some papers charge non-profit groups a mini-mal cost. But fees for nationally syndi-cated photos (AP, for example) amount to $85 or more a shot.

Example C · Bar charts

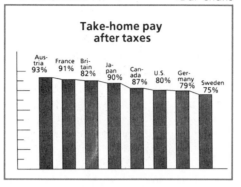

Take-home pay after taxes

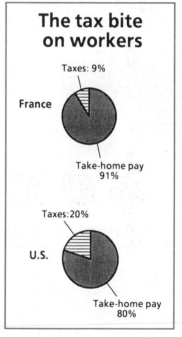

**Take-home pay after taxes**

Austria 93%
France 91%
Japan 90%
Canada 87%
Britain 82%
U.S. 80%
Germany 79%
Sweden 75%

Line graph

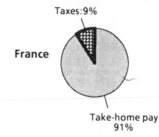

**Tax burden on workers**

Pie charts

The tax bite on workers

Example D

Example E

Putting the same cartoon to different uses

STILL NO COVERALLS?

THIS WAS US HALFWAY THROUGH OUR LAST CONTRACT

Carol Simpson cartoon

DON'T WORRY—IT'S AN OFF-THE-ROAD VEHICLE.

THE ECONOMY

Example F

**James Leo Rises Again**

## the People Pledge!

Example G

Standard photo given new meaning

Example H

Example I

Work of a head-collector

## TAX DEBATE!

High-contrast line shot

If you can't get the original, don't enlarge a photo clipped from the daily paper; the dots get ridiculously big. And don't ask the printer to halftone a clipped photo. You could end up with a crazy pattern, like example H.

### Fiddling with an old stand-by

Grab an old photo from your files, and transform it into an exciting new graphic by pasting your own commentary right on top. That's how examples F (p. 159) and G were born. Or collect heads – newspaper photos of politicians, landlords, polluters and others who deserve ridicule. Make editorial cartoons from stick drawings topped by the appropriate heads (example I). All you need is a clever idea. (If you're worried about libel, consult p. 29.)

# Make the photos work for you

### Oh no! We used color film

This isn't the disaster it used to be. Today, a good printer can make a decent black-and-white print from a color photo – with one big exception: red comes out looking like black. That means a dark face with redish highlights will be solid black. If you can't print in full color (p. 62) and key elements are red-against-black, find another photo. When in doubt, ask your printer.

### Crop, crop, crop

• **To improve a bad photo.** Many decent photos look boring because the photographer was too far away. The main character or event looks miniscule, while the photo's full of distracting details and dead space.

Don't despair. You can make a winner out of almost any photo by *cropping* away everything that isn't needed.

• **To improve a good photo.** Crop to give the viewer a real close, intimate feel for the subject. Once you've zeroed in on the bare essentials, blow them up as big as possible.

You'll also crop to make photos the right shape for the page layout.

• **How cropping works.** When you crop, you slice extra inches from the top, bottom and/or sides of the picture – without damaging the photo itself. You'd be surprised how much you can cut. Keep the faces and gestures, and just enough of the surroundings to put them in place. But chop off legs, pot-bellies, and even backs and tops of heads, and no one will miss them.

Keep handy two "L's," cut from cardboard. Lay them over each photo to see what it looks like cropped various ways (example J). If that's too much trouble, just place blank sheets of paper over each edge of the photo.

• **Grease pencils.** Use these to write crop marks or other instructions in the margins of photos. They write easily on photographic surfaces, and the writing can be wiped off when you re-use the photo (53¢ each).

• **Make crop marks.** If the photo has no white margins around it, paste it onto a large white sheet of paper.

First decide where to crop the photo. Then place a ruler over it, either straight up and down or straight across, marking where one side should be chopped off. But *don't* massacre the photo by cutting or drawing across the image. Just put a little mark alongside the photo area where the ruler hits the margin. Do the same for the other three sides.

You'll end up with four marks, one on each side of the photo. Point little arrows toward the picture area you'll keep, as example L illustrates.

To keep an edge of the photo as is (uncropped), you still need a crop mark – just continue the edge of the photo into the margin, like example M on p. 163.

### Halftone or high contrast?

Most photos are set aside to be *halftoned* (p. 60) so the greys will show. But how'd you like a dramatic black-and-white version of a dancer or basketball play? Just paste a photo directly on the layout sheet without halftoning it, and the greys will disappear. Or ask the printer for a *line shot* (p. 162).

Warning: You're taking your chances if the photo isn't simple and dramatic. If you're not sure how high-contrast will work, run the photo through a copy machine (without the "photo" setting) first, and see how it looks.

### Stupid backgrounds

Want to erase the background? Or

make part of the photo – someone's head, for example – pop right out of the background, like example K?

• **For photo offset printing,** you need a custom-made *silhouette*. If your printer handles the paste-up, tape a sheet of tracing paper over the photo, and sketch an outline of the area you want. Add a note, explaining that this area should be lifted (or isolated) from the background (with a silhouette).

Then figure how much the photo must be reduced or enlarged (p. 162) so the outlined area fits on the page. P. 165 explains how to save money by making the silhouette yourself.

• **For other kinds of printing,** get rid of an annoying background by cutting the figures out with a sharp X-acto knife (p. 152). Or paint typing correction fluid over the whole background. To avoid ruining the original photo, make a copy (on a copier with a "photo" setting) or *velox* print (explained below) before you attack it, and tinker with the print. Use typing correction fluid labelled "for copies." Good luck!

### If you're sending the photo to a printer

Attach this information to each photo: 1. Where it goes (page, placement); 2. Name of your publication; 3. *H-T* if it'll be halftoned. Otherwise it's a line shot. 4. Percent reduction or enlargement (100% or *s.s.* means same size); 5. Should it be cropped? Where?

### For mimeo, copiers, etc.

Once you've cropped the photo, have a copy made the right size.

• **Fancy copiers** like the Xerox 5028 have a "photo" key that helps them pick up the greys in photos – including color shots. If the page is full of paper edges and non-repro blue lines, copy the page first without the photo setting, so those distractions disappear. Then reduce or enlarge the photo, paste it down, and print the full run using the "photo" setting.

• **Paper or plastic plate offset and mimeo machines** won't pick up grey tones unless you have the photo *halftoned* (p. 60). Some stencil-cutters (p. 57) can halftone photos.

Otherwise, your best bet is to stop by a printer or photocopy shop to get a *velox* print. (Make sure you've *sized* each photo before making a print – p. 162.) A 5"x 8" velox costs around $8. If

Example J

Photo's too complicated

Background removed

Cropped version

Example K

Example L

Original photo    Cropped photo

crop marks

Cutting the photo or xerox to fit the layout

you'll be printing with an offset printer (p. 60) on good paper (not newsprint), ask for a velox with a 110-line screen. Otherwise, an 85-line screen will do.

• **To paste a cropped photo** on the layout sheet  you must – gasp! – physically cut the photo (or velox print). The crop marks will guide you. Use a ruler to measure and draw a light line straight across the photo where it should be cropped. That's where you'll cut.

Hold a metal ruler steady along that line, and cut with a sharp X-acto knife (p. 152). (Hold the ruler on the *inside* of the line, so it covers the good part of the photo. Then if your knife slips, it won't slash someone's face.)

### Sprucing up photos for copiers & mimeo

Photos are so valuable, it's worth printing them with mimeo and copier machines, even when the quality is embarrassing. You'll get the best results from simple photos, with sharp black-white contrasts.

The worse the quality is, the more you can doctor the original without being obvious. If the photo shows a light coat in front of a white wall, the subtle

Original

Printed with a cheap method

How it can be spruced up

Line shot

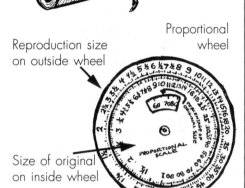

Grease pencil

Proportional wheel

Reproduction size on outside wheel

Size of original on inside wheel

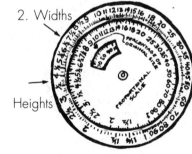

1. Measure the widths

6⅝"

8"

Layout sheet

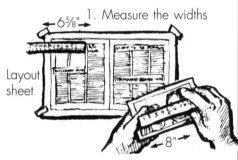

2. Widths

Heights

3. Checking the heights

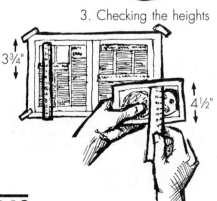

3¾"

4½"

difference between the coat and wall could disappear when printed. But not if you draw a tiny outline around the coat, with a fine black pen. Consider darkening the letters in picket signs, too.

Likewise, dark hair might merge into a dark background – unless you scratch a tiny white outline around the hair with an X-acto knife.

If you clip a black-and-white photo from a magazine or newsletter, your machine might not pick up all the tiny dots. If you enlarge the clipped photo a bit, it'll do better.

# Making graphics fit

### Leave space in the layout

Chances are, you'll blow up or shrink graphics to make them work just right on the page. Most modern office copiers can reduce or enlarge graphics, so if you've got the right kind of copier handy, experiment with different sizes as you do layout. If not, p. 162 shows how to use a *proportional wheel* to *size* each graphic. Put it aside, with a note telling the printer how to reduce or enlarge it.

How do you know how much space to leave on the layout sheet? The rule of thumb is: If the graphic – or the part of it you plan to use – is tall, leave a tall space. If it's fat, leave a wide space. If it's square, leave a square-ish space. To be more precise than that, you must do some figuring. (See box below.)

### Line shots

These are cartoons, drawings and type you reduce or enlarge without making a halftone. Printers charge around $5 to $10 per line shot or *photostat*. It may be worth taking line shots to a quick-copy shop instead – they'll reduce or enlarge them on a copier for around 10 cents a shot. But first, see if they make high-quality copies.

### Try a proportional wheel

Although you could also use a hand calculator, this wheel is custom-made to help you quickly figure the exact percentage photos and other graphics must be reduced or enlarged to fit in the layout. It costs $4 at an art supply store.

---

## How to use a proportional wheel

**1.** Measure widths of the photograph (or other graphic) and the layout sheet space. To use the proportional wheel, consider the photograph (or graphic) *size of original* and the space on the layout sheet *reproduction size*. If you cropped the photo, the *cropped* dimensions are the *original size*.

Since you normally must line up photographs within one or more columns, figure widths (the least flexible measurement) first. *Reproduction size* width will be one, two or more columns plus the *gutter* (p. 68) between columns.

Let's suppose the *original* photo (or cropped area) is 8" wide and the layout (*reproduction*) space is two columns, which for your style means 6⅝" wide. Write down and label each measurement so you won't get confused.

**2.** Match up the two widths on the proportional wheel. Find the photograph width (8") on the inside (*size of original*) wheel. The varying distance between numbers may throw you off at first, so take your time.

Hold that place while you find the 6⅝" (*reproduction size*) on the outside wheel. Turn the wheel until the numbers are up against each other.

Now look in the window at the *percentage of original size* arrow, and write down that number – in this case, 83%. This tells you the percentage the photo should be reduced.

But if the width is reduced to 83%, the height is reduced to 83% also.

**3.** Check the heights at the percentage. Keeping the wheel steady at 83%, measure the height of the original photograph (or cropped area). Find that number on the inside wheel. What number is directly above it on the outside wheel? You'll find that if the photograph is 4½" tall (*size of original*), its height on the layout sheet (*reproduction size*) at 83% comes to 3¾".

Measure the 3¾" height on your layout sheet to see if this fits. If not, either rearrange the layout, or re-crop the photo. P. 163 explains how.

## Does a cropped photo fit?

First, crop the photo as tightly as possible. Be brutal. Then use a proportional wheel to see if the cropped photo will fit perfectly in the space you left for it. If it doesn't, here's what to do:

3½"

4½"

Only 3½ inches space

---

### What if a cropped photo is too tall?

You'll have to shrink the photo a little more and crop the sides a little wider to make it line up evenly with column edges. Here's how:

Suppose the cropped area of your photo is 4½" tall. It'll end up 3¾" tall after you reduce it 83% to fit within two columns. But the space on the layout sheet is just 3½" tall.

**1.** Reduce it smaller to fit. Find 4½" (the height of the photo's cropped area) on the *size of original* inside wheel, and move it around until it matches up with 3½" (the height of the layout space) on the *reproduction size* outside wheel. That gives you a new *percentage of original size* – in this case, 78%.

**2.** Look up the width of the layout space at that percentage on your wheel. If a two-column space on the layout sheet is 6⅝" wide, hold the wheel steady while you find 6⅝" on the outside *reproduction size* circle. What number does it hit on the inside *size of original* wheel? In this case, 8½".

**3.** Re-crop the width of the photo. Since you now know that an 8½"-wide photo will fit evenly into the layout space, crop the sides of the photo again, to 8½" wide. That means adding more width than you wanted. If the photo is too narrow (8" wide, for example), rearrange the layout or find another graphic.

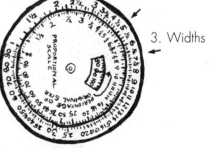

5"

1. 5" tall space on layout sheet

---

### What if the cropped photo is too short?

**1.** Try to re-crop the photo to make it fit. Suppose the layout sheet space is 5" tall, but the cropped photo will be only 3¾" tall when reduced 83% to fit a two-column space. Hold the proportional wheel steady at 83%, and look up the 5" tall area on the *reproduction size* outer circle. What does it hit on the inner *size of original* wheel? In this case 6". Is the original photo at least 6" tall? If so, crop it again, adding height to make the cropped area 6" tall. That's it. Skip steps 2 and 3.

**2.** If the original photo is too short, then start all over again, matching the heights. Look up the 5" height of the layout space on the outer *reproduction size* wheel, and match it against the entire height of the photo on the *size of original* inner wheel. If the whole photo is 5½" tall, they match at 91% (*percentage of original size*).

Hold the wheel steady at 91% while you look up the width of the layout sheet area – 6⅝" – on the *reproduction size* outer circle. What does it hit on the inner wheel? Just about 7¼".

**3.** Crop the width of the photo mercilessly to make it fit. In this case, you must make the photo area just 7¼" wide. You may have to leave out a person or two to get the photo that skinny, but your only other choice is to completely re-do the layout.

Short photo

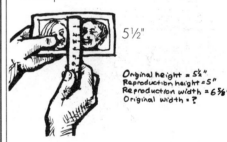

5½"

Original height = 5½"
Reproduction height = 5"
Reproduction width = 6⅝"
Original width = ?

2. Matching heights

3. Widths

---

## Special tricks for photo offset printing

These techniques work only with metal plate offset printing, because they involve a *negative*. Review p. 60 in the printing chapter to see how it works.

In each case, tape tracing paper over the page layout, and on the tracing paper sketch out exactly where everything goes and how it's shaped. If you're pasting up yourself, p. 165 explains more.

### The bleed

Suppose you want a photo or other picture to go right off the edge of the paper. Or how about putting a grey or colored background over the whole page, including the margins? Normally a printer must keep all ink at least ¼"

<u>Example M</u>
Photo with crop marks

For p. 11
Top left
Make halftone
at 91% +
crop as
indicated

7¼"

5½"

Necessary information

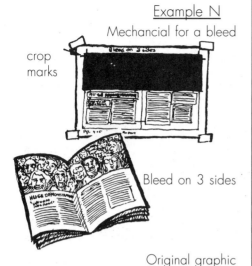

Example N
Mechancial for a bleed

crop
marks

Bleed on 3 sides

Original graphic

Reverse                    Flop

Screened at 30%

Screen abuse

---

from the edge of the paper.

But pages are often printed on large sheets that are later folded and *trimmed* (cut) to the right size. Find out from your printer if this is the case. On the side(s) that'll be trimmed, a picture or colored background can *bleed* to the edge. How? If the picture or background extends slightly beyond the page area, it'll be printed that way. It's then chopped off when the paper is trimmed.

Caution: Anything you plan to bleed must stick out ⅛" beyond the page area – going right across the margin and ⅛" beyond. If a photo will bleed, crop it at least ⅛" from its edge, so there's ⅛" extra to trim.

● If you're doing your own paste-up, use layout sheets bigger than the actual page, and mark the page edges with *crop marks* (example N).

### The flop

Ask the printer to *flop* the negative of a halftone or line shot, and it'll be turned around so the image is backwards. It costs nothing, and may help your layout. Warning: don't flop anything with type in it, because it'll come out backwards.

Don't get a flop confused with a *reverse*. A reverse gives you a negative image like a camera negative.

### Screens

To make type or graphics come out grey instead of black, ask the printer to *screen* them – to replace the black with a dot pattern that looks grey (p. 60). But first, check the cost – some printers charge $8 per screen. If you're printing with colored ink, screens give you lighter shades of the color (p. 147).

How about getting a screen slapped over boxed type, or over the whole page? On tracing paper taped over the page, outline and shade the areas to be made grey. Specify how dark the screen should be – 10% or more. So people can read the type, don't use a screen darker than 30%.

### Beware of screen abuse

Sooner or later, someone in your group will look with despair at a page full of article type, grumbling that there's no room for a graphic, and then be struck with a brilliant idea: Why not just *screen* the graphic and print it over the type area? This is proof positive that a little bit of knowledge is dangerous. Printing a screened graphic over an arti-

cle will destroy both. You won't see the graphic clearly, and you'll make it hard – or annoying – to read the type.

Yes, there's an exception or two. If the type is headline-size and short and the screened graphic is a simple symbol or shape – and you have space on the page to keep it all from looking crowded – it can work.

## Dropouts, knockouts & overburns

These can make your paper look super, but they do cost extra.

● **Dropouts.** Wouldn't it be nice to throw a white headline into the dark background of a photo? Or to put white type within a screened or black band for *topic heads* (p. 74)? Have the type set normally – black on white – and ask the printer to *drop* the type *out* from the dark or screened area. Just make sure the whole area is dark, so the white type will stand out.

Think twice before dropping out small type, however. It could be mighty hard – or annoying – to read. If you take the plunge, use a bolder version of type than usual, so the ink surrounding the words won't fill in the letters. As for small serif type (p. 69), forget it. Little serifs and other skinny areas of the type could disappear.

● **Overburn or doubleburn.** How can you slip black type (or a dark image) into a light area within a photo or graphic? Ask the printer to *doubleburn* both images into the same plate – like a double exposure. Show exactly where the type goes on tracing paper taped over the photo or graphic.

● **Knockouts.** Suppose you're printing with black plus a colored ink (p. 146), and want a colored headline stuck into a black-and-white photo or a screened background. Since printers' ink is transparent, the background will show through the colored headline – unless you *knock it out* of the background. That means the printer *drops* it *out* of the background first so it's plain space, then prints the type into that space with a colored ink.

## Special shapes

To make a photo circular or any other shape, sketch the shape you want on tracing paper taped over the photo. Put *crop marks* (p. 160) on the photo itself, showing where the shape's outside edges will fall; Or make the top of the photo follow the line of a chart, so the

**164**

photo becomes part of the chart, like example B on page 158.

# Paste-up for special tricks

## Extra supplies you need

● **Acetate.** This plastic sheet is the Cadillac of overlays (p. 166). You could use tracing *vellum* (p. 152), but acetate is sturdier and completely transparent. ($5.25 for 25 9"x12" sheets.)

● **Rubylith or amberlith.** This is a big sheet (or roll) of expensive acetate, with a transparent colored coating that peels off. Amberlith is orange and rubylith is red. Use either one for special overlays and silhouettes – It's beautiful stuff to work with. ($2.50 per 20"x24" sheet.)

● **Special marker that draws on acetate.** It also repairs scratches on rubylith or amberlith ($2.25 each).

● **Register marks.** These marks help position overlays more accurately than drawing your own. One roll will last forever ($4.50).

## To isolate a figure from its background

As p. 60 explains, photos are *half-toned* separately and added to the page at the negative or plate stage. If you put a black or red *silhouette* (p. 60) on the layout sheet, it's photographed as a *window* on the printer's negative. The printer places the photo negative onto the page negative and the photo shows through the window.

Normally the window is the size and shape of the cropped photo. But if the silhouette is the shape of just one figure in the photo, the window will be, too. The black of the printer's negative will block out the rest of the photo.

To silhouette part of a photo and/or get rid of the background, tape down the photo (or other graphic). Cut a portion of amberlith (or rubylith) big enough to cover the whole photo. Tape the amberlith securely on top, with the dull side up. (To make sure the dull side is up, scratch a corner; the colored coating should come off.)

With a sharp X-acto knife, trace the exact outline of the figure you want. Cut lightly enough to scratch the top coating without going through the acetate.

When you're done cutting, peel off the colored coating, starting with outside edges. If you've cut correctly the

Type dropped out of photo

Good registration

Bad registration

Type burned into photo

Rubylith sheet

Special marker

Roll of register marks

Acetate pad

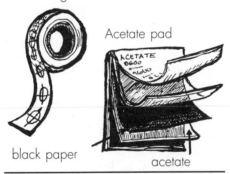

black paper

acetate

Silhouette made from rubylith

Rubylith

Special shape original photo

Printed photo

silhouette

inside will stay put, becoming a colored sihouette of the figure. Repair scratches with an acetate marker.

Paste this silhouette onto the layout sheet, and if you must snip off excess acetate, don't cut close to the figure. If it's the wrong size, have the silhouette reduced or enlarged. Mark on the original photo that its size must be changed by the same percentage.

## Special shapes

Put a black or red *silhouette* (see above) the shape of a "2" where a photo goes on the layout sheet, and the printed photo will be shaped like a "2." Make it a filled-in circle, and you'll get a circular photo. The photo must be enlarged or reduced to cover the whole

When screen or color doesn't overlap with black

transparent paper guide

Layout sheet for 2 colors

When screen and/or color overlap with black

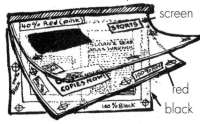

Overlays for second color & screen

Color separations

yellow

blue

red

black

Full color

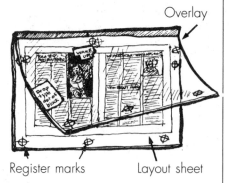

Overlay

Register marks          Layout sheet

shape. The part of the photo that doesn't fit into the "2" or other fancy shape gets blocked out by the black of the negative. So make sure your fancy moves don't block out something crucial, like the head of your group's president.

### To get burns, dropouts & knockouts

• **Use an overlay.** Fasten tracing vellum or acetate (p. 165) over the layout sheet with masking tape. The printer makes a second negative from the overlay, so there's an extra cost. Write clear instructions in the margins of the overlay.

• **Register marks.** Put black or red *register marks* in several places on the layout sheet, just outside the page area. Register marks are crosses you buy (p. 165) or make yourself with a ruler and marker (or fancy computer program). Put identical ones on the overlay, positioned exactly on top of the ones on the layout sheet.

The printer keeps those register marks lined up on the negatives and plates, so everything is in the right place. This is how you get proper *registration*.

• **Put the type or image** on the overlay, pasting it exactly where it belongs. Specify whether it'll be double-burned, dropped out, or whatever.

If it goes over a photo, you'd better get a copy of the photo made the right size for the layout sheet, so you can see what you're doing. If it's just a xerox, write "Position only" or "FPO" in red on the xeroxed photo. Now you can see if the type on the overlay runs across someone's nose, for example.

### Screens & colors

Remember, the printer will add the actual screens and colors. Everything that will be screened and/or printed with colored ink is still black (or red) on the layout sheet (or overlay).

• If a screened area will touch or overlap on anything else on the page, put the type or graphics you want screened on an overlay. If a large area will be screened, you could cut its shape from a sheet of amberlith or rubylith the same way you'd cut a *silhouette* (p. 165). Use a metal ruler to get the edges straight on the area to be screened.

Write instructions clearly with an acetate marker, or tape a sheet of instructions onto the overlay.

• When screened areas don't touch anything else, paste them onto the layout sheet itself. Then mark whatever's to be screened (with the exact percentage screen you want – p. 145) in non-repro blue on the layout sheet. To make sure the printer gets the message, mark it again on tracing paper taped over the page.

• Treat colored areas and colored screens the same way as regular screens. Remember, the actual color isn't added until the printer rolls colored ink onto the plate (p. 62). Use a PMS guide (p. 146) to find the exact color each area should be printed in, and mark the proper PMS number on the layout sheet or overlay.

### Paste-up for full color

To add one or two colors, you'll make a separate overlay for each color ink, and the printer makes a plate from each overlay (p. 62).

But to print photos in full color and get other subtle color mixtures, you can't make the overlays yourself. All those shades can be made by blending just four primary colors (p. 62), and the inks for those basic colors are cheaper than ink for special PMS colors. Have the printer make *color separations* (p. 62) for about $85 a shot, and you'll get four plates, one for each color.

With fancy computer programs like *Photoshop,* a desktop publishing system can also make color separations; but you need a color *monitor* (p. 46) and a small fortune to pay a *service bureau* (p. 54) to print it all out.

### Just to make sure

Whenever you do anything fancy, make sure the printer notices and understands the marks on your mechanical. Repeat all special instructions in a cover letter, and go over them with the printer when you deliver the paper.

# 19. Distribution: getting the paper out

This is the last and most important step. After all, if no one sees your publication, it doesn't matter how beautifully it's done.

## Handouts & drop-offs

Recruit volunteers who'll blanket the town, shop or office as soon as your paper's off the press.

### Community drop-offs

Print sturdy signs or stickers saying your paper is "available here." Then visit potential drop-off sites and ask permission to leave the sign in the window.

Look for storefronts and offices your audience (p. 3) is apt to visit. Try cafeterias, variety stores, restaurants and supermarkets; social service centers and waiting rooms; schools; beauty and barber shops; laundromats and city hall; housing coops and clubs. Think of other places people meet, talk or best of all, wait.

• **The wrong way to drop off papers:** Just leave a pile of copies without talking to anyone. They'll get scattered around or disappear on a dusty back shelf. Someone will get tired of seeing them sitting around and throw them out.

• **The right way to drop off papers:** Divide your area into routes and, as soon as the paper is off the press, rally a troop of volunteers. Keep a master list of all the routes and tell people to keep track of how many copies they drop off and where. This list will also help prove the paper's circulation to potential advertisers (p. 26).

Talk to the merchant or office manager at each spot, and ask whether all the papers got snapped up. Tactfully suggest stacking them where people will see the paper as they enter or leave. Make spot checks a week or so later to see if the papers are still there.

### Door to door

This makes sense when your news concentrates on certain neighborhoods. It's illegal to put hand-delivered mail in the mail box. Instead, roll up each paper and attach it to the door handle with a rubber band.

### Special deliveries

When you write a big story on a person or situation, make sure the people involved see the paper.

### Delivering a union paper

Ask for volunteers to hand papers out at the front door or plant gate – see p. 33 for legal guidelines. And get the company to provide literature racks in non-working areas.

# Discount mailing rates

Mailing costs have skyrocketed, especially for non-profit groups. What follows are ways to avoid paying First Class postage. However, expect mail delivery to take up to two weeks. Local mail will move faster, and Second Class may be a little speedier than Third Class, especially if you mail more often than once a month. In Canada, mailing discounts are harder to come by – see p. 170.

## It's downright confusing

Post office rates are about as easy to follow as IRS tax forms. They're always changing, so double-check everything with your post office. When your local postmaster gives you a hard time, ask to see the regulation in the Domestic Mail Manual.

Unions have another valuable resource: Edwin Schmidt, AFL-CIO Director of Reproduction, Mailings and Subscriptions, vigorously defends the mailing rights of non-profit groups. Unions can contact Schmidt at (202) 637-5041 or at the AFL-CIO, 815 16th St. N.W., Wash. D.C. 20006.

# Third-Class Bulk discounts

It used to be that Second-Class rates were cheaper than Third, but today it's really a toss-up, depending on countless details. If you don't publish on an exact schedule or the paper is mimeoed, Bulk Third-Class is the *only* way to go. Chart D on p. 170 shows the savings.

## You can mail Third Class if you:

- Mail at least 200 identical pieces or 50 pounds at a time.
- Mail either your own group's publications or those from a group approved for Third-Class rates at the same post office (called a *cooperative mailing*). If you're non-profit, they must be non-profit too.

(You can mail other groups' materials under your permit, but *only* when you make them yours by reproducing them and adding your letterhead or your own page set-up information – p. 74 – and return address.)

- Sort the mail by zip codes before it's delivered to the post office – (p. 171).
- Carry only advertising that's part of your publication, *not* inserts.

## Apply for one of these:

Third Class costs $75 a year. Pick one of three possible permits:

- Authorization to mail with your own "indicia without affixing postage." This is both the most expensive and the most useful permit. You'll pay an extra one-time $75 indicia charge to get the permit; then typeset and print your permit number in a box where the stamp would normally go. Example A shows the proper form for non-profits.

The post office will keep a bulk account in your name. Before each mailing, deposit enough money in the account to cover the postage.

To apply for this permit, send the post office a letter like example B (assuming you're non-profit – p. 170), along with yellow Form 3601.

- Authorization to mail. This saves you the $75 indicia fee, but all you get is the right to let another group (such as the printer) mail your materials with its Third-Class permit. Print its indicia on each piece. However, if that group isn't non-profit, you don't get a non-profit discount (p. 170).
- Authorization to mail and pay postage by pre-cancelled stamps or with a meter. This also saves you the $75 indicia fee. Buy a roll of pre-cancelled stamps or pre-cancelled stamped envelopes from the post office.

Or use a metering machine. Buy one from a dealer and then rent a *fractional meter head* from a mailing machine company. Every time you need postage, take the machine to the post office, lay down cash, and they'll adjust the machine.

## Preparing for a Third-Class mailing

If it's self-mailer, see p. 12 or 76.

- Print the name and address of the organization that owns the permit in the upper left-hand corner of the mailing space or envelope.
- To figure your postage, fill out the right post office form – 3602PC for pre-cancelled stamps or a meter or, for a

printed indicia, form 3602R or 3602N (non-profit). Bring that to the post office with the mailing.

Second-class discounts

# What is Second-Class mail?

## Consider Second Class if:

- You mail the paper on a strict schedule, at least four times a year. When you apply for the permit, tell the post office your "frequency" – even if it's as bizarre as "every January, February, October and November."

(You can probably foul up on the frequency once; and you can add special editions if they're timely, and you tell the post office in writing.)

- The paper is printed, not mimeoed.

- Readers either request or pay a substantial price for at least half the issues you mail out. If the paper's supported by dues money, then it qualifies as a paid-for paper.

- It gives public information, or is devoted to a special industry.

- All advertising is an "integral part" of the paper. You can't insert a business circular.

- You pre-sort each mailing by zip code (described on p. 171).

## Advertising

The less advertising you have, the more you can save.

*Publisher's Own* are free ads boosting your organization or a good cause – such as fund-raisers or a credit union, or the sale of educational goodies.

*General advertising* means paid ads. As soon as you put a single general ad in the paper, you must:

- Limit the number of free copies sent to libraries, the press, prospective members, etc. to 10% of paid subscribers. If you don't, you pay higher rates.

- Deal with more red tape. If you're a union or other membership organization, your executive board must adopt a resolution saying this paper is the group's official publication, that subscriptions are paid through dues, and that a certain portion of dues money is set aside for the paper.

- Show a "financial transaction" for every name on the mailing list. Each should be on a dues list, subscription form or other record.

- Pay a higher postage rate if all advertising – general plus publisher's own – takes up more than 10% of the paper.

## Second-Class rates

As chart E on p. 171 shows, you pay according to the number of papers mailed, how far they travel, the weight, the folded size, the amount of advertising, and how you sort the mail. If you don't have a Nobel Prize-winning math scholar on your staff, you might find these complexities somewhat terrifying.

## How to apply for a permit

The post office must see the paper before it approves anything. So print an issue with the right information, and send two copies to the postmaster.

## Every issue must include:

Either on the front page, or in a masthead box (p. 75) within the first five pages, print the:

- Volume & number. Vol. 2, No. 6 means this is your second year of publishing and the sixth issue this year.

- Date. Tell the month (Sept. 1992) or the exact date (9/14/92) or the season (Fall 1992).

## To get the biggest postal discounts

Rates vary widely, depending on how easy you make it for the post office to handle your mail. Here are ways to save:

• **Get letter-size discounts** by folding your newsletter or leaflet until it's between 5"–11½" long, and 3½"–6⅛" tall, and no more than ¼" thick. Folding an 8½"x11" newsletter in half will do the trick.

• **If you seal open edges** with peel-off dots or spots of glue, you can get the discounts that require machine sorting, such as zip+4 and barcode (explained next).

• **Add zip+4** to a computerized list. These four digits are tagged onto the end of the regular zip code to show each neighborhood. But it won't work for handwritten addresses, and for typed addresses check with the post office to make sure the computer can read them. Bring your list to the post office on a floppy disk and they'll add zip+4 codes for free – but only once.

• **Add barcodes.** If you mail 250 pieces at once, this will, by 1992, offer the biggest savings. Those funny little lines on the mailing label stand for the zip code and/or zip+4 in a form post office machines "read" to sort mail faster. To use them you can't print anything else in the bottom ⅝" of the mailing area. Eventually barcodes will even be used to sort the mail to the exact address, offering the biggest savings if you send lots of mail to the same streets.

A mailing service will barcode your list for a fee. Some computer programs claim to barcode mailing labels, but make sure the post office accepts their format – or you won't get the discount. Barcode rates also vary depending on how you sort the mail. There's a barcode rate for basic sorted mail, then another rate for sorting into packages by the first three digits and another for sorting down to all five digits.

• **If at least 125 pieces** in a sack go to the same first three zip code digits, you get the *3/5 digit* discount. Rules differ for Second- and Third- Class, so check with the post office.

• **Carrier route coding,** which sorts mail for each letter carrier, offers the biggest savings for 1991, and you needn't seal open edges with dots or glue. But by 1992 these rates will be undercut by the barcode discounts explained above.

• **A firm package** discount applies only to Second-Class mail when two or more copies go to the same address.

• **If you use a mailing service,** ask about added discounts for combining your mailing with another group's and/or trucking mail directly to far-away post offices (*drop shipping*).

• **Find out how much** a brochure or newsletter weighs by buying a small postal scale; or bring a sample to the post office.

• **Identification statement** like example C (p. 168) giving the paper's name, its frequency, the name and address of your group, the price (or that it's supported by dues), and the city.

• **Every page is numbered,** including advertisements.

• **Where to send** address changes (example F on p. 172).

### From then on

As you mail each issue, figure your postage on Form 3541R or 3541N (if you're non-profit).

Getting Second-Class approval takes time. If you already have a Third-Class permit, mail at those rates first. As soon as the Second-Class permit comes through, you'll get a refund.

# Special non-profit rates

Whether you mail Second- or Third-Class, you'll get the best deal when you convince the post office your group is non-profit. Labor unions as well as religious, educational, scientific, charitable, agricultural, veterans' and fraternal organizations can qualify for this discount.

To apply, get the right form from the post office and send it in along with a letter like example G. Enclose evidence that you're non-profit – including your group's charter, constitution, etc. If you're a local union or a local chapter, always use the constitution of the international union or other parent group.

If the IRS considers your group tax-exempt, get a copy of your *Certificate of Exemption from Federal Income Tax.* If your group isn't tax-exempt, you may still qualify for *special non-profit* rates under post office rules. Ask for their criteria. Apply for non-profit status with a Second-Class application by filling out Form 3502. When applying for Third Class, use Form 3624.

While you're waiting for your non-profit application to be approved, insist that the postage you pay be put in escrow. Once you get the nod, you'll get a refund.

# Canadian mailing discounts

When you mail 5,000 copies or less, you may have to use *Lettermail* (which

---

Chart D

## Third-Class postal rates

Permit fee: $75 a year (plus optional one-time indicia charge of $75 – p. 168)
*Letter-size* rates (see above) are for pieces weighing up to 3.3 ounces (or 2½ or 3 ounces if zip+4 or barcodes are added). If you go over size or weight limits, you must mail at the *flat-size* rate.

|  | Letter-size regular | Letter-size non-profit | Flat-size regular | Flat-size non-profit |
|---|---|---|---|---|
| Basic Sort | 19.8¢ | 11.1¢ | 23.3¢ | 12.5¢ |
| with zip+4 | 18.9¢ | 10.4¢ | ** | ** |
| with barcode* | 17.9¢ | 9.4¢ | ** | ** |
| 3/5 digit | 16.5¢ | 9.8¢ | 18.7¢ | 11.1¢ |
| with zip+4 | 16.1¢ | 9.4¢ | ** | ** |
| sorted by 3 digits & barcoded* | 15.4¢ | 8.8¢ | ** | ** |
| sorted by 5 digits & barcoded* | 14.6¢ | 8.1¢ | ** | ** |
| Carrier route | 13.1¢ | 7.4¢ | 14.2¢ | 8¢ |

\* By 1992 barcode rates are expected to drop below carrier route rates.

\*\* Discounts not available until 1992.

used to be First Class) – and pay a whopping 40¢ (plus 3¢ tax) a piece. You'll pay more if you don't include the postal code, or if the folded newsletter measures more than 5⅞"x9⅝". (You're safe if you fold 8½"x11" sheets in half.)

● **The Addressed Admail category** (formerly Third Class) can save you plenty – but only when you send at least 5,000 pieces provincially or 10,000 nationally per mailing. Apply for the permit from Canada Post, and you can use it for all your publications. You'll print your permit number on each piece you mail.

You must pre-sort the mail by postal code, using a master list from the post office which shows the exact sorting order. You'll also need to bundle, bag and label the mailing into sacks just as the post office tells you to. But the savings are worth the effort – Admail can cut the Lettermail rate in half. Rates are based on the total weight of your mailing, so it costs more to send a 12-page newsletter than an 8-page one.

● **Publication Mail** (formerly Second Class) is the cheapest way to go, offering savings of up to 75% off Lettermail rates. But getting this permit can be difficult, and it can be used only for the publication on the application. Unions must set up independent "publishing societies" to get around the rule that excludes them from this category. Other groups have to prove their publications give general information and don't exist solely to promote any individuals or organizations.

There are other requirements too – you must publish at least four times a year, and carry only a limited number of ads. Rates vary by weight and classification within the Publication Mail category. Unlike Admail, you don't have to send a huge number of pieces; but you must pre-sort the mail.

● **Consider using Parcel Mail** to send a bundle of publications to each location. Rates vary depending on how far the parcel will travel, and whether it's sent via air mail.

# Sorting by zip code

The trick is to keep your mailing list carefully arranged by zip code. After publications are addressed, divide them

Finding out new addresses costs 35¢, or $1 in Canada

Chart E

## Second-Class postal rates

$275 one-time fee to apply

To get discounts that require machine sorting (barcoding or zip+4), follow the requirements for *letter-size* (p. 170). Otherwise, there are no size limits. To figure the full postage, add the per-pound rate to the per-piece rate and deduct any non-advertising discount you have coming (see below).

|  | Regular rate | Non-profit rate |
|---|---|---|
| **For copies mailed within the county only** *if at least half your mail is distributed in-county:* | | |
| per pound rate | 11.6¢ | 11.6¢ |
| *plus* per piece rate | 3.3¢ to 7.7¢ | 3.3¢ to 7.7¢ |
| | (variations depend on how the mailing is sorted) | |

---

| | Regular rate | Non-profit rate |
|---|---|---|
| **For copies mailed out of the county** *(and in-county, if most of your mail goes out-of-county):* | | |
| Basic per-pound rate for publications with less than 10% advertising *or* for the non-advertising portion of the paper: | 14.7¢ | 10.6¢ |
| When your paper carries more than 10% ads, apply this per-pound rate to *the advertising portion of the paper only:* | 19.6¢ to 36.7¢ | 14.1¢ to 35¢ |
| | (variations depend on the distance the paper travels out of the county) | |
| *plus rate per piece, sorted:* | | |
| Basic sort | 20.1¢ | 16.9¢ |
| with zip+4 | 19.2¢ | 16.2¢ |
| barcode (with zip+4)* | 18.2¢ | 15.2¢ |
| 3/5 digit | 15.8¢ | 12.6¢ |
| with zip+4 | 15.4¢ | 12.2¢ |
| sorted by 3 digit & barcoded* | 14.7¢ | 11.6¢ |
| sorted by 5 digit & barcoded* | 13.9¢ | 10.9¢ |
| Carrier route | 11.9¢ | 8.8¢ |
| *minus non-advertising discount:* | | |
| If you carry no ads, subtract from the above out-of-county per-piece rate: | 5¢ | 3.5¢ |
| (If you carry ads, you get part of this discount for the non-advertising portion of the paper.) | | |

*By 1992 barcode rates are expected to drop below carrier route rates.

These all go to the same state

into bundles of ten or more. You'll pay several different rates depending on how narrowly each package is sorted (see boxes on p. 170 and p. 171). Here's how to do a basic sort:

**1.** First, pick up free stickers, rubber bands, labels and mail sacks from the post office.

**2.** Full zip code. When ten or more pieces go to the same zip code, tie them together with a rubber band and put a red "D" sticker on top.

**3.** Then arrange the leftovers into stacks by the first three numbers in the zip code. Rubber-band each stack that has ten or more pieces, and attach a green "3" on top.

**4.** State. Rubber-band any ten or more leftovers that go to the same state, and stick an orange "S" on the top.

**5.** Mixed states. Rubber-band the remaining pieces and put a brown "MS" sticker on top.

**6.** Stuff the bundles into sacks and label each one with your group's name, the class of mail, and the post office the sack is going to. Every sack must have at least 125 pieces or 15 pounds.

# How to address each mailing

Here's how to avoid writing the address on every single envelope:

## Xeroxed peel & stick labels

This is the cheapest method, especially for a one-shot or small mailing. Pick up 8½" by 11" sheets of peel-&-stick labels at an office supply store for about $10 a package of 25. Each sheet has 33 labels (three abreast).

Take the lined sheet of paper (called a *matrix*) that comes in each package, and type a name and address into each of the 33 spaces. If the matrix lines are thick and black, put a blank piece of paper over it and insert both in your typewriter. The black lines will show through, giving you a guide to type the names in the right spot. This is your "master."

Then xerox each master onto several sheets of labels. Peel those xeroxed labels apart every time you do a mailing.

To mail by Second- or Third-Class, type all the names in zip code order. Names you add later and addresses you change will be out of order, however; you must sort those extras into proper bundles by hand each time you do a mailing. That can be a major hassle. When you've got more than 500 names, try something else.

## Let the computer do it

Whether you have a simple word processor (p. 37) or a fancy computer, use it to set up your mailing list. The names and addresses you enter into the machine and save in its memory are called a *database*. When you're ready to do a mailing, call up the database and a special *program* (p. 50) tells the machine to print it all out in zip or postal code order. The same database can be used to keep track of dues, phone numbers, etc. – if you have the right program.

• **Word processors** do a fine job, but your mailing list is limited by the size of the machine's *memory*. If, for example, the memory holds up to 50,000 *characters* (p. 36), your list can't run longer than around 700 names. Get around that limit by breaking the list into smaller sections and storing each on a *disk* (p. 37) – if the machine can handle disks.

Most word processors are set up to use peel-and-stick labels that come 33 to a sheet. Usually you can also merge all or part of the mailing list with form letters, so that each letter comes out individually addressed. Keeping track of things like phone numbers is also possible, but for detailed record-keeping you'll need a computer.

• **No-frills computer programs** like *LabelPro* for IBM/compatibles ($49 discount) and *MacEnvelope* for Macintosh ($89.95 list; $57 discount) do everything a word processor does, plus they can handle bigger mailing lists. More expensive programs will also weed out duplicate addresses, let you add more information and even print out postal *barcodes* (p. 170).

• **Use a full-fledged database program,** and there's almost no limit to what you can keep track of — mailing lists, members' dues, financial reports, or finding out how many paid subscribers you have in Dallas, Texas. Make a list of all the record-keeping and office tasks you do, and then see which program can handle those jobs. A *relational database* program keeps track of several lists at once. For example, if you delete deadbeats from the dues list, they're automatically deleted from the mailing list, too. That's harder to learn and use than a *flat* database program, which keeps each list separately.

*DataPerfect* ($299 discount) is a relational program for IBM/compatibles (p. 49), while *File Maker Pro* is a flat database program for Macs (list: $229; $218 discount). It might be worthwhile to instead ask a computer specialist to create a customized program to handle all your database needs – from mailing lists to union grievance forms. Try PC Labor Union Software: (517) 799-3000; or Union International Systems: (617) 770-3800. They specialize in programs for unions, but they'll also handle the needs of other groups.

## Labels for computers

● **Peel-and-stick labels** come in all sizes and shapes, to suit each machine. If you have a dot-matrix printer (p. 52), try buying a long, continuous strip of single labels. You can buy labels for as little as $11 a box.

● **A labelling machine** is worth buying if your list has more than 1,000 names and you do a lot of mailings. Models range from simple ones that just peel off each label to auto-feed, belt-driven babies that'll peel, and stick and stack. Prices range from $350 to over $3,000. Look in the yellow pages under mailing machines and equipment.

● **Print addresses onto wide computer paper,** four or five across a sheet, instead of sticky labels if you'll be taking the job to a professional mailing service (explained next). Their *cheshire machines* will cut apart the labels and paste each where it belongs.

## Mailing services

Just drop off your mail and mailing list, and they do the rest – labelling, sorting, bagging and tagging. For most jobs, it'll cost $18-$20 per thousand pieces, plus postage. Give them mailing lists printed on computer paper as explained above. If you instead bring them peel-and-stick labels, it could double the cost.

These companies know all the fine points of getting mail delivered quickly and cheaply. With the confusing jumble of postal regulations and rates, a mailing service can save you headaches – and money.

Some mailing services offer *list management*, which means they'll keep your names and addresses on their computer and make labels for you. It'll cost 15¢-25¢ per name; and you'll be charged again for every change, deletion or new address. If they add *carrier route* or *barcoding* (p. 170) to your list, it could save you money.

Some printers run their own mailing services, saving you from the hassle of delivering your publications to the mailer.

Typing the master for gummed labels

This machine runs off mailing labels

---

# Updating your mailing list

● The U.S. post office won't forward Third-Class mail to a new address, and Second Class is forwarded only for 60 days after an address changes. When someone has moved and mail comes back to you with a forwarding address scrawled on the envelope, it costs 35¢ a shot, even if all you find out is "address unknown." Adjust your list as soon as you get a correction.

For Second-Class papers, you'll get address corrections every mailing. But with Third Class, finding out new addresses is optional. When you plan to clean up your list, print "Address Correction Requested" in the mailing space underneath the permit box or stamp.

● **In Canada,** address corrections, if you request them, cost $1 apiece in the Admail category. Publication Mail is forwarded to a new address; but "address unknown" pieces are returned, if you request them, for 80¢ each.

## Or better yet . . .

Explore cheaper ways to find out who's moved. For example, a box in the paper could urge people planning to move to send you their new addresses.

## Zip & postal codes

Every address must include a zip or postal code. Buy a zip code directory for $12 at your post office. Order Canadian postal code directories for $10 through the post office or by calling 1-800-565-4362.

---

# Index